STRESS
IN
ISRAEL

Edited by

Shlomo Breznitz, Ph. D.

Lady Davis Professor
Director, Ray D. Wolfe Centre for
Study of Psychological Stress
University of Haifa, Israel

VNR VAN NOSTRAND REINHOLD COMPANY
NEW YORK   CINCINNATI   TORONTO   LONDON   MELBOURNE

Manufactured in the United States of America

Published by Van Nostrand Reinhold Company Inc.
135 West 50th Street, New York, N.Y. 10020

Van Nostrand Reinhold Limited
1410 Birchmount Road
Scarborough, Ontario M1P 2E7, Canada

Van Nostrand Reinhold Australia Pty. Ltd.
17 Queen Street
Mitcham, Victoria 3132, Australia

Van Nostrand Reinhold Company Limited
Molly Millars Lane
Wokingham, Berkshire, England

15 14 13 12 11 10 9 8 7 6 5 4 3 2 1

Library of Congress Cataloging in Publication Data

Main entry under title:

Stress in Israel.

   Includes bibliographical references and index.
   1. Jewish-Arab relations--Psychological aspects--
Addresses, essays, lectures. 2. Israel-Arab War, 1983--
Psychological aspects--Addresses, essays, lectures.
3. Stress (Psychology)--Addresses, essays, lectures.
4. Israelis--Mental health--Addresses, essays, lectures.
I. Breznitz, Shlomo. [DNLM: 1. Stress, Psychological--
Occurrence -Israel. WM 172 S9155]
DS119.7.S75   155.92   82-2661
ISBN 0-442-24422-3   AACR2

"Next year we shall sit on the balcony
and count the migrating birds.
Children in the grove will run and play
between twilight and dusk.

You will see, you will see, how good it will be
next year, next year."

A popular Israeli song
by Naomi Shemer

Contributors

Shlomo Breznitz, Ph.D. — Lady Davis Professor, Director Ray D. Wolfe Centre for Study of Psychological Stress, University of Haifa.

Shmuel N. Eisenstadt, Ph.D. — Professor of Sociology, The Eliezer Kaplan School of Economics and Social Science, and The Truman Research Institute, Hebrew University, Jerusalem.

Yohanan Eshel, Ph.D. — Senior Lecturer in Psychology, University of Haifa.

Gideon Fishman, Ph.D. — Senior Lecturer in Sociology, University of Haifa.

Reuven Gal, Ph.D. — Colonel, Head of Behavioral Sciences Unit, Israeli Defense Forces.

Louis Guttman, Ph.D. — Professor of Psychological Measurement, Hebrew University, and Director of the Israeli Institute of Applied Social Research, Jerusalem.

Michael Inbar, Ph.D. — Barbara and Morton Mandel Professor of Cognitive Social Psychology and Education, Hebrew University, Jerusalem.

Avigdor Klingman, Ph.D. — Lecturer in Education, University of Haifa.

Shlomit Levy, Ph.D. — The Israeli Institute of Applied Social Research, Jerusalem.

Amia Lieblich, Ph.D. — Associate Professor in Psychology, Hebrew University, Jerusalem.

Raphael Moses, M.D. — Israeli Institute of Psychoanalysis.

Amiram Raviv, Ph.D. — Lecturer in Psychology, Tel Aviv University.

Nitza Yarom, Ph.D. — Lecturer in Psychology, Medical School, Tel Aviv University.

Foreword

I am very glad to learn that *Stress in Israel,* first published as a chapter in Selye's *Guide to Stress Research,* Volume I, will now appear as a volume to be distributed by Van Nostrand Reinhold, Inc.

I am sure this study will become an immediate success, because the reports herein are based on timely research. They detail the effects that successive wars, threats to life, and continuous tension — which are so much a part of Israel's special conditions as a country under a high level of stress — have on Israeli behavior. The theoretical and practical aspects of some of the most pressing problems in contemporary Israeli society are dealt with: combat reactions, stress reactions of women and children, widows and orphans, and physical disability, all of which would have a decisive influence on the quality of life in any society.

There are few people who would be better qualified than Professor Breznitz to write a book of this kind. Professor Breznitz and I have collaborated in the past and the continued affiliation between the Ray D. Wolfe Centre for Study of Psychological Stress in Haifa and the International Institute of Stress have always been, in my mind, the model of cooperation for institutions of higher learning. The association has been inspired and is flourishing.

I was honored to be asked by Professor Breznitz to write this brief Foreword for a volume that certainly represents a great contribution to current stress research.

Hans Selye
C.C., M.D., Ph.D., D.Sc.
President, International
Institute of Stress
Montreal, Canada

Preface

I can think of at least four reasons why I should never have started a book on the topic of stress in Israel. First, the amount of reliable existing information about stress in Israel is quite limited. This necessarily leaves the field open to a great deal of speculation, much of which will on hindsight probably turn out to have been premature.

Second, all of the contributors live in Israel and we are too close to the subject matter. Personal involvement is surely a critical limiting factor to scientific objectivity. One wonders whether it is at all possible to deal in a detached way with something that touches so deeply.

Third, the topic is not without some important political implications. Whenever the thin line between expert analysis and politics is crossed, the implications must be spelled out as explicitly as possible.

Last, but not least, since all Israelis hold themselves to be experts on stress, I am putting myself in great danger by trying to claim something that to many will inevitably seem entirely unacceptable.

With these reasons in mind, however, I still think that the risks are justified. It is my firm belief that by studying Israeli society we can learn something new about coping and adjustment. Furthermore, the hope that this book may encourage future research into this complex issue by itself warrants its publication.

It all started with a chapter on the same topic written for *Selye's Guide to Stress Research,* edited by Hans Selye and published by Van Nostrand Reinhold in 1980. Upon receiving the manuscript of that chapter, the publishers thought that the topic deserved to be treated as a separate volume. I hope that they will be vindicated. My teacher, colleague, and good friend, Hans Selye was more than encouraging in connection with this project, and I owe him many thanks.

Special thanks are due to the contributors, who often had to bear with me for the numerous "final deadlines" that I unsuccessfully attempted to impose. Without their thoughts and efforts there would have been, of course, no volume to publish. The satisfactory delivery of articles on short notice by Dr. Lieblich and Drs. Raviv and Klingman is particularly commendable.

The administrative staff of the Ray D. Wolfe Centre for Study of Psychological Stress was very kind and forebearing. Ruth Maos is the only person in the world (myself included) who can read my handwriting. Dina Katz, somehow, managed to unscramble my dictations. To both I am in great personal debt. The figures were prepared by Edna Baksi.

As the British say, "When it rains it pours," and the hectic period near the end of the project somehow always manages to coincide with many other projects, and such extras as: a school strike, my daughter's flu, a long-awaited and cancelled vacation, etc., etc. The only way I could cope was by asking my wife Tzvia to be even more considerate "just this time." With her help I weathered the storm.

SHLOMO BREZNITZ

Contents

Introduction
The Many Facets of Stress

Shlomo Breznitz
University of Haifa

Ever since Selye introduced the concept of stress into experimental medicine, thousands of studies have demonstrated its central role in the development of disease. Irrespective of whether the stressors are physical or psychological, or whether their outcomes are problems in somatic health or psychological health, the one dominant theme running through what has by now become a tradition of research, is the perception of stress as a negative, destructive agent. Anything that is alien to the organism, anything that is new, whether minute or dramatic, changes the equilibrium, the biological homeostasis, and starts a process that can ultimately lead to maladjustment and illness. Stress, in short, is the ever-present inescapable intruder on peace.

Rarely have a concept and the research tradition associated with it achieved such quick recognition and acceptance. Indeed, the argument that stress is the culprit for everything that is wrong with people has reached such a high degree of acceptance that, rightly or wrongly, some people view this as the *age of stress*. Oddly enough, it is not so long ago that we were supposed to be in the *age of anxiety*. Everything was anxiety. Our problem was how to deal with it, how to discover it in ourselves, and how to avoid it if possible. Where did anxiety go? How come we moved so quickly from the age of anxiety to the age of stress? The answer, I believe, is directly related to some of the predominant differences between the two concepts. While anxiety is internal, stress is external. While anxiety is often unconscious, stress has a specific cause in the environment. While anxiety is often the outcome of certain difficulties during the earlier years of development, stress always relates to the here and now. And finally, while the only way to get rid of anxiety is through serious, difficult, and time-consuming soul-searching, stress can be reduced by ecological intervention, or through simple techniques of stress management that one can acquire and master over a weekend if necessary.

It is much easier to consider all our problems as being the outcome of stress rather than anxiety. It is more comforting to think they are due to outside factors, where we are not to blame, rather than internal factors, with all the implications of personal responsibility and even feelings of guilt. In a nutshell, the transition from anxiety to stress plays a functional role in the evolvement of our own perception of the world. It is the externalization of the internal, the perfect excuse. How can we be expected to properly cope with problems when the stress with which we have to deal is so tremendous? How can we be held accountable for our failures and lack of self-control when the provocation of stress is so high? Just as we blame the emotions for unwanted behavior, so do we take comfort by using stress to explain away our failures and inadequacies.

One of my research assistants told me the following story: Having just finished her shopping in the supermarket, she approached the cashier. She was quite taken aback to find that the cashier, for no obvious reason, was very agitated and crude to her. She asked for an explanation of this behavior; the reply was, "Didn't you hear the latest news?"

This is a true and rather typical Israeli story. As this volume illustrates, it is not easy to live in a country that is continuously exposed to high levels of stress. At the same time, however, the story gives a very simple example of the function of stress as an excuse. It is not our claim that stress is only an excuse; but for too long it was seen only as a source of difficulties to adjustment. What we do claim, however, is that in addition to being just that, it is many other things besides.

Among other things, stress is a great integrator. Under duress, people close ranks and support each other more than during so-called normal times. There is abundant evidence from studies of communities in disaster (e.g., Baker and Chapman, 1962) pointing to the integrative function of stress. In difficult times, particularly if they are acute and involve entire groups of people, the social barriers between individuals are often dramatically reduced. It is in the midst of disaster and suffering that many people, often for the first time, sense a true closeness to other people without the artificial barriers of social conventions. On a smaller scale the same phenomenon often takes place when there is a death in the family and the different members close ranks and support each other more than they did before. How disappointing then their return to "normal." With the distancing from a disaster comes the reinstatement of social barriers and inequalities between men. Thus, what are bad times in one sense are often the best of times in another sense.

Stress is also an opportunity. When faced with personal problems of exceptional magnitude, individuals sometimes gain a better perspective of their own lives. Dangerous, perhaps life-threatening situations may cause us to have second thoughts about the direction our lives have taken. It is not uncommon for people who have barely escaped an accident or some other kind of personal calamity to undergo fundamental changes of lifestyle. The basic realization of the human condition, namely, that one's days are numbered, has a far-reaching impact on most of us. For, as the poet Wordsworth said, "The world is too much with us," and rarely do we have the occasion to see ourselves in true perspective. Stress often gives us just that. As such, it provides an excellent existential opportunity.

In addition to being a cause of disease, an excuse, an integrator, and an opportunity, stress can also serve as an amplifier of latent or mild tendencies. This is particularly true of intense stressors. Whereas in mild stressors one often finds a great deal of individual differences, the higher the stress the less prominent these individual differences tend to be (e.g., Lazarus, 1966). It is as if a major stress had a way of extracting from people the most essential way of behaving, the common denominator, the main effect. Paradoxically, individual differences can sometimes *best* be seen in their fullness when the person is confronted with a stressful situation. A good example of this was the attempt to categorize individuals into Type A versus Type B categories by subjecting them to what is known as the stress interview (Friedman and Rosenman, 1974).

During exposure to stress it is often easier to separate the essential from the secondary, the important from the unimportant, the signal from the noise. Stress can serve as a probe, as an essential research tool even in areas unrelated to it. As we shall see, this theme occurs throughout this volume, which concentrates on the stress of life in Israel but often deals with nonstress-related topics.

Finally, this list of the various facets of stress will not be complete without mentioning that stress can also be a social phenomenon. Instead of focusing on the single individual, it is possible to look at larger units such as families, communities, and even entire nations exposed to particular stressors. For a variety of theoretical as well as methodological reasons, such an approach provides tremendous research opportunities. It is precisely with this in mind that the writing of the present volume was undertaken.

ISRAEL'S LONG LIST OF WOES

Life everywhere is often visited by difficulties, misfortune, and tragedy. We ought to bear in mind that the Israelis are not exempted from "the thousand natural shocks that flesh is heir to." In addition, they have their own special problems. What follows are short descriptions of the "extras" that are borne by the Israelis.

Primary among these is the continuous state of war between Israel and its Arab neighbors. Since its establishment thirty years ago, Israel has fought four major wars, but it could easily be described as one continuous "thirty years war." In addition to the major outbreaks, there have been two long wars of attrition and a ceaseless chain of hostilities.

Terrorist activity inside the country has added to the sense of insecurity. The continuous need to take precautions and be on guard keeps the people aware of omnipresent threat to their daily routines. If there is gradual habituation, the occasional explosion and loss of life remind one of the realities of the situation.

Israel is the immigrant country par excellence. The overwhelming majority of its citizens were born elsewhere. Immigration is a major stressor even when the immigrant's condition is improved by it. Leaving relatives, friends, and familiar surroundings, customs, and language is no small matter. Often the immigrant was allowed to leave only after a long period of uncertainty and without family or possessions. To complicate matters, the immigrants are not of a single origin. On the contrary, their diversity makes the country a true melting pot of languages and cultures.

Economic hardship constitute another facet of stress. With an inflation rate of about 120 percent per year there is little trust in the economy and few ways to safely provide for present and future.

In addition to active military service of three years for young men and two years for young women, married women excepted, every Israeli serves reserve duty. In "normal times," that is, provided there are no special emergencies, eligible Israelis serve reserve duty for approximately one month a year until the age of fifty, then switch to civil defense. Reserve duty often totally disrupts the reservist's usual activities for long periods of time.

Last but not least, it ought to be remembered that Israel is a small country with a small population. This implies that whatever is happening there becomes, to a great extent, a personal affair. For instance, when somebody is injured or killed, there is a good chance that he would be known by randomly chosen individuals or by one of his friends. This smallness makes everybody tuned to names and details and effectively amplifies the impact of casualties.

It is, therefore, of no surprise that Israelis live by the news. They start their day with the news, go to sleep with the news, and listen to it many times in between. Their state of mind can be described as one of continuous vigilance.

The personal history of many Israelis includes the tragedy of the holocaust in Europe. Sole survivors of entire families harbor a hypersensitivity to personal loss that is augmented by psychological wounds of dimensions unprecendented in modern times. The spectre of another national holocaust exponentially magnifies the subjective experiences of the various objective stressors of the community.

These are some of the specific causes of stress in the lives of many Israelis. Add to them the important dimension of time, the prolonged exposure to these stresses, and the central question concerning our theme comes into focus: Which of the aspects of stress will predominate in Israel? Are the lives of Israelis best described as one continuous wear and tear, or as an exciting challenge? Do the Israelis show signs of exhaustion, or of exceptional vitality in sense of purpose? And further, is there anything that the theory of adaptation can learn from the Israeli experience?

This book does not and cannot attempt to give a comprehensive answer to the above questions. At best it tries to illuminate the richness and the fascinating complexity of the concept of stress. To illustrate the different aspect of stress, this book is divided into four parts:

Part I focuses on stress as an opportunity. It deals with how the acute stressors of war can be potential turning points in the lives of young adults. In the first chapter, Yarom presents data based on intensive interviews with young men who were in combat during the Yom Kippur War. That war, which has often been described in Israel as an earthquake, left its mark on all Israelis, but particularly on the soldiers, many of whom were confronted with death for the first time. Fortunately, Yarom lets the men speak for themselves, and she presents the data in their own language. The terrifying ordeal is revealed as a vehicle for personal change. The soldiers report on the transformation that has taken place in their attitudes toward themselves, their families, their friends, and to the entire issue of life and death.

In Chapter 2, Lieblich presents a sensitive document about the more intimate levels of experience of those who lived through the Yom Kippur War. In Gestalt therapy groups, the influence that the various facets of the trauma had on the personalities of those involved found meaningful and interesting expression. Here again, the stressful experience provided an impetus for seeking deeper self-knowledge.

A systematic attempt to analyze the personality and situational components of acts of special bravery is presented in Chapter 3, which closes the first part of the book. Again the dominant factor appears to be the situational one. In other words, dramatic situations in battle provided opportunities for dramatic affirmation of personal values through acts of extraordinary heroism.

Part II deals with stress as a social phenomenon. It is difficult to exaggerate the pitfalls and dangers in jumping from the individual level of analysis to the social level. At the same time, however, it should be kept in mind that when an entire community is subjected to essentially the same stressors, synchronized individual stress is produced. In other words, while the stress, or much of it, still affects each individual separately, there is temporal synchronicity with all the other individuals in the community who share essentially the same problem. In addition, there are some purely social elements in the stress invovled. A trauma such as the Yom Kippur War is focused on the danger to the actual existence of the entire State of Israel.   This transcends the individual level and adds to it a particularly social element.   It should also be emphasized that in a situation of stress, at least to the same extent as in "normal" situations, there is a great deal of social influence that affects the way people cope with the situation.   Modeling, social support, conformity, leadership − these factors become more prominent during emergencies.   These are, of course, purely social psychological phenomena.

In Chapter 4, Eisenstadt presents the thesis that the evolvement of Israeli society has to a great extent been influenced by the way that the society defined its situation.   More specifically, he claims that Israeli society perceived itself and defined itself as a society under stress, and this in itself led to a variety of social and psychological consequences.   True to the best of traditions in sociological theory, Eisenstadt claims that the definition of the situation is essentially more important than the objective aspects of that situation.

Exposure to prolonged and varied stress makes the issue of national morale one of paramount importance.   In their analysis of the various facets of morale, Guttman and Levy, basing their ideas on a great deal of information taken from longitudinal comparisons of representative samples of the Israeli population, make the case for a multifaceted approach to the issue of morale.   It is of particular interest to note that in the assessment of the Israeli situation, the issue of coping and the question of mood need not covary together and, in fact, exhibit some interesting idiosyncratic features.

In Chapter 6, psychoanalytic theory is applied to Israeli society. The recency and actuality of the events that are analyzed perhaps make the label of psychohistory too presumptuous in this particular instance, and I prefer to think of the analysis as a "national case history."   In his chapter, Moses presents some subtle and intriguing insights into the behavior of Israelis, using essentially a psychodynamic approach.

Chapter 7, by Raviv and Klingman, is about children under stress and closes the second part of this volume.   Raviv and Klingman make it quite clear that an event's impact is felt far beyond the locality where it took place.   Children in every part of Israel are influenced by the events there, as are their parents, their teachers, and the entire educational system.   It is this centrality of the children in the society that turns their issue into a major social issue.   A close inspection of the many studies done on the effects of stress on children in Israel gives some insight into the variety of psychological costs that are involved.

For a variety of reasons, Israel has been seen by many behavioral scientists as a natural laboratory for studying stress and coping. Part III of our volume thus deals with general-interest stress research that attempted to take advantage of the Israeli situation for methodological and theoretical reasons. Consider, for instance, the question of crime during national emergencies. Since in Israel there were two major wars within a span of less than a single generation, there is a basis for comparing and analyzing the crime rate in the same society under different circumstances. Fishman's data are relevant not only to criminology, but also to issues of morale, social cohesiveness, and coping with stress.

Chapter 9 presents the current status of the "vulnerable-age phenomenon." Inbar discovered that immigration has particularly detrimental effects on children between the ages of 6 and 11, a finding that appears to run contrary to most of the thinking in this area. While the study used Israeli subjects, it could be extrapolated to other populations, leading to essentially the same results. The vulnerable-age phenomenon is an illustration of research of general interest that took advantage of one particular characteristic of the Israeli population, namely, the high frequency of immigration. As Inbar himself points out, however, the vulnerable-age phenomenon need not be restricted to the issue of changing location, and might very well influence children's adjustment to other kinds of stressors.

The idea that recent life events play a major role in the development of physical or psychological illness has become very prominent in recent years. In Chapter 10, Breznitz and Eshel take advantage of the fact that many Israelis are exposed to exactly the same life events, even some dramatic ones, in order to pose certain general questions. Chief among them are what effect does the frequency of life events have on the subjective definition of an event? the importance of those events? and, the weights allocated to those events? Also, to what degree do recent life events interfere with previous ones? The chapter also deals with the issues of motivational control of perception, and the role of memory in major life events. Last but not least, Breznitz and Eshel raise the issue of "experiential age." It is implied that rich and varied exposure to life events, even stressors, can have a positive effect on individuals. In the empirical section of the chapter, they test for a positive correlation between life events and successful coping under subsequent stress.

Finally, Part IV of the volume looks at stress as a way of life. The concluding remarks of Chapter 11 suggest some common integrative themes that run through the entire volume, as well as some directions and needs for future research.

REFERENCES

Baker, G. W. and Chapman, D. W. (eds.), *Man and Society in Disaster.* New York: Basic Books, 1962.

Friedman, M. and Rosenman, R. H. *Type A Behavior and Your Heart.* New York: Knopf, 1979.

Lazarus, R. S. *Psychological Stress and the Coping Process.* New York: McGraw-Hill, 1966.

Part I
Stress as Opportunity

1.
Facing Death in War—
An Existential Crisis

(Soldiers' reactions to their combat experience)

Nitza Yarom [1]

Tel Aviv University

"War is a negative thing, that created in me something that is good for me."

H. R., an ex-combatant.

For the people of Israel wars have unfortunately been a part of living. Going through a war and then having to go on with the effects of such an experience is difficult. For men who have to fight and face death in combat, the threat is greater and the effects may be more dramatic. This study attempts to show the effects that front-line fighting has upon subsequent behavior. The author interviewed 34 men who had participated in the Yom Kippur War, with the idea of finding out the range of the possible effects of facing death in war.

Soldiers' reactions to their combat experiences have received much attention both in fiction and in professional literature. A thorough historical background of military psychiatry was provided by Bourne in his article "Military Psychiatry and the Viet Nam War in Perspective" (1969). He claimed with pride that "over the years combat psychiatry has evolved from a barely recognized entity to a sophisticated science with ramifications in every area of military planning.

---

[1]With gratitude to the 34 young men who contributed accounts of their war experiences, and to Dror and Judith Wertheimer, whose help was indispensable.

Beginning with the Civil War each subsequent conflict has led to a refinement of treatment techniques and has added progressively to our understanding and conceptualization of man's ability to deal with the stresses of combat" (p. 221). He also emphasized the point that "many distinguished psychiatrists served the military during World War II, and several utilized their talents to apply scientific research methodology to the data they obtained on casualties . . . . Particularly, the work of Grinker and Spiegel, described in their book, *Men Under Stress* (1963), represented a major advance in the systematic evaluation of man's psychological responses to combat" (p. 224). Bourne concludes this account of the great advancement of military psychiatry by presenting the percentages of psychiatric casualties evacuated in two wars separated by a generation: 6% during the Viet Nam War as compared to 23% during World War II.

There is no doubt that military psychiatry has gone a long way. Up to now we have had many psychiatric and psychological reports on the percentages of psychiatric casualties in various wars, the recommended techniques for treatment, and the speculations on the causes of those casualties. What is apparent is that military psychiatry has focused on the soldier who "breaks down" and deals with him in psychiatric terms (neurosis, symptoms, etc.).

However, theorists and practitioners in the area of stress and crisis offer a different view of the soldiers' reactions to their combat experiences. In his 1963 survey on the status and implications of the concept of crisis, Miller made the following statement: "Many of the studies of the reactions of soldiers in combat also fall within the category of crisis responses. At the time they were labelled as 'war neuroses', but it was recognized that they were distinct from typical neurotic manifestations especially with reference to the time factor" (p. 198).

Bourne, Sabshin (1972), and other representatives of military psychiatry admitted that the achievements and findings of military psychiatry can benefit stress and crisis research and the area of crisis intervention. Can the analogy be drawn both ways? Can we consider war another stressful event?

Golan (1978), in her book, *Treatment in Crisis Situations,* distinguished between personal crises and community crises (including, besides war, a great variety of civilian disasters). It is interesting to note the difference in the reported percentages of people affected in military and civilian crises. For example, Fritz & Marks (1954) reported that almost 90% of the survivors of a tornado disaster in Arkansas had suffered from acute anxiety or from psychosomatic reactions on the day after the disaster, and 75% had reported these symptoms to last for several days. Simultaneously, in a study done by Star (reported in Janis, 1972), of 1,897 soldiers who fought in the front line in World War II, 48% exhibited symptoms like tremors, insomnia, nervousness, etc. The difference in the reported figures may, on the one hand, be due to differences between the events, but, on the other hand, it may also be due to a lack of willingness on the part of the soldiers to admit their symptoms or to a lack of willingness on the part of military authorities to recognize them.

What seems apparent is that investigators of civilian disasters perceive a continuum of certain symptoms that are common among people who go through a particularly stressful event, with the possibility of an increase in duration and intensity in some of them. Investigators of reactions to military stresses, however, tend to perceive a dichotomy and differentiate between those who break down and those who cope. Again, one wonders about the reasons for this difference in approach.

If war and other community disasters are basically crisis situations, maybe the comparison can be extended even further. Can the effects of a war on soldiers be compared to the effects of other situations, where a threat to life or personal integrity, or any personal loss is involved? The literature that deals with death in the family (Pincus, 1974), for example, illustrates well the point that if the loss is adequately dealt with, it can enrich the life of the survivor and improve both his ability to cope with further stresses and his concept of himself as a person and a "coper." The vast body of literature on various personal stresses makes it clear that stress involved both negative and positive effects; it can either make or break the person, or both.

How come, then, only negative terms have been used in the discussion of the effects of war upon participating soldiers? The interest of the military mental-health professionals in the soldier who "could not make it" is well understood. This kind of soldier has either to be returned to the battlefield or compensated. In both cases the interest is to "repair" the man and minimize the damage. It is, therefore, partially due to practical considerations that the negative effects of war upon soldiers have been focused upon. The soldier who went through his war experience without pronounced problems in functioning — or perhaps even benefited from the war experience — is thus of no concern to the military health professionals.

Theoretical orientation can be another possible explanation for this state of affairs. Military psychiatrists seem to lean basically on psychoanalytic principles. The motivational principle of psychoanalysis is homeostasis, which implies that the organism functions only when the equilibrium is disturbed, in order to reconstruct it. Therefore, a war is an event that upsets the system, and treatment should be given in order to get rid of the symptoms and bring the person back to his prewar balance (Grinker & Spiegel, 1963). The alternative motivational model is the one advocating growth, and it has been the core of humanistic and existential psychology. The model of growth assumes that a person is motivated to grow and develop. Why can't a person who fights a war grow and develop, and not only break down?

Only recently a few professional reports have come out that relate the reactions of soldiers to their war experiences regardless of psychiatric labeling. These reports focused on the effects of the traumatic war experiences on the inner world of soldiers rather than on their overt behavior, as was traditionally done. R. J. Lifton's book, *Home From the War* (1973), thoroughly investigates the effects of the Vietnam War on those who participated in it. The soldiers Lifton met and listened to in the rap groups he organized were simply soldiers who wanted to get together and talk about their war experience. In his discussion Lifton showed that out of the war came young men who suffered from excessive guilt feelings as a result of killing and surviving. At the same time, the war and the rap sessions made them reexamine their perceptions of themselves and their relationship to the norms and conventions of the society they were part of. The end product was, according to Lifton, young men who were more morally and socially conscious, with a clear antiwar commitment. Those, to Lifton, were positive effects on the one hand, and personal growth on the other.

Another very interesting document is the book *Tin Soldiers on Jerusalem Beach,* written by Amia Lieblich, a psychologist from Jerusalem. She presented the accounts, dreams, fears, and fantasies of young Israelis, including men who had participated in the Yom Kippur War as soldiers, as they came up in their gestalt groups.

Again, a soldier was portrayed as a person in search of his inner world. Dr. Lieblich noted that being in touch with one's feelings seemed the only way sanity could be maintained in a country where war has been a way of life.

It is becoming apparent that the impact of a war experience upon men who go through it as soldiers is broader than what can be dealt with in terms of symptoms. It is important to systematically explore the areas of life that can be affected positively and negatively by a war experience, and this is the aim of the present study. Due to the abundance of material, only findings that relate to the general effects of the war experience and their implications will be discussed.

METHOD

Subjects

The sample consisted of 34 young men who were interviewed between the years 1974 and 1976. They had one common denominator — having been in the front line — and thus having been exposed to enemy fire during the Yom Kippur War (October 1973–March 1974). When interviewed, however, all of them were civilians. They were between the ages of 22 and 42, with 25 as the median age. Many of them were students at the University of Haifa, were otherwise known to the author and her collaborator, Dror Wertheimer, or were referred to them by whoever knew that the study was in progress. It is by no means a representative sample; however, representation and generalization were not the aims of this study. The aim, rather, was to find out the range of possible effects of a life-threatening war experience on a person's subsequent life history and development.

Procedure: A Therapeutic Interview

The interviews were structured and included items concerning all the possible areas of life that could have been affected by life-threatening experiences in war. It should be stressed that the assessment of the effects was subjective, being given by the men themselves. The reason for this is that the author was interested in the way the soldiers were affected by the war, and not in the kinds of changes they actually underwent.

The process of interviewing turned into a story in its own right. The interviews were one to six hours long and were colored by intense emotionality. The interviewed men were occasionally carried away by their associations, which sometimes were not directly related to the questions asked but to elements of the combat experience. Some issues provoked resistance or denial in some men, and contradictions about the same issues were quite common.

As already mentioned, the emotional tone of the interviews was rather intense. It was apparent that the soldiers talked about an important and painful personal experience. Expressions of grief, anger, relief, euphoria, and other emotions were rather common. There were a few men whose depression and apathy seemed quite pronounced. The good feelings were associated with the relief of "getting things off one's chest," and, perhaps, also with the joy of remaining alive. In spite of the painful process of the exploration, the general level of motivation to tell and explore was very high.

The attitude toward the interview was not always uniform. There were men who, when the interview started, were open and cooperative, but as the interview progressed and touched upon specific topics (death, a future war), they became withdrawn and irritated and even wished to terminate the interview at that point. At the same time, there were others who at the beginning were reluctant and tense, but gradually opened up and demonstrated that they enjoyed the interview greatly.

It was quite common for the interviewed men to look for reassurance and evidence that the way they reacted to the war was normal. One common way of doing this can be seen in the following examples: "Other guys I know also started getting interested in other people," or "I am less self-confident. Other people are less self-confident too," or "I am more political minded. It is (a) nationwide (phenomenon)." Some asked for direct reassurance from the interviewers, that is, they wanted to know if their inclusion in the study was an indication that they were "spotted out," or if their confusion during the first part of the interview was exaggerated.

The attitudes toward the confrontation of traumatic material in the interview varied. Some exhibited apparent motivation to explore certain aspects of their war experiences that had not been completely worked out yet, two subjects expressed a wish or a need for professional help, and three came to the interview expecting professional counseling. Several men were rather ambivalent toward the process of exploration. They expressed a preference for avoiding issues dealing with the war, but seemed to enjoy the opportunity to talk about them. Two men strongly advocated forgetting. One of them said: "I want to forget. The interview brought up memories . . . . It causes tension." The other said: "Today the war is part of history and I don't want to . . . it is only history."

Another trend worth noting is that for some of the men it seemed important to prove that the war had changed them, implying that the change was for the better. Others rejected the possibility of being affected by the war and left the impression that they tried to shield themselves from the possibility of being negatively affected.

It seemed that the men who were interviewed during the first year of the study were more often carried away by their associations and exhibited more overt depression than the ones who were interviewed during the second year. The latter seemed somewhat more organized.

When asked to evaluate the merits of the interview, many of the men admitted that it was helpful. D. W. said: "It helped me to organize things within myself. On my own I would not have managed to organize things in all the areas." For many of them the interview was an opportunity for self examination. Some wanted to explore exactly what happened to them during the war. A. D. said: "I don't like to talk about it at all, but I try to help myself reduce the tensions. Therefore, it is better if I talk than if I keep quiet." Others tried to find out whether or not they could talk freely about the war issues. E. M. said: "Today I can see that I speak about the assault on Mount Hermon* like (one speaks of) eating candy. It shows that I worked things out. I am glad that (today) I speak about it freely." And others yet left the impression that it was important for them to present a positive picture of themselves for their own conviction.

Another use of the interview was "to get things off one's chest." M. E., who was elated throughout the interview, said: "I never happened to talk (about it). It is a very good opportunity. I think it will help (me)." And H. E. said: "I never told anyone about it, except my wife. I decided long ago that I need to tell (it) to somebody."

---

*The battle on Mount Hermon was a very fierce one.

RESULTS

General Effects

Before discussing the results it is important to examine the issue of data analysis. As pointed out earlier, the process of data collection was not an ordinary one. Since the issues covered in the interview were emotionally loaded, it seemed impossible to make a good and valid quantitative analysis or to analyze the responses to each item (completely) separately. Furthermore, it also seemed that narrowing down the richness of the interviewed soldiers' own expressions into numbers would not necessarily bring about the best assessment of the war impact. Since the aim of this presentation was to point out the overall psychological changes in the soldiers, we refer here only to the material collected under those items that deal with the more general impact of the war, and analyze the trends of the changes as reported by the soldiers. The orthodox experimental and clinical methods were used only to a limited extent. The soldiers' reports were translated verbatim from Hebrew.

Positive and Negative Effects of the War

One of the questions presented to the soldiers was: How do you evaluate the effect of the war upon you in positive and negative terms? The answers appear in Table 1-1.

These findings suggest that the war experience did, in fact, have both positive and negative effects upon the soldiers who participated in it, just as the theoretical model suggested.

Before making a more thorough analysis of the nature of the changes, it is worth examining both the men who were affected more positively and those who were affected more negatively. Unfortunately, data concerning the 34 men's prewar or preinterview personality characteristics or life histories were not available. However,

Table 1-1. Positive and Negative Effects of the War.

Positive, but also Negative	= 16
Negative, but also Positive	= 10
Positive only	= 3
Negative only	= 1
No Effect	= 1

it may be of interest to indicate that the ethnic background did seem to make a difference: Of the 16 soldiers who admitted "positive, but also negative change," 12 were of European origin (Ashkenazim) and 4 of Oriental origin (parents born in Iran, Iraq, Yemen and Greece). But among those who admitted "negative, but also positive change," 9 were of Oriental origin and 1 was of European origin.

There are several reasons why the young men of Oriental origin tended to be more negatively affected by their war experiences. The tendency among Oriental Jews to live in extended families may lead to a greater dependency of the individual upon the group and therefore lessen his ability to cope as an individual. Another possible factor may be that because many Oriental Jews belong to the lower socioeconomic classes, daily economic stresses lower the individual's ability to cope with further stress. Other factors like level of education, attitude toward authority, and external versus internal orientation may also play a part here. In order to arrive at scientifically based conclusions, a proper study of this particular aspect should be carried out separately.

Another finding that may be of interest is that out of 8 soldiers who did receive psychological help during or after the war, 7 indicated that the effect of the war experience upon them was "negative, but also positive." This may provide support for the statement made earlier, that it is the men who "broke down" that are seen by the military mental-health professionals. Even then it is interesting to note that in spite of the fact that those soldiers broke down, the war had some positive impact upon them too.

Factors like age, previous combat experience, and function during combat (fighting versus services), did not seem to make a difference. The present sample is of course not large enough to come to any conclusion with regard to the actual contribution of such factors. Additional situational factors should be included in order to better understand the sources of psychological gain and loss due to combat experience.

Existential Crisis vs. Combat Neurosis

The first question that was presented to the soldiers was designed to stimulate a spontaneous account of the effects of the war upon them. Their answers were grouped into a variety of categories of positive and negative change. It was found out that there was one central positive change and one central negative change.

The central positive change can be referred to as an existential change. This change consisted of a reevaluation of personal values and priorities, and it was expressed by some of the men in statements about how they had acquired more maturity, a more serious approach to life, a change in the priorities in life, a broader perspective, a soul search, etc. Nine soldiers reported such change in response to the first question, and eight more referred to it in answers given to other questions.

The overwhelming sense of this existential change was marked both by intense feelings of elation and pride and by the richness of expressions used to convey those feelings:

> D. S.:   I have a more comprehensive view of the world now; I see things from all angles.
>
> Y. H.:   I learned to differentiate between the more important and the less important things . . . [I learned] that much worse things can happen to you. The proportions between the more important and the less important have changed.
>
> H. E.:   The conditions of danger made me think intensively about problems that I otherwise would not have considered . . . . It emphasized the fact that what I had chosen before was right. Now I am willing to fight for it.
>
> E. M.:   I went through an enormous improvement. I matured by a million years. The war pushed me to greater extremes . . . to search myself . . . to judge people for better or for worse.
>
> N. E.:   More maturity. Maturity — this is the key word. A more realistic perception of things, more perspective . . . ."

What we see here is a reevaluation of one's self and one's relation to life and to the world around. As N. E. put it: "The war changed me a lot. There is in me much more self-awareness, openness, desire to look more deeply into more significant things. The war operates in many directions in terms of influence. An admission to a university, for example, influences only one area. The war influences more areas."

The most pronounced negative change category included symptoms like fear, tension, nervousness, nightmares, etc. To the first question, about the general effects of the war upon the soldiers, there were seven answers that spontaneously described such symptoms!

H. R.: What is left of all the influences that were upon me in the [combat] situation is only the fear. I am left with a fear of those things that I don't want to happen again.

Y. S.: I have dreams and nightmares . . . . Every noise startles me . . . .

A. D.: I think that the war ended only two months ago. It is hard for me to digest the fact that it ended two years ago. I think that I am still in 1973, because the whole time I remember the [battle] field. I live it more intensely. I hear a name that resembles a name of someone who was [there] with me, and it again revives the memories of that period. Or even the weather [report]. They say [on the radio] in the Golan Heights there will be so many degrees, or skiing conditions — and it brings back the memories of the Hermon.

Apparently, the most pronounced effects of the war are, on the one hand, the existential change or crisis, and, on the other hand, symptoms that are traditionally associated with combat neurosis, existing side by side, sometimes within, the same person.

"The Place of the War in Your Life"

As part of question 10, "What did you learn about yourself from your war experience?" the soldiers interviewed were asked to identify the place of the war in the continuum of their lives. It seems appropriate to deal with these perceptions here, as part of the general impact of the war experience. Thirteen men identified the war as a very remarkable event in their lives:

H. N.: The war is one of the most important points in my life, not the most important one.

R. S.: The war experience is prominent beyond any proportion . . . beyond the time it lasted.

Y. S.: [The war is] very important, traumatic event.

Y. D.: It stands out very prominently, it is hard to say in what way . . . in the feelings, in the fear, in whatever happened . . . an intense experience.

D. W.: A sad joke . . . . The war is something that does not resemble anything else . . . . The toughest stress situation I have ever gone through. It can't be compared to anything else.

H. E.: In a certain sense the war was a peak in my life. A certain peak. Since I grew up in a society whose ideal is the war . . . all the examples and the games were war . . . . And I wanted to experience war — and I did. Now all the things seem less intense. It [the war] is a criterion according to which I compare other experiences.

I. Y.: It is a stage in terms of the feeling of insecurity. The most central stage . . . .

A. D.: It will be the peak of the curve. And after it — [there is] nothing. The line does not go any further.

M. G.: The war is one of the most important landmarks . . . . It is not simply [there] in the continuum [of my life]. From it I started a new development.

R. M.: The war changed a lot . . . . When I think of the past, I see it [my life] as a very even plateau until the war period [came]. It is like I see myself only from the war period on, because I changed. To me, the war is a very big, black thing and it protrudes sharply [from the plateau] when I look back.

A. B.: If I went through crises in my life, this [the war] is definitely the most difficult of the latest period.

E. R.: The highest [in influence].

A. E.: It sticks out but it is not the most dominant. I prefer not to include it. When I talk about periods [of my life], it is until the war and after the war. The war [itself] is an isolated, out-of-the-ordinary period.

Even with those who assigned the war a minimal place in their lives, one cannot escape the feeling that a different, stronger truth lies behind the spoken words:

E. E.: It fits in like [a chapter] in a story, in installments: school, the draft . . . just like the other things. It is like a pause in

> [my] life. I feel the war upon me because of the injury.
> I have an invalid's card. I went through the war and it left
> a mark . . . .
>
> D. A.: I would speak [about it] in a few words: I participated.
> I would go over it briefly. I would not emphasize. It is a
> negative concept.

The general sense is of an event that was traumatic, but not necessarily negative.

SPECIFIC EFFECTS

Since we established the existence of the existential crisis, we shall
now review the effects of the war experience on psychological areas
that directly relate to such a crisis. The three areas chosen were:
the soldiers' perceptions of themselves, their relationships with others,
and their attitudes towards the issues of life and death.

Change of Self-Concept

Self-confidence and Self-esteem.   Going through the war experience made
many of the men change their perception of themselves and some of
their ways of relating to the world. Many of them reported changes,
both positive and negative, in self-esteem and self-confidence. There
were soldiers who were surprised by their own competence and
adaptability during combat and became convinced that they could
cope with life stresses better than they ever suspected.

D. S., who served as a tank commander during the war, reported: "I
learned to appreciate myself more. I would not have believed that I am
capable to hold out the way I did." Elsewhere he said about himself:
"During the combat I was very careful. I acted according to all the rules
I had learned. If I were injured, it would have been a shame for me. I
was very active. I took upon myself more tasks than was expected
from me." And he gave as an example how, after his gunner had become
"shell-shocked," for seven days, in addition to being the tank commander, he was also the gunner. Apparently, for D.S. the way he carried out
his tasks as a fighter, his ability to play the game as he understood was
expected of him, perhaps even overestimating his criteria of good
performance — all of it served to increase his basic sense of self-worth.

E. M. also reported feeling more worthy as a person after his combat experience: "I did not run away, . . . I proved myself. *To me* it was important."   R. M. drew a sense of self-respect because he handled his fear during combat with more dignity and self-control than the other people around him. Y. D. felt better about himself because he volunteered to join his battalion and fight. He said: "I discovered about myself [that I could volunteer] and I am rather proud of myself, because I never thought I would do it, without being called for, and with my family putting pressure on me [against it] . . . ." Again, we saw how one's ability to function under pressure or in spite of pressure was an important discovery to the soldier and reflected upon his self-image as a competent and worthy person.

The perception of the war experience as a test for one's psychological strength was either directly or indirectly communicated by several soldiers. Y. H. said: "I tested myself. In one respect I proved [myself], and in another respect I did not . . . . On the whole I fulfilled my expectations; most often, I functioned above and beyond, but the performance was not [always] perfect."

Apparently, we cannot escape Erikson's (1968) notion that the formation of one's self-identity is influenced by the communal identity. Thus, it seems that in a country like Israel, where war has been a way of life, going through a war without breaking down might be perceived not only as a personal victory of competence but also as passing the society's "initiation rite" and finally belonging to it as an adult. H. E. put it very clearly: "In some sense it [the war] is a peak in my life . . . . Since I grew up in a society whose ideal was war, all the examples and games were war . . . . And I wanted to experience war — and I did . . . ."

One's standards for self-evaluation are a product of the culture that one belongs to, and are shared by others of that culture. Another reported source for increased self-esteem was, therefore, the respect one received on return from the war. Because someone was a soldier where the action was, people treated him both as a hero and as a reliable source of information. A. S. said: "My status improved, especially because of [my] severe injury. People treated me differently, and it made me become more self-confident in conducting my affairs." D. S. then said: " [My brothers] always respected me as the oldest brother, but now my status among them improved a lot. They see me as a hero, [they] come to me for advice, [they] say that I am a man. It is sometimes embarrassing . . . . Girls and friends respect me more now . . . ."

Failing to prove oneself in combat seemed to have a severe meaning for some of the fighters. A. N. said: "I would say that I should not have been in the paratroopers. It is possible that I asked of myself more than I should have, and I took upon myself too much. It is possible that inside me I had felt all along that it was not for me. I should not have been a fighter because of fears and because of guilt feelings that I send someone else to get killed.   I think I knew it and the war had proved it more definitely. With all the will and everything, it proved that I am not strong enough for such a mission." A. N.'s conflict was a very difficult one.   Being the eldest of 10 children and the first paratrooper* from his development town could have been great boosts to his ego.   But, at the same time, he could not regard his fears during the war nor his concerns about sending his men to imminent death as either normal or positive feelings. As a result, he suffered considerable depreciation of his self-esteem.

A similar conflict was expressed by Y. H.: "I did not expect myself to cry, but I could not stop myself. I know that if I did, I would have gone into a much deeper crisis."

Unlike A. N., M. M. presented a different approach toward his own fears during the war and, consequently, his self-esteem did not seem to suffer. He said: "I am not a hero. I am afraid. I did not experience fear before [the war]. Today this is a general phenomenon. I am not ashamed that I am afraid, it is a natural reaction . . . ."

The loss of self-confidence was not only due to performance failure with respect to one's own standards and those of the society, but also to a carry-over of the sense of helplessness felt during combat. Y. C. said: "I learned that I see myself as [a] weaker [person], less capable to stand up in life, without self-confidence, and it bothers me."   And M. N. said: "I am still helpless in facing things . . . ." E. M. reported that feeling insignificant during the war left him with a tendency to depreciate himself. He said: "I don't care if I die . . . . Man is a nothing . . . [until recently] the lack of consideration for myself was rather pathological . . . [during the war] there was [in me] indifference to death. Why should I care if I die? Why should I appreciate myself?"

---

*A highly prestigious military corps, similar in prestige to the American Marine Corps.

I. Y. said that the war was significant because of the sense of in-security it introduced. He expressed his loss of faith in the strength and the future of Israel. The realization that his country may not be a stable support could have contributed to his loss of self-confidence. At the same time, it is also possible that the worry about the future of the country was a projection of his personal feelings of vulnerability.

Spontaneity and self-assertion vs. impulsiveness and aggression. As a result of their war experiences, some of the soldiers interviewed found themselves to be more open and direct in expressing their ideas and feelings and in daring to say what they really thought. They reported less self-consciousness about the reactions of other people to them. E. M. reported a new kind of spontaneity that he was pleased with. He said: "I am more spontaneous, freer (Q: How does it show?) In my work with the team, we laugh more, we talk more. I can more easily give compliments, something which used to be very hard for me." One gets the impression that his new spontaneity is an expression of the desire to enjoy life more, as a counterbalance to what he went through during the war. It may also be that with the heightened value of life there is less willingness to waste energy on pretending and conforming.

Along with spontaneity new attempts at self-assertion were also reported. Y. A. said: "The war contributed to my self-confidence. People respect me more. I dare to speak with people openly." D. W. said: "Today I do whatever I feel like doing. I say unpleasant things in company . . . ." A. E. said: "Today I criticize and get angry. At home I criticize my mother more. I am more critical toward her, toward everyone in the family. It was a taboo [before]. In the past I used to sit with the family. Today if someone irritates me, I get up and leave. It's all right."

In the above three cases it is difficult to differentiate between expressions of self-assertion and spontaneity, or between impulsive-ness and aggression. It may be concluded that there was an increase in self-confidence, but there also appeared a tendency to less self-control, more tolerance toward one's own aggressiveness and use of aggression as an outlet for feelings of frustration and depression. Y. S.'s words demonstrate the latter very clearly: "I have discovered in me personality traits that I did not know existed – aggressiveness, inability to delay gratification. Today I don't delay gratification. I don't save money. I don't make long-range plans. Whatever I can do at the moment I do. It is not nice because it opposes the values that I had been brought up with. It creates conflicts. Before the war I was a restrained person. But on Shavuot Eve (a Jewish holiday) I beat up someone until he went to the police. My threshold to anger got lower . . . ."

Y. S. seemed to feel proud of becoming less restrained, but at the same time this kind of behavior contradicted his previous values. His ambivalence was also related to the fact that his inner boundary between self-assertion and aggressiveness was not well defined, and he was concerned about it. The ambivalence conveyed by Y. S. toward the changes that took place in him was often expressed by the other interviewees as well.

Opening the Eyes: Skepticism vs. Suspicion.   A response given in almost every interview and spontaneously brought up by 10 of the 34 soldiers was that the war had opened their eyes and made them see things as they really are. They came to realize that what they had believed in before was false, and thus they lost faith in all authority, civilian as well as military. H. R. defined this kind of reaction as follows: "It [the effect] is positive because the war opened my eyes rather than closed them." Y. S. said: "It was an awakening from all kinds of ideas and conventions that I used to think were important."

Naive ideas about different facets of life in Israeli society were discarded. Some lost a naive belief in their leaders' intentions and ability to end wars. N. E. put it: "[It is negative] that we have to go on fighting after we lived with the illusion that everything was all right." Others, probably the ones that had fought in a war for the first time, awakened to the realization of what war was all about. Y. A. stated: "I am not in the garden of fools I was [in] before. When I was on reserve duty [lately], I was more tense. When I use a gun, it does not seem like a toy anymore." The loss of naive beliefs resulted in growing suspicions and increased vigilance against such things happening again.

The mistrust was mainly focused on the leaders. They were blamed for the war; theirs was the responsibility for what had happened. When leadership was discussed, anger was always added to the mistrust. D. A. said: "The war made me hate leadership. People sit at the top and send other people to get killed. This is why I hate them. Until today I don't trust them and I don't care what happens to them." R. S. said: "When you participate in combat you ask yourself, Why? What do I fight for? Today I am more curious to know the reasons and [find out] who are the people responsible."

This process of "opening the eyes" seemed to range from alertness and realism, which the men regarded as positive changes, to suspicion and excessive criticism, which they sometimes felt restricted them. Concerning the possibility of coexistence of these elements, A. K. said: "I question more, I am careful, [I am] more calculated. Once I was more cheerful. I had my head in the clouds. Today I have my two feet on the ground." About being overly critical, Y. D. said: "It could have been good if I were less critical. The world would have seemed rosier. I would have been more successful in giving of myself, while now I am [too] careful."

There seems to be a relationship between the increase in skepticism and an increasing interest in politics, which many of the soldiers reported. E. E. said: "I became more interested in politics. I care more. I feel more [of an] Israeli. I listen to things and analyze them. It was not [this way] before [the war]. You find out certain things. You try to scream, to say that you saw it . . . . I am more of an Israeli because I say that as a citizen of this country I have to protect its interests. We have gone through wars and we will go [through more wars]. Whether it is me or them, we will have to fight." Apparently, E. R.'s interest in politics was a means to ensure that the ruling political party would make appropriate preparations for the next war. For H. R., however, turning to politics seemed to serve the opposite purpose: "(I want) to try to do everything that I can in order to prevent the next war."

The tendency toward mistrust of authority was a reaction that Lifton (1973) reported existed very strongly among the Vietnam veterans. He wrote: "There is something special about Vietnam veterans. Everyone who has contact with them seems to agree that they are different from veterans of other wars. A favorite word to describe them is "alienated." Veterans Administration reports stress that veterans' sensitivity to issues of authority and autonomy. This group of veterans is seen as having greater distrust of institutions and unwillingness to be awed by traditional authorities." (p. 35). Wolfenstein (1957) also described it as a common reaction after disasters, and enumerated possible explanations for it.

Vigilance and alertness are also reactions that are common after experiencing a stressful event (Janis, 1971). They seem to help one cope with, or even prevent future stress. Janis presents the problem of maintaining a state of "discriminating alertness," that is, to avoid apathy on the one hand and paranoia on the other. The same problem seems to hold true for Israeli society on the whole.

Change in Interpersonal Relations

Attitude Towards People in General. The general attitude towards people changed too. There was a pronounced expression of a greater need for closeness, a more tolerant attitude toward people, and deeper relationships with others in 16 out of the 34 subjects. The growing tolerance for others was explained by R. S. as follows: "When [one's] life is in a perpetual danger, when you see how meaningless you are, you learn to appreciate other people, to be less critical of them."

Of course, the realization of one's meaninglessness on the battle-field, where man's life seems worthless, made others lose confidence in human value and power. R. M. said: "The most pronounced thing [influence] is [the realization that] human life is of no value, neither my own life, nor anyone else's." The quick transition from an alive and active person to a lifeless mutilated body, and the sight of a great number of bodies lying around could not leave one indifferent. The interesting point, however, was that the same experience affected people so differently.

Y. B. found himself to be more tolerant with people after the war. He did not dare to express anger at them, as he had been used to before, because "I happened to kill people. I started thinking: What is my right to kill him? . . . He is human . . . ." But as a result of this realization and guilt, Y. B. turned against himself, and, he reported, he was a different, less adequate person: "If I was a closed person before, now I am twice as closed. I think more. I isolate myself more. I became difficult to befriend."

Unlike Y. B., most of those who felt more tolerant to others also sought their closeness. E. E. said: "I am closer to people. People are closer to me. I seek closeness much more: friends, family. Above all — family. I don't feel like being alone." E. E.'s description of his growing closeness to people may also imply growing dependency on them in a restricting sense.

A. D. also reported a growing need for friends and closeness, but his feeling was associated with a different component of the experience of the war, one of loss and grief. He said: "I need more friends. As many as possible. If one goes, you don't remain alone. There is an alternative. But if there are [only] a few . . . if one isn't there any more, then we are finished [as people]."

A. D. himself attributed his change with regard to people to another factor: "I help more and want to help more. And when I see people who don't help, I get angry. (Q: Why?) Maybe because this is the way I was educated in the army, to help." A. D. was 22 when interviewed, and 18 when drafted. This period consists of the formative adult years. (Erikson, 1968; Lifton, 1973). Thus, one can acquire new values and behaviors both in the military service and in war. However, since we have dealt with young people, people who are changing and growing anyway, it is sometimes difficult to determine which effects can be attributed to the war and which to the normal process of growing up.

The change in attitude towards people and its roots in the war experience is demonstrated by I. Y.'s words: "I noticed that the field of [relations with and services to] the older people was neglected in the kibbutz and it preoccupies me more. In the past it was possible [for me] to say: "Those old bores." Today I understand them better . . . . As a result of the war, you see them [and realize] that those [who fell] were their sons . . . ." I. Y., like Y. B., demonstrated the survivor's guilt. Unlike Y. B., I. Y., who is an older fellow (42) with a more secure background and personality, managed to sublimate his guilt and involve himself in a useful and gratifying activity — taking care of the old people of his kibbutz.

As commented on earlier, some men reported "closing up" and becoming more critical of people; they were, however, fewer than the ones who reported more closeness and tolerance towards others. The loss of interest in people seemed to be one aspect of a more general process. Martha Wolfenstein (1957) reported that during the impact phase of a disaster people tend to grow more narcissistic; there is a constriction of emotional concern, a transfer of mental energy from the outside to the inside, in an attempt to reorganize and to compensate oneself for being hurt. Wolfenstein claims that while this kind of reaction is most typical at the time of impact, if maintained it may be due to difficulties in handling one's own aggression, ambivalence, or strong identification with the dead.

The attitude toward this growing criticism toward others varied among the men. There were some who felt embarrassed by it and wished they acted differently. In two young men the impression was that they grew more exclusive and liked it. D. W. said: "Today I am a little bit more demanding in my requirements. In the past I could stand stupid people. Today I either cut off or kick . . . ." And A. E. said: "I respect a man who went through an experience like mine." The first demonstrates more tolerance to expressing aggression, while the second one seems to use his "heroism" as a source of worth, and perhaps of compensation.

Attitude Toward Wife or Girlfriend. The present sample included 19 single and 15 married men. Twenty-four of them reported transient or continuous changes toward their partners.

Impact upon the single men. Five men got married after the war and one was about to marry the girl he met during the war. We don't know how representative these figures are nor how good the marriages are. One man admitted that having someone waiting for him gave him strength, and meeting with the beloved person whenever possible during the war was important to "recharge the batteries." Another man said that the ability of a woman to understand what he had gone through helped him to select his future wife: "[During the war] I wrote many letters . . . . I found myself writing to some girl and not sending [the letters] to her . . . . When I told her, she did not understand. But my wife did understand. My wife is a more sensitive and a warmer person than the other girl. I *needed* to share feelings." For H. R. the act of marriage was a symbol, a celebration of life: "I think that the war influenced the date of the wedding. I wanted to live. The marriage symbolized the continuation of life."

E. M. did not get married but he has developed a desire for a permanent relationship, which he did not have before the war: "If in the past I was looking for a screw, today I am looking for something permanent. I don't have the energy to play around. The mere fact that I have a steady girlfriend is a novelty. I want to settle down and she is someone that you can settle down with." Again, it is difficult to determine how much of a 24-year-old-man's wish to settle down is a function of his war experience or simply of growing up.

There were four other men who admitted that they wanted to get married right after the war, or at least form a close relationship then. M. N. explained the process of forming a close relationship with a woman after the war and then giving it up: "I became attached to a girl during the war and went through a strong emotional experience. I wanted to get married right after the war, but it did not materialize. Today, I deliberate more, I want to experience more, I am looking for a greater variety of things in a woman . . . ." On the one hand, this may be a rationalization for trying to maintain one's independence in spite of all, but, on the other hand, M. N.'s consideration is a valid one: that for a marriage to succeed one should seek in a partner for more than the characteristics relevant in a relationship during or immediately after a war.

Three men stated categorically that the war reduced their motivation to get married. D. W. said: "Among the guys we used to say: it is not worth getting married, because later there will be orphans. In the coming three to four years I have no plans to get married. I am not for a steady girlfriend. Beforehand I was considered as more serious in this respect." A. D. said: "After the war I said to myself: there is no point in making a wife and children miserable. It is better alone . . . ." This, of course, may reflect both the fear to hurt others but also the fear of being hurt again by getting closer to people and then losing them.

An altogether different line of reasoning was presented by R. M.: "Most of the girls did not go through such an experience. An anti attitude has been formed in me. Why is it men who have to die? I have something against society's legitimizing the death of young men. I have formed [an] identification with young men."

Impact upon married men.   Of the twelve men who were married at the time of the war, five reported greater closeness to their wives and a general increase in the importance of the family in their life. The relationship between the war experience and the growing closeness with one's wife was clearly expressed by M. M. who said: "[The war affected me] favorably. She [the wife] discovered that I am important to her. This was a chain reaction. I discovered that I am more attached to her. Today we feel closer to each other. We fight less. But this impact is gradually decreasing. In the war, when I talked with her on the phone, I felt good. Later I started feeling down, I felt that I was far away and I could get killed. I told my wife about my war experiences. She was happy that I came back. That helped me. The fact that I could tell her made it easier for me."

N. E. and R. S. demonstrated the way that this process of getting closer evolved and gave more specific expressions of this change. N. E. said: "We should distinguish between the period that came right after [the war] and between today. Right after the war there was a retesting of the relationship. Today the relationship is of a better quality, [it is] deeper. We have more conversations, more honesty [between us]. Right after the war I was growing distant from my wife. Today [there is] more closeness. Today I am more willing to compromise [when there are] things that I don't like . . . ." R. S. said: "The family gave me a very good welcome when I came back. Everyone knew that it was going to be a common job to re-build the family life. At first it felt somewhat artificial. Today there is more consideration, more talk between my wife and me . . . . We learned to appreciate, understand, forgive more. It is not an ideal situation, but there is more cooperation."

N. E. made it clear that on his return from the war there was a period of growing distance between him and his wife as he with-drew and was less available to her. A. B. also reported this kind of difficulty in relating to his newly wedded wife, a fact that gave a bad start to the marriage: "The war introduced a certain tension [between us]." Both N. E. and A. B. reported that the growing apart period did not last and was followed by a lasting period of growing closer. At the same time, M. M. reported that the initial closeness started to deteriorate with time. A. N. and E. R. reported being distant from their wives, a result of a process that started after the war. In A. N.'s case, he came back from the war in a state of shock. As a result, his wife grew more independent. This disturbed him and put a strain upon their relationship. He said: "I am more critical [now]. Before the war I did more around the house. I did most of the shopping according to my taste. After the war I let her be more on her own. Today she does the shopping by herself. She does whatever she wants. She went out to work. It relieves me from many responsibilities, but why does she need a separate bank account? Maybe she will buy something that I would not like? It stands against the tradition I come from. In spite of the problems I see that she does her duties and the kids are well taken care of."

E. R. who got injured during the war, reported feeling very dis-appointed with himself for not being able to satisfy his wife's wishes: "Especially when she comes back from work and says, 'Let's go for a walk.' " He was also very angry with her for coming to him with demands that he could not fulfill. Consequently, he felt the marriage was on the edge of a breakdown.

We have seen so far that each man's participation in the war affected not only his personal balance, but also the balance of his interpersonal relationships. In some cases the new balance was conscious, mutual, and perceived as positive. In other cases the new balance involved a change in one partner [physical or psychological] that alienated the other partner, and a deterioration in the marriage followed. As mentioned before, it is difficult to assess the actual change only on the basis of what the men said. For example, if someone reported growing closer to his wife after the war, it is possible that in actuality he grew more dependent upon her.

Attitude Toward Children. Primarily, the men showed increased con-cern for their children's future. They fear that their children's lives would be threatened by another war or that they would grow up without fathers. The intense concern for the children's welfare can, of course, be a projection of the men's concern for their own lives and futures.

Among the single men there was an objection in principle to hav-ing children because "later they would not have fathers." Among the married men there was concern for the future of the children they already had. E. M. said: "Before the war I saw myself [in the future] when my children will be older. But today a doubt [about my survival] is creeping in. [When] I see my daughters happy, I think: How sad it will be . . . . I also give more time to my daughters."

In spite of the worry and concern about the future, there were several men who expressed a strong desire to have more children and greater closeness with those they had. A. E. explained his desire for a child as follows: "This is the reason why we are getting married, because we want a child. I don't want a child. I want a *son*. In my view a son can carry his father's name. I don't want an end to the family's continuity. In the war it bothered me a lot." H. E. said: "I had always wanted a child. My child is not a direct result of the war, but in my thinking he is. The child is important to me because [during the war] I wanted home and continuity. I wanted that something of me should remain. The thought that haunted me in difficult times was: How it is that I disappear like that . . . ." A. E. and H. E.'s expression of their desire "to leave a mark" through children is a common human expression in the face of death and the realization of human finiteness (Shneidman, 1974).

Wanting "to leave a mark" brought R. S. closer to his children. He said: "I always felt close to the children. Now, I feel closer. I want to give more . . . I can die . . . I think more about the close people [relationships] I want to leave behind. I want to give more of myself. I want to leave a mark on the relationships." M. M. also felt that he grew closer to his son, but he attributed this process more directly to what he went through during the war: "I thought much more about him [during the war]. Now I love him more. When I came on leave he was very attached to me. It hurt me to see the look on his face when I went back." E. E. was hospitalized during the war and as a result got the necessary perspective to reexamine his relationship with his daughter. He said: "In the convalescent home I had time to think. My daughter was three and a half years old then. I felt that I did not behave with her the way I wanted. I did not understand that she was just a child. I demanded from her things I would demand from an adult . . . . Today I changed my attitude. I began to take more interest. I read more in this area, and it helps."

The men expressed special considerations with regard to sons. All of a sudden they were perceived as future soldiers, and this realization was frightening. H. R. wished he had girls instead of the son he had. I. Y. found himself treating his son differently: "Today I would not push him as hard. I prefer him happy rather than pushed. I am more tolerant with the children. You realize that life does not have much value, so why push him so hard?" I. Y. illustrated how his war experience affected the values that he transmits to his children. He also spoke of what it is like to be an Israeli parent and bring up children with the apprehension that they too will have to go through war as soldiers.

Issues of Life and Death

In one of the questions, the soldiers were asked about the effects of the war upon their attitudes and feelings concerning the issues of life and death. This kind of discussion led to a wide range of emotional reactions, from a factual, emotionless report, to elation, sadness, and overt anger and restlessness. Two or three men even attempted to terminate their interview at this point.

The general effect of the war experience with regard to death was either a greater tendency to avoid the topic or greater preoccupation with it. A more specific analysis showed that, since the war, 12 men reported not having or not wanting to have any preoccupation with this matter, while 15 reported being preoccupied with it in different ways. Simultaneously, there was a pronounced tendency to evaluate life more and enjoy it better after the war. There were 8 reports of growing appreciation of life and 12 reports of enjoying life bettter or wanting to get as much as possible out of it. At the same time, 6 subjects reported that they were growing indifferent to many things in life.

Attitude Toward Death. Encounters with death apparently had definite impacts on the later lives of the soldiers. G. T. defined it as follows: "I don't think that a person who went through the experience of facing death can ever get rid of it entirely. It does not affect my daily performance, and yet there is some unclear state of mind, a state of anxiety . . . of what can happen."

Facing death in war made many of the young men realize, all of a sudden, that one can die, that they can die and that dying is an irreversible process. R. M. said: "Before the war I was quite innocent and took life for granted. Killing a person was something that was unfamiliar to me. But when you see dozens of dead and when you can get killed in no time – it is different. Now I feel that death is more probable . . . ." H. R. said: "In this war death became more concrete . . . I saw death face to face . . . I saw how easy it is to pass from a state of being to a state of not being, and this easiness frightens me." Apparently, the war experience not only made one more familiar with death but also more afraid of it.

There were also frequent thoughts about the possibility of an untimely death, about the fact that one can die, and not necessarily of old age. A. N. said: "Before the war I used to take life for granted. Now I realize that death can arrive in the middle of adulthood. This does not fit the ideas I previously had about life and death." D. W. said: "If I lived in Canada or Sweden, I could have the chance to live up to the age of 120, but here it is a professional hazard." Not only can death happen any time, but in Israel it is especially possible for a young man to die. D. W. seemed to refer to this point with resignation, and even with a touch of pride, while E. S., with a sad expression on his face, said: "I wish I were born in another country, where there are no wars."

While there were some men who admitted that after their war experiences they became more fearful of death, there were others who felt that facing death in the war was actually a strengthening experience. The mere fact that during the war they were close to death and came back alive proved their invulnerability. The explicit reasons for this effect varied. Y. A. saw in the fact that he could have died but did not — a proof that he was invulnerable. N. E. claimed that since he had seen death, it was not a stranger to him and he did not have to imagine it any longer. Therefore he has been less preoccupied with it since the war. For him, as often reported in the literature, reality, however threatening, was easier to deal with than fantasy. For D. A. the encounter with death made dealing with this issue easier because of a yet different reason. He said: "Once I used to be afraid for myself. To me death was something very frightening, because you don't know what will happen afterwards. Maybe I was afraid because I believed that there was hell. Today I don't believe in it. When I saw people die, maybe I got the courage to die."

The subjects reported different ways of coping with the fear of death. Twelve claimed denial or conscious avoidance of the topic. Some of them simply said that they did not think about death or did not want to think about it. A. E. said: "I reached the conclusion that I don't want to mess with it." Y. S., however, had an explanation for his avoidance behavior: "I try to think about it as little as possible . . . I try to avoid it . . . I have achieved a certain balance when I don't think about it." There were also other reasons for not thinking about death. A. B. said: "I am not looking for an explanation. I used to try, but I came to the conclusion that there are things that I have no answer for." M. A. said: "I don't think why I am alive. What is it good for? This kind of philosophizing is not going to save me."

Five of the soldiers said that they did not think that they would die. The belief in the impossibility of one's death seemed to be supported either by personal or collective invulnerability ("I don't think I will die" vs. "It is impossible for it to happen because we are strong").

An attitude of indifference to death ("I don't care if I die") was brought up by two men who felt either a great fear of death, disguised by depression or apathy, or an acceptance of the role of sacrifice. An example of self-sacrifice accompanied by a feeling of worthlessness is the case of A. D. He said: "I am a small screw in the world around me. To myself I don't attribute any significance. And the proof for it are those who died. Everyone is like a screw. It does not make any difference to the society. (Q: Why is it better that you die?) Because they are many and I am one. It is better that I die than them . . . I respect the lives of others, not my own. When the examinations come, it does not matter to me if I don't prepare and give my notebooks to someone else . . . I get by with a minimum."

A. D.'s need to sacrifice his own welfare as an expression of fate touches upon the guilt feelings of the survivor. As in the various accounts of Lifton on this matter, we also met here expressions like "Why am I alive?" with a strong flavor of guilt concerning one's own survival, and the perception of the deaths of others as having made it possible ("Maybe they died for me"). This raised the need to make some sacrifice.

There were still other soldiers who talked about death not in terms of indifference but rather in terms of acceptance. In both cases the reasoning accompanying the expressed attitude was similar but the emotional tone was different.

An active attempt to master death was expressed by H. E. who said: "It interests me. It seems like a topic that people ignore. I tried to confront the experience of death. I read a lot about people who committed suicide. I think I am calm." H. R. reported a similar attempt at mastery: "The thoughts about death come periodically. I don't try to suppress them. I try to express myself. It comes out in my poetry." M. M. seemed to simply come to terms with his fear of death: "I am not such a hero. I am afraid. I had not experienced such fear before the war . . . . But I am not ashamed that I am afraid . . . . Fear is a natural thing."

The encounter with death left four soldiers preoccupied with suicide. M. N. said: "I don't think of death in war. Of suicide, I do think. I admire those who deliberately commit suicide, because they act their wish out. I had not thought this way before the war. In the war your fate is not in your hands. In suicide, yes. I myself am not capable of committing suicide."

Another trend that came up was the tendency of some men to become more careful after the war. In the war they became aware of the fact that a certain act could easily terminate one's life. Therefore, some young men reported consciously trying to guard against this happening. D. W. said: "I look left and right when I cross the street, so it wouldn't happen to me." And A. N. said: "The mere fact that I don't change my low medical profile is because it is in the army that my life can come to an end." Although A. N.'s passivity with regard to his low medical profile could increase his chances of remaining alive in the future, he was quite depressed about it. Apparently, he did not live up to his own expectations and the social norms.

Others projected their concern about their own deaths onto their families. This kind of concern was reported to occur either during the war or afterwards. E. E., A. N. and E. M., with regard to their possible deaths, were greatly worried about their children's welfare and future. Concerns about wives or fathers suffering breakdowns were also expressed.

Several soldiers reported preoccupation with their dead comrades. I. Y. said with great sadness: "I get to think about them very often." R. M. said: "You are aware of the fact that the others died. You go on having conversations with people who are not alive anymore. . . . I feel comfortable talking freely about the dead, instead of saying that it is forbidden to mention them." Whenever this issue came up it was apparent that there was a great amount of grief experienced by the interviewed soldiers. Some let themselves feel the grief and express it, whereas a few others were either overwhelmed by grief or tried to cut short the discussions about it.

Attitude Toward Life. The value of life definitely increased. Many of the soldiers emphasized the fact that life had more meaning for them after the war. Often the reference to the heightened value of life came in one and the same breath with its opposite — death — as faced during the war. A. K. said: "My attitude toward death did not change. The attitude toward life changed. So many soldiers fell in the Chinese Farm.* Today I appreciate life enormously. I have a fantastic desire to live. I don't believe I will die. My faith in life was not shaken even when I saw all the atrocities, the torn bodies, etc." Of course, the value of one's own life increased because one was very close to losing it. Y. A. said: "Life that was taken for granted before all of a sudden seemed like something special, like a gift."

With the realization of their own vulnerability, many of the soldiers emphasized that they wanted to get as much enjoyment and meaning as possible out of their lives. R. S. said: "I want to take more advantage of life, to enjoy more. I look around more, I pay more attention, things taste better to me, instead of always being in a hurry. My hierarchy of priorities has changed in favor of the present and the enjoyable." Y. B. said: "I enjoy the smaller things — landscapes, sunset. Before the war I did not like the sea at all. All of a sudden I found out that it is peaceful and good." H. N. said: "I simply enjoy myself more and want to take more advantage of life. I travel more because the country is beautiful, and I want to see beautiful things. I also enjoy more listening to music."

Coming back from the war with the commitment to enjoy life more was not easy in practice. E. E. got disheartened: "It is difficult to carry out in practice the wish to take advantage of life. Only if one had a lot of money is it possible to fulfill one's dreams. In the meanwhile, I can dream, it does not cost me anything."

Besides the wish to have more enjoyment in life, many soldiers expressed the desire to make their lives more meaningful, to use their potential to the full, to achieve actualization. Few reported on concrete steps taken in this direction. Z. H. said: "I remember that after the war I was convinced that I had not achieved anything. If something had happened to me, I would have felt that I had not achieved anything, that I am a nothing, that I am losing out . . . . I started to wish that things will be more meaningful, the work that I do will be more meaningful. I know that what I am doing now [studying social work] is meaningful." H. E. said: "I now regard more favorably the attempt to change what I don't approve of, in order for things to be better. This is why I decided to study."

---

*A famous battle on the southern bank of the Suez Canal, where many Israeli soldiers fell.

Whereas many of the soldiers reported with elation their growing appreciation of life, some expressed the opposite, disillusionment and despair: life lost its meaning as one realized how easy it was to die, and how meaningless death was. M. A. said: "I don't care much about life. I live from one day to another . . . . I know that there will be another war, and who knows if I will survive it. The probability for a tank driver to live is high." This growing sense of vulnerability following a near-miss experience, the experience that one could have been killed, is widely reported in the literature (Janis, 1971).

Some soldiers did report a feeling of senselessness and apathy. E. E. said: "After the war I became lazier, more apathetic. My wife takes care of everything. I don't think about the war at all. Before the war I was scared of war, today I am not. I know what awaits me. I know there will be another war, that thousands will be killed, but we will go on existing. Before, I used to take things personally. Now, I don't. After the war, when I came back to civilian life, I heard that this guy fell, that that guy was left with no leg or hand, and I started to get apathetic . . . ." This sense of apathy seemed to stem both from the traumatic experience of the past and from a threatening and insecure future. If what happened can happen again, then one's efforts to fight fate are senseless.

It is interesting that facing death under similar circumstances led some people to optimism and action, and others to pessimism and resignation.

DISCUSSION

At the beginning we took it upon ourselves to examine the scope of the impact of war upon soldiers whose lives were endangered. The data indicate that the war was a very significant life event for many of them, and that their reactions to it touched upon the core of their existence, including both positive and negative reactions. Many of them went through an existential crisis and reported to have come out of it with greater personal strength and appreciation of life.

How can we explain, then, the existential changes and personal growth resulting from the soldiers' war experiences? Today there exists a rich body of literature concerning death and death realization. Kastenbaum (1971) described the following effects of facing

death: "In the face of death our experience can be grouped into two classes: The first group consists of emotions of anxiety . . . .
The second group consists of a reevaluation of our values, our
relations to other people and to ourselves, and a reassessment of
the total plan and meaning of our life. This response is sustained
in any serious confrontation with the reality and realization of
our death" (p. 259). Eissler (1955) claims that: "The knowledge
or the vague feeling that the end is approaching may enable some
persons to step aside, so to speak, and view themselves and significant sectors of their lives with humility and also with insight into
the futility of so much passionately living in it" (p. 53).

What both Kastenbaum and Eissler described as the effects of
facing death resembles very much the reactions to their war experiences reported by our thirty-four young men. They did report a
reevaluation of their values, their relations with other people and
with themselves, and a reassessment of the total plan and meaning
of their lives. They also reported a change in perspective with regard
to which are the more important and the less important aspects of
life.

The basic point of view of both existential psychology and phi-
losophy is that since death is inevitable, it is better if man learns
to accept the fact that our existence is "existence toward death."
The realization of the possibility of dying becomes undeniable in
certain situations, like war, where death and its implications are
close and visible. Therefore, realizing the possibility of dying and
coming to terms with it may be a source of personal growth and
psychological well-being (Kubler-Ross, 1970).

Burton (1971), as a representative of the psychoanalytic approach,
is more skeptical about the growth potential of the realization of
death. Freud made it clear that "the idea of one's own death is
unacceptable to man's unconscious." Thus, Burton argues that
facing death can only make a person feel trapped in despair and
alienation: "Death . . . makes no creative contributions to the
living, but torments the individual with an unseen burden" (p.
295). According to him, the only chance man has in relation to
death is to defend himself psychologically against it. One of the
ways of doing this is through compensation, by attributing extra
meaning to life as a means of protecting the ego against the excessive anxiety evoked by the realization of one's possible death.

The accounts of our subjects show that the encounter with death in war produced two kinds of effects. Some claimed an overall sense of psychological gain, while others claimed a sense of psychological loss, and yet others claimed both losses and gains. The question, of course, is what accounts for these differences? We saw the use of a variety of defense mechanisms and coping strategies such as the use of denial, displacement, bargaining, rage, depression, and acceptance. They clearly resemble the reactions of terminal patients as reported by Kubler-Ross (1970). There are major differences in the degree of one's success in protecting the ego against excessive anxiety and in one's ability to grow.

The encounter with death could also activate the wish for immortality. Among our soldiers many reported changes that signified this wish to "leave a mark." Some tried to achieve it by getting involved in more meaningful activities such as studying, and others by establishing a family, having children, and evolving deeper relationships with people. Many representations of the two orientations toward immortality, the self-orientation and the service-orientation, as specified by Shneidman (1974), could be found throughout the interviews.

Explaining Existential Change

Throughout the interview many of the young men stressed the point that the war only accelerated already ongoing processes. In other words, as young adults they were in a process of change anyway, and the war only helped them in testing themselves out. Adult change was Erikson's (1968) response to the psychoanalytic claim that the formulation of personality is completed within the first six years of life. Erikson came to the realization, while working with veterans of the 2nd World War, that adults do change. He discovered that they lost a sense of personal sameness and historical continuity because of their war experiences. He spoke of a loss of Ego Identity. This conceptualization brought about the realization that each age has its own identity crisis, resulting from the new demands and roles imposed on the person at that stage. Erikson, however, admitted that "we cannot separate personal growth and communal change, nor can we separate the identity crisis in individual life and contemporary crises in historical development because the two help to define each other" (p. 23). The interplay between the psychological and the social aspects could be responsible for the identity crisis and formation of a new identity that some of the subjects of this study reported to have gone through. The Yom Kippur War was a historical event that led them, and possibly other Israelis who went through it, to "open their eyes" and reevaluate their own values and attitudes toward the norms and conventions of their society.

Caplan (1974) argued that a crisis situation upsets the internal balance of forces within the individual, and a new balance can therefore form. The new balance can imply a better organization of the personality.

Stress theorists claim that stress can serve not only as an incapacitating force but also as a challenge. Selye (1965) wrote: "The stress of using our mind and muscles within the limits of their capacities is healthy, pleasant and indeed indispensable to keeping fit" (p. 98). War experience may serve as a challenge and bring about a positive change. Selye makes it clear, however, that strain beyond the capacity of the human organism is its worst enemy.

War as a Facilitator of Personal Growth

Lifton claims that only those soldiers in the Vietnam War who let themselves be aware of their guilt, particularly towards the people they killed, grew as a result. According to him this kind of guilt, which he calls "animating guilt," "propels one towards connection, integrity and movement . . . . The animating guilt is a source of self knowledge . . . . In illuminating one's guilt, one illuminates the self . . . ." (pp. 127–128). He bases this claim on Buber's perception of guilt as a "wound in the order of being."

A question may arise about the generality of the guilt feeling as a central emotional element in the personal growth of soldiers. In the soldiers of this study, the element of fear of death seemed more prominent than that of guilt. Basically, it is possible for both guilt and fear to be motivating forces. Every war, like every stress situation, can evoke feelings of fear, guilt, grief and anger (Janis, 1971), but the intensity and the manifestations of each emotion may vary.

The difference in the emotional reactions of the two groups of soldiers can be, above all, attributed to the difference in the nature of the two wars, the Vietnam War and the Yom Kippur War. The characteristics of a war and its meaning for the society and for the soldiers determine its impact upon them. It is well possible that the Yom Kippur War touched upon the fear of death and annihilation, whereas the controversiality of the Vietnam War contributed to the arousal of guilt.

The present study did not intend to view the reactions of the thirty-four soldiers comprising our sample as a paradigm of change for all the soldiers who fought in the Yom Kippur War or for soldiers in general. Our central aim was to delineate the scope of the possible effects of a war experience.

Concerning the durability of the changes observed, according to Kastenbaum (1971), the encounter with death facilitates not only reevaluation of life, but also creates an urgency to act with no delay, as one realizes the finiteness of one's life. Therefore, it is possible to assume that this sense of urgency pushed some of the soldiers into putting their new ideas and feelings into action, and actually changing their lives for the better.

Changing one's life is not, however, a simple project. The accounts of two of the soldiers may help to illustrate the difficulties involved. M. D., who was a medic during the war, told the following: "The war strengthened me . . . . I volunteered to take care of the wounded men under fire . . . . There was a big mess and at a certain point the doctor did not function. He did not want to come and treat the wounded. Then I stayed with the doctor in the trench and helped the wounded . . . . After this incidence my status went up in my squadron . . . . Beforehand the men saw me as an indifferent fellow. Now they have great respect for me . . . . A friendship developed between me and the doctor . . . ." With a strengthened ego and heightened expectations of himself, M. D. applied to medical school after the war, but was turned down. He said: "I feel humiliated. My disappointment now is greater than it was before the war."

E. E. returned from the war with the intention of leaving his old town and settling down in a new Kibbutz, because he felt he wanted to do more for the country. But his wife did not go through the kind of experience that he went through; she did not reevaluate her life, and therefore refused to cooperate. His father-in-law was also not too encouraging. He said to E. E.: "You are crazy. There is no security in what you are going to do; you will fail." As a result, E. E. became disillusioned and apathetic.

To turn the experience of confronting death in war into a source
of change in life, the availability of internal and external resources
seems indispensable. Otherwise, the existential crisis remains at most
just a vivid memory.

In spite of realizing the growth potential of a war experience, it
will be most appropriate to conclude with Janis' suggestion that "we
need a moral equivalent of disaster which would provide a stimulat-
ing and unifying outer challenge without the unfortunate side
effects." We agree with Allport (1968) that "constructive peace
time projects may be . . . both exciting and satisfying."

REFERENCES

Allport, G. W. The role of expectancy. *In,* L. Bramsen & G. W. Goethals (eds.),
  War: Studies from Psychology, Sociology, Anthropology. New York: Basic
  Books, 1968.
Bourne, P. G. Military psychiatry and the Viet Nam War in perspective. *In,*
  P. G. Bourne (ed.), *The Psychology & Physiology of Stress* (With reference to
  special studies of the Viet Nam War). Academic Press, 1969.
Burton, A. Fear of death as countertransference. *Omega,* 1971, *2,* 287–297.
Caplan,G. *Support Systems and Community Mental Health.* Behavioral Publica-
  tions, 1974.
Eissler, K. R. *The Psychiatrist and the Dying Patient.* New York: International
  Press, Inc., 1955.
Erikson, E. H. *Identity: Youth & Crisis.* London: Faber & Faber, 1968.
Fritz C., and Marks E. The NORC studies of human behavior in disaster. *Journal
  of Social Issues,* 1954, *10,* 26–41.
Golan, N. *Treatment in Crisis Situations.* Glencoe, Ill.: The Free Press, 1978.
Grinker, R. R., and Spiegel, J. P. *Men Under Stress* (second edition). New
  York: McGraw Hill Book Co., 1963.
Janis, I. L. *Stress and Frustration.* New York: Harcourt Brace Jovanovich, 1971.
Kastenbaum, P. The vitality of death. *Omega,* 1971, *2,* 253–271.
Kubler-Ross, E. *On Death & Dying.* London: Tavistock Publications, 1970.
Lieblich, A. *Tin Soldiers on Jerusalem Beach.* New York: Pantheon, 1978.
Lifton, R. J. *Home From the War.* New York: Simon & Schuster, 1973.
Miller, K. The concept of crisis: Current status and mental health. *Human
  Organizations,* 1963, *22,* 195–201.
Pincus, L. *Death and the Family.* New York: Pantheon, 1974.
Sabshin, M. Twenty five years after men under stress. *In,* D. Offer & D. X.
  Freedman (eds.), *Modern Psychiatry and Clinical Research.* New York:
  Basic Books, 1972.
Selye, H. The stress syndrome. *American Journal of Nursing,* 1965, *65,* 97–99.
Shneidman, E. S. *Death of Man.* Penguin Books, 1974.
Wolfenstein, M. *Disaster: A Psychological Study.* Glencoe, Ill.: The Free Press,
  1957.

2.
Between Strength and Toughness*

Amia Lieblich
Hebrew University, Jerusalem

The present paper attempts to examine the notion of the so-called toughness of the Israeli man as it expresses itself in Gestalt therapy groups in which both men and women have participated since 1970. We will present some background material, describe the nature of the data that will be discussed, and give numerous examples of the phenomenon under discussion.

THE MESSAGE OF HEROISM

People who meet Israelis for the first time often comment on the tough front they are presenting to the world around them. This impression, which has become an integral part of the Israeli stereotype, is probably based on physical appearance, manner of speech, dress and movement, some impoliteness in interpersonal situations, and frequently observed blunt, aggressive behaviors. It draws additional force from the frequent encounters with men in uniform and the number of guns one can see in a normal day in town. On a less superficial level, the above stereotype may be formed and reinforced by the Israeli norm that respects independence, achievement, and performance above words and feelings, and the sacred value that

---

*The present chapter uses some excerpts from the author's book, *Tin Soldiers on Jerusalem Beach,* published by Pantheon Books, 1978. Pantheon Books were kind enough to permit the use of these excerpts.

gives priority to the state, the nation, its security and its future, rather than to the individual and his private needs and aspirations. Although this stereotype is usually attached to Israelis in general, it is more often associated with Israeli men than women. This naturally parallels the generally accepted differences of feminine versus masculine behavior, according to which men are strong, instrumental, and independent, women soft, emotional, and dependent.

Although a comprehensive study of the Israeli stereotype, its validity and origin, is beyond the scope of the present paper, we will attempt to demonstrate that strength is of tremendous importance to Israelis and their identity as individuals. Moreover, the need for power is so central that any signs of weakness are regarded as threats to the identity-as-a-whole and are, therefore, concealed from view.

Two major antecedents may account for the central position of individual strength in the personality of Israelis. From a historical perspective, this trend can be understood as a reaction against the former Diaspora-Jewish stereotype: the weak Jew, rich in spiritual assets but poor and oppressed in all worldly aspects of life. The perceived helplessness and passivity of this type of Jew has, in the past, been associated with many tragic situations, culminating in the holocaust in Europe during World War II. The revolutionary ideology of the pioneers of the modern movement of settlement in Israel has resulted in a new image of the Jew. This ideology is reflected in many aspects of the national identity, but for our concerns it, simply stated, created a strong Israeli instead of the helpless Diaspora Jew.

Since the Jewish existence in Eretz Yisrael has always been threatened by the Arabs, the second source for the focus on strength in the Israeli identity has been the sheer need for survival. The drive to excel in the military realm has grown and developed through the declaration of the Independent State in 1948, and the many wars fought in the area up to this day.

These two sources create a pressure toward heroism that is transmitted both on overt and covert levels. People are educated to dedicate their lives for public goals and to forsake their individual plans for national needs. This educational pressure is always accompanied by the message to be strong. In the process, it is internalized and many feel it as their own inner demand. Strength in this context is both physical and spiritual. Unintentionally, perhaps, this ideal is also understood to demand the denial of emotionality and sensitivity, the development of a tough, harsh facade, and scorn for weakness of any sort.

Naturally, the message of heroism is transmitted primarily to men in Israel. Since men are usually perceived as the more instrumental among the sexes, they are also the main target for the various educational and social pressures in this area. Furthermore, men are the soldiers who fight the wars, they serve more often in the military reserves, and thus they are trained and retrained to play faithfully the heroic role. The price Israeli men are paying for this internalized social role, in terms of the denial of a rich, emotional life, is also much higher. Women, however, do not completely escape this influence. They are, perhaps, also shaped to be stronger than women elsewhere, in the sense of readiness to support — and sometimes sacrifice — the men around them in their military role. Yet our main concern in this paper is the psychology of men facing war in Israel.

Although the main source of data for the present paper is the author's group records, it is interesting to note that several Israeli psychotherapists have expressed similar views. Most of their working hypotheses or models have been expressed only orally. One of the few exceptional attempts, summarized in writing in this area, is in the work of Alon and Omer (unpublished). As psychotherapists in a mental health center of the Israel Defense Forces, they have treated a number of chronic post-traumatic men. They found the syndrome, as well as the pre-morbid personality, to be highly consistent over individual cases. They reported that most of the men suffering from the syndrome have an extreme need to perform well and succeed in competitive situations and a tendency to assume responsibility very early in life. These traits, which seem part of the strong-Israeli image, are, however — according to the authors — a superficial facade covering a basic problem with masculine identity. The trauma, which is, objectively, sometimes only a slight injury or accident, receives this tremendous impact because of the inability of this sort of personality to face feelings of helplessness or of lack of control. In fact, in this personality there are hidden wishes to be weak, passive, dependent, and taken care of by others. In terms of this report, Alon and Omer describe a situation where only one extreme pole of the strong-weak continuum is developed, and the other end is completely denied. The significance of such an inner split of the personality will be clarified below.

SOME THOUGHTS ABOUT LAING, FRANKL,
AND THE ISRAELI EXISTENCE

In searching for a meaningful theoretical frame of reference for understanding the effects of the ongoing stress of living-with-war on some personality traits or processes of Israelis, two theoretical contributions seem to stand out. These are Laing's description of the *divided self* (1959), and Frankl's presentation of the *will to meaning* (1959). Both theories belong to the broader existential school (which also reflects my personal preference), and both date after World War II and have — so it seems to me — man's tenuous security in the world as an underlying assumption. However, these two theories are leading toward completely different, even contradictory, implications.

Starting from Laing's general approach, living constantly with the threat of war may produce the psychological condition of basic insecurity along with the psychological conditions that result from this insecurity. On the other hand, from Frankl's point of view, it may facilitate the development of a sense of mission and meaning to one's individual existence. Let us examine these two approaches more closely.

Several psychologists have presented views on the possible relationship between inner fear and insecurity and an exterior of rigidity and interpersonal insensitivity. One approach is, of course, the famous psychoanalytical notion of reaction formation: Those who fear inside will present a "heroic" front to defend against their inner panic. This "front" will be differentiated from "true bravery" by its extremist and inflexible nature. A somewhat similar trend of thought is expressed by R. D. Laing in one of his major works, *The Divided Self* (1959). As the central problem in the development of human personality, Laing is presenting what the existentialists call ontological insecurity, namely, the feeling that one is threatened by nonbeing. He describes three modes of ontological insecurity. One is that of *engulfment,* or loss of identity — every social contact threatens to overwhelm a very tenuous sense of self, and only in isolation can it somehow be maintained. When the individual senses that at any moment the external world may rush in and obliterate one's individual identity, he experiences what Laing calls *implosion.* Subjectively, this experience is also felt as being empty like a vacuum. Finally, *petrification* is a form of terror that one will be turned into a machine, a robot or stone, an object without feelings or awareness. Other terms used by Laing to describe this last mode are *depersonalization,* or the doubt of being alive. It is also accompanied by treating others as not human, as objects, not as beings.

Although it may seem that the above describe extreme cases of abnormal behavior, Laing himself assessed these conditions to be rather prevalent, and in minor forms exist in most individuals.

The splitting of the self is seen by Laing primarily as a normal reaction to abnormal stress. For the normal individual, the false self, the external facade, is a convenient social necessity that covers the authentic self from threatening influences. Highly insecure persons, however, such as the schizophrenics, develop a massive discrepancy between their behavior, experience — their "real" self — and body.

In trying to use Laing's concepts for understanding some aspects of the Israeli reality, it will be necessary to draw a parallel between his concept of ontological insecurity and what seems to be, superficially, "only" a state of physical, or political insecurity. Laing's basic concept referred, indeed, to the feeling that one is threatened by nonbeing, not to fear of death. Death would be one way of losing one's being, but other ways are more prominent in Laing's thought, mainly the fear that what is most essential to oneself as an individual might be lost.

It is my claim that the stress of the political reality of life in Israel in the twentieth century, as well as the strong reminders of the Jewish holocaust in Europe, may have created for Israelis, especially Israeli men, a situation in which insecurity, in the general meaning of Laing's theory, is rather prevalent. One of its products, on which the present paper will be focused, is the Israeli men's tough front, and the frequent impression of an alienation between their acts and their feelings.

Before dwelling in length on this point, let us return to a different theoretical approach. Rather than seeing the constant struggle we are living through as a negative human condition, some may claim that it provides those who identify with the Israeli state a challenge, a sense of mission and significance, or a feeling that here one may live a worthwhile, meaningful life. In his famous work, Victor Frankl (1959) claims that man's search for meaning is a primary force in his life. This meaning is unique and specific to each individual, and must be discovered by the person himself. It differs from man to man, from day to day, and from hour to hour. There is no meaning to life in general, but rather the specific meaning of a person's life at a given moment. However, Frankl himself believed that the meaning of our existence is not invented by ourselves, but rather "detected." Healthy, meaningful life is always based on a certain degree of tension between what one has already achieved and what one still ought to accomplish. What man actually needs is not a tensionless state, but rather the striving for some goal worthy of him. When this goal, value, or meaning is missing in one's life, life is experienced as futile and boring, an "existential vacuum." Discovering the meaning of life may take place in various ways. Among them, the way of achievement or accomplishment, the way of love for another human being, or the way of suffering. According to Frankl, discovering the meaning of unavoidable suffering, and accepting the challenge to suffer bravely, are perhaps the most profound ways of understanding life's meaning even while facing death.

Although Frankl stressed the individual route one must take towards the discovery of one's meaning of life, it seems plausible that certain cultures, political climates, or social organizations may provide the individual with ample opportunities for the "detection" of values or meanings. Consequently, it may be claimed that life in Israel, with its mission and commitment to defend and maintain the Jewish people and tradition, and with its daily struggles for survival, may provide many individuals with a sense of value, a dedication to a goal, and an awareness of a worthwhile life. This would then lead, according to Frankl's theory, to a better life, from the perspective of criteria for mental health — a hypothesis certainly also including aspects of a richer, warmer, and more mature emotional life — for more individuals.

We are, therefore, faced with two alternative formulations. Life in Israel, with its inescapable stress, may produce in people ontological insecurity on the one hand, or a more meaningful existence on the other.

This report concentrates only on negative psychological consequences of the political situation, and even then not on all of them, but specifically on the "toughness" of the Israeli man. However, it may possibly be true that for some individuals and/or for some of the time, the present political tension has positive beneficial effects. (For a demonstration of what may be interpreted as such a case, see Lieblich, 1978, pp. 253–260.) Since this report is not based on a representative survey or an experimental test, our focusing on the negative aspects of the current situation should not be taken as a refutation of the positive aspects.

THE ORIGIN AND NATURE OF OUR CASE STUDIES

In the following pages we will present several clinical case studies to demonstrate some of the psychological effects described above. The material is based on transcriptions of Gestalt therapy groups and workshops that I have conducted in Israel since 1970 (Lieblich, 1975, 1978, 1980). The majority of the groups were undertaken within the framework of training for the mental-health professions, namely, clinical psychology, adult education and social work, and the participants were advanced students or young practitioners in these fields. It is important to stress that the participants in these groups can be characterized as normal, young individuals whose primary motivation for joining the groups was learning rather than therapy. This implies that the themes and problems that prevailed in the groups cannot be considered "sick" or deviant from the norms of the total population. On the other hand, this sample is more representative of people of Western origin, people with higher education, and, because of their professional activities, perhaps of people who are more sensitive to the situation and its psychological consequences. Whereas I believe that the contents of the group sessions reflect normal problems of living in Israel, specifically men's problems of adjustment to the prolonged stress of the war, it may very well be that in the area of emotional expression of one's inner experience and interpersonal sensitivity, men of Eastern origin (Asia and North Africa) have greater facility than men of Western origin. Casual observations and some research seem to indicate that Israelis of Eastern origin are less alienated from their feelings than Western ones (Amilianer, 1979). Although they do try to exhibit the popular male heroic front, their inner experiences "behind the mask" are easier to discern. However, the norm and stereotype of the Western "Ashkenazi" is by far the more dominant one in Israeli society, both as we see ourselves and in the eyes of foreign observers. The readers should, however, beware of overgeneralizing from the material and creating a stereotyped Israeli, male or female, of Western or Eastern origin. We are actually dealing with an area of vast individual differences and a great deal of within-person variation.

The groups were conducted by Gestalt therapy method. Although the focus of this chapter is the content of the sessions, our ability to unravel the specific emotional difficulties of Israeli men should be, at least partly, attributed to the method of conducting these groups. Following, therefore, is a shorthand presentation of some principles of Gestalt therapy. Recently, there has been a growing number of books and reviews that provide comprehensive explications of Gestalt therapy (Fagan and Shepherd, 1970; Polster and Polster, 1973; Stephenson, 1975; Hatcher and Himmelstein, 1976; Simkin, 1976; Smith, 1976). The following outline should be considered mainly as a simple aid for the understanding of the following parts of the paper.

Gestalt therapy is a variant of the existential-humanistic approach to psychotherapy, innovated by Fritz Perls (Perls, 1969a, 1969b, 1968c, 1973; Perls, Hefferline, and Goodman, 1951). Gestalt is a German word meaning "whole" or "configuration," which is used in the context of Gestalt-therapy approach to convey the belief that people are total organisms functioning as a whole, and that human needs continue exerting influence as long as they are not met. Therefore, unrecognized, unexpressed needs become "unfinished business" that tie down attention, thus reducing the flexibility of the person and his ability to cope with and adapt to new situations and demands. The aims of Gestalt therapy are to finish the unfinished business, and, in more general terms, to lead to an integration of the various personal elements or "parts," which results in a person becoming a centered being who is smoothly functioning and flowing. The basic methods used to achieve these aims attempt to focus awareness in the now and lead people to experience how they block themselves. Broadening awareness is, in fact, both the basic technique and one of the major goals of Gestalt therapy.

Gestalt therapy is usually conducted in groups rather than individually, and is characterized by direct communication between an active therapist and a responsible participant who volunteers to "work." The therapist may use various games and techniques designed to enhance awareness and bring external situations into the here-and-now of the group. These techniques have become the trademark of the approach although they are quite external and derive their significance only from the assumptions mentioned above.

Two techniques should be specifically mentioned since their use was of major importance in uncovering some of the hidden themes of war in Israel. One may be named "centering," and it involves working with splits and polarities. It is based on the assumption that as long as the person experiences only one extreme of any continuum, he has no center, and there is a repeated struggle without resolution. The therapist leads the person to experience his polarities (e.g., the weak part and the strong part), and then, using a dialogue technique or a similar "game," aims at a better integration or reconciliation of the opposing parts.

Another technique involves working with dreams. Dreams and fantasies are considered to provide the dreamer important existential messages in disguise. In order to get the message, the person is directed to relive the dream as if it were happening in the present, and then to identify with several of the items that appear in the dream (people, objects, landscapes, etc.) by becoming each one in turn or by enacting encounters between them. In this way people may advance toward an understanding of their various parts, and begin the process of reowning projected, missing aspects of their personality, which is the essence of psychological growth.

In both techniques mentioned above, as well as in all other interventions undertaken by the Gestalt therapist, there are no preconceived ideas of stages, causes, or the meaning of symbols. Rather, the therapist follows or accompanies the person into the inner space of his dreams, fantasies, or conflicts without predetermined hypotheses as to the contents of the individual's private world.

The cases that would be presented below are excerpts of records of group sessions conducted in the last ten years in Israel. They were selected in order to demonstrate the multifaceted phenomenon of the need/habit of the Israeli man to adapt a harsh, tough front that gradually leads to alienation of essential parts of his inner experience and true self.

THE NEED TO BE STRONG

The extreme need of Israelis, especially men, to be strong, found different expressions in the groups. It is most evident in the following examples.[1]

David was born and educated in Europe. He has served in the Israeli army for the last six years, but he did not receive the "toughening"

---

[1]If not otherwise stated, all the following citations are from Lieblich, *Tin Soldiers on Jerusalem Beach*, 1978. Page numbers appear in parentheses.

Israeli education.   In one of our sessions, he presents the following dream, which, he says, is a repetitive dream:

"In my dream I am standing in line with many soldiers since we are supposed to start our march to the battlefield any minute. The order to start is announced, and I begin to put on my gear. As I try to assemble the various parts, I feel very clumsy and inadequate. It takes me a long time to get ready, and in the meantime the whole unit is gone. I am alone in the desert. I have a very strong sense of my obligation to join my unit in the battle, but I don't know the direction they have taken. I feel lost. Inexplicably, a command car with an unknown driver shows up and takes me through the desert to a camp where I find my unit. However, now I realize that my gun is missing. I go to search for one in the storage area and cannot find any. Finally I find a pistol, but as I try it I discover it does not work. All this takes a while, and in the meantime I hear that two thousand six hundred soldiers were killed in the first day of the war. I realize that my unit, for which I was searching, does not exist any more, and I missed the war" (pp. 30–31).

Following are some parts of our work on the dream:

Interviewer: What is the dominant feeling of this dream for you?

David: My feelings of inadequacy, my clumsiness, and my anger at myself for being that way. This is a feeling with which I am very familiar. In the army, even in officers training course, I often felt clumsy, slow, and, in general, inadequate. I am the schlemiel type. I keep daydreaming or solving a problem in my head, and in the meantime I don't manage to accomplish what is demanded with the necessary speed — or, at least, I have to put lots of extra effort into being as efficient as necessary.

Interviewer: Be the unknown driver of the command car.

David: I am a soldier like you, but I am completely adequate and can perform my tasks successfully. I never get lost. I am well acquainted with the desert, and have my bearings. I have all my necessary equipment with me, my firearms and a well-functioning car. In short, I am very competent, and I can save you.

Interviewer: Can you have the two, the unknown driver and the schlemiel, talk to each other?

David: Yes, I'll start with the schlemiel.
— I have lost my unit. Can you help me find it?
— Sure I can, just hop into the car.
— Thank you. I don't know where you have come from exactly when I need you so, but I know you very well. You're this famous Israeli type who can function under all hazards and hardships. You don't think too much, but you act swiftly and effectively. You're one of those people whom I encounter in the reserves time and again. You can take the military service in your stride.

Interviewer: What does the competent driver say?

David: He says: "Don't be so clumsy. Don't stay behind. Come on, I'll give you a hand."

What David described as his personal dilemma is the basic polarity between the strong and competent, popular Israeli type, and the helpless, somewhat clumsy, Diaspora type. Although, at the beginning of the session, David gives all respect to the strong type, later he finds some advantages in the rather helpless type.

Talking to the strong command-car driver, David says:

"Actually, I am not sure I even like it so much, being like you. Do you read poetry? Do you like classical music? Do you enjoy philosophical debates?" (p. 33). Here we start to encounter some of the shortcomings of the strong Israeli type: he may be limited in his ability to experience aesthetic joy or intellectual interests if they do not contribute directly to his immediate task.

A similar concern is expressed by Ron (p. 138–142), an American who currently lives in Israel. Working on a dream, he describes an encounter between himself and Joel, his Israeli childhood friend. About Joel he says the following:

"You are strong and confident, while I feel weak and ashamed . . . . You are morally superior. You faced hardships silently and proudly. I see you as a man . . . . You, Joel, seem to know very well the road you're traveling on; you are firmly anchored in your identity as an Israeli . . . . You had been in two wars and in other battles; your closest friend had been killed and you had been wounded . . . ."

About himself he says:

"Standing in front of Joel, I feel weak and ashamed . . . I feel guilty . . . . It is guilt over my life being easy . . . . I feel that you see me as a boy, still awkward, still immature . . . . I lived a relatively sheltered life as a student."

Interviewer: What do you feel?
Ron: Guilt, shame, the feeling — in contrast to Joel — of being a pampered child . . . .

And again, later, talking to himself, Ron says:
"You are a half-baked dreamer. Get out into the world and *do* something."
The contrast here is between the Israeli soldier — who fights wars, is strong, confident, and is *doing* things — and the child, who lives a sheltered life and *dreams* about things. Yet, surprisingly, in Ron's dream, which opens the session, Joel is terribly deformed, his arms thin and twisted, and he is crawling on the ground, while Ron is healthy and upright, watching him from above. Again we are given hints about the hidden deficits of the Israeli male stereotype, and the ambivalent feelings — of jealousy and a sense of superiority — it provokes in outsiders. Is toughness necessarily strength? Are dreams absolutely unnecessary? We will have more to say about this in the following pages.
Before going on, however, it should be noted that our aim in the group work is to integrate the conflicting polarities. In both of the above cases, this means to find a middle way, a center, of being both strong and weak, a doer and a dreamer. This therapeutic work, however, does not concern us here directly, and we will return to it toward the end of the paper.
This need to be strong in the limited sense of succeeding in the military role, preferably as a combat soldier, finds its clear expression in a recent work of Nir, a young man who participated in my 1979 group. Following is Nir's monologue:
"I, who in my appearance look like the stereotype of an Israeli male, was, during my military service, a "jobnick," and have never participated in a war. Even today, six years after the war, I am trembling with shame just writing these words.
"In high school, I was a sportsman and my brother was a pilot. I looked forward to — and felt others expected me — to volunteer to one of the elite units. I even considered parachutists as jobnicks.

"During my basic training I was wounded. Then I turned into a real jobnick. For two and a half years I returned to my parents' home every single evening. I did not study in my free time. I did not even read. I was out after entertainment all the time. Not to think. I was overwhelmed by guilt feelings and shame. I tried to convince myself that there was no choice. It was an order. There was medical indication. Actually, however, I was not sure. Perhaps, after all, I am a coward, or I had to continue and be a fighter, even at the price of my health.

"I was jealous no end of my friends, and combat soldiers, who had mostly become officers. They were jealous of me, of my comfortable situation. I encouraged this attitude, hoping to convince myself as well.

"Then came the war. Later, my mother told me that during the first days she was more worried about me than about my brother, the combat pilot. She was certain I would run into the battlefield just so, alone, without a unit. She knew a tiny bit of my feelings. She worried about me, while I stayed in a well-protected place, whereas my brother almost got killed so and so many times.

"I did not go to fight. We had much work and I was a good boy. I was also afraid to go down, just like that, to the combat area. But I used to imagine how I arrive, save the world, perform all sorts of heroic deeds and receive medals and citations.

"I arrived at the university with the veteran classes, all the combat graduates who scorned the women and men who stayed behind in the home front. I arrived with the heroes.

" 'Where did you fight?' they asked me, whose appearance is so misleading. I turn all red in my face, clear my throat: 'In the center. It is good that the Jordanians didn't open fire,' while I know that even if they did, I am not sure whether it would make a difference in my case.

"To this day I give this answer to the frequent question posed before me here. Abroad as well, asked by all these Diaspora Jews and their children who want you so much to be one of those fighters who provide them with their pride vis-a-vis the Gentiles. When you answer that you do not belong to the rank of those heroes, they believe you are modest. Or perhaps I am partly responsible myself for this double message.

"I can analyze how social pressure causes people to lose the strongest survival instinct, the instinct to live, and they volunteer to dangerous units, increasing the probability of their death. I can scorn the tremendous conformism which characterizes this country, mock the closed, square stereotype of the Israeli commander. But I know that deep down I am dying of envy; that, like a child, I stare at these heroic soldiers, and I admire them, and that I regret the fact that I did not fight, I was not wounded, I was not taken as a prisoner of war.

"What will I tell my unborn son when he asks me, 'Daddy, where did you fight in the war?'

"Today I am serving as a psychologist in a unit of the armored forces, and still waiting, waiting and hoping for a war in which I may participate, stand out in public and prove my masculinity and my courage. So that I, too, would be able to say that I experienced war. I fought.

"As I say this I am aware of how infantile and irrational this is. I cannot believe it is me who feels this way, yet it is stronger than me." (Unpublished personal records.)

A man whose war experience led him to a complete breakdown, or, one might say, to a temporary abandonment of his brave, external facade, is Zoe, who suffered shell shock during the 1973 war. From his therapy, which was conducted individually and not in a group (see pp. 123–132), we may learn more about what lies behind the exterior of the warrior.

Zoe, a tanker, fought for three days in miserable battles in the North until his tank suffered a direct hit. He managed to escape physically unharmed, but was diagnosed as shell shocked and was incapacitated for two weeks. Later, working with me at the Students' Counseling Center, he gradually made a complete recovery. Yet, his personality underwent a profound change, a change of values and priorities, which may be interpreted, in Laing's terms, as a breaking through of his inner self. Since his "normal," external self was collapsed by the trauma, the first self-image Zoe reports is that of a crazy man:

"Didn't I tell you I am going crazy? I think I should go back to the hospital right away" (p. 125).

The emotions that underlie his "crazy" experience are extreme terror and guilt. His fear is the basic fear of death and injury. In a fantasy about a mirror facing him he says:

"Mirror, I am afraid of you . . . . I am afraid of a thing I may see . . . . I don't want to see" (p. 128).

And later, he simply summarizes:

"You know, I am a coward. I know that for sure. And I have learned in this past month that I can live with it, with this knowledge. So what? So I am a coward who wants to live . . . survival, you know" (p. 129).

While this fear is very basic, it has provoked guilt feelings for his not being brave enough during the war. Talking to his dead friend, a crewman from his tank, Zoe says:

"Gadi, I wish I had a nonflammable suit for you. I wish I had something to protect you, to save you. I wish it were not too late. If I had been stronger, if I hadn't run away from the tank, maybe you wouldn't have burned to death, there" (p. 126).

This guilt is so strong that, simultaneous with Zoe's fear of injury is his wish for physical injury and, thus, punishment, atonement for his guilt, and a chance to save "face":

"I would have felt better if I were wounded, you know that, don't you? It would have been so much easier. I'd be safe in the hospital, taken care of. Everybody could understand what had happened to me, they wouldn't ask me all these questions. I wouldn't be the weakling, the failure, the misfit, the crazy impotent" (p. 131).

Much later, recovering from his trauma, Zoe learned to live with his fear and part of his inescapable guilt. It was a long process of getting reacquainted with his own feelings. By this he lost his harsh exterior and became, to my judgment, much stronger in the true sense of the word.

THE PRICE OF HEROISM

Supposedly, people could go to the army and perform their role, then return to their family and profession and shed their strong-hero facade together with the uniform. However, the social demands seem to get somehow generalized to many different areas, and thus, when men in Israel do adopt the strong, heroic front, it usually implies a certain style of life, experience, and behavior that is broader than their limited military role.

This may also reflect the basic insecurity that permeates life in many spheres, the awareness of constant danger, of limited freedom and resources, which lead to the various phenomena described by Laing. The price of heroism is apparent mainly in a certain emotional bluntness, in respect for doing rather than feeling, in lack of sensitivity to oneself and others, and in an excess of so-called "objectivity" in one's life. Following are several demonstrations of these phenomena.

When Yuval returned from the Yom Kippur War, he described his existence in the following manner:

"The group started a few days after I was released from half a year of reserve service in the army. I came back to Jerusalem feeling totally alienated, in the streets as much as in classes at the university.

"I can recall my feelings then: I felt detached from my surroundings, from the activities I had been participating in, and from people, even those who had been close friends before the war.

"To be open to my being and my memories could produce only pain and fear. For the first time in several years I consciously, intentionally, tried to repress things — not to be in touch with myself.

"As I tried to relate to the people around me, I discovered I was seeing them through glasses recently acquired. They were not human beings; they were categories. First, I looked at the soldiers, those who had actually fought on the battlefield, with appreciation, from a distance, as if saying: "You and I know what it is really all about, we know the truth. And we know we cannot share this knowledge with anyone, so we stay engulfed in our silence and solitude. Each of us will maintain his own seclusion.

"For the men who did not fight, I felt contempt, sympathy, and a willingness to relate, to demonstrate my superiority.

"My feelings toward women were mixed. Sometimes I felt hostile and accusatory. Sometimes I felt protective.

"A few days after the cease-fire, I had a dream in which I was an astronaut flying through space. As I left my spaceship to check something from the outside, the door slammed shut and I could not get back in. I had an oxygen tube and a radio, from which I heard that I would never be allowed to return to the spacecraft but would remain alive, getting oxygen from the tube and being able to communicate through the radio. I could talk with people through my radio, but I would feel completely alone. This feeling of loneliness scared me, and I woke up.

"I know there are two of me: one inside the spacecraft and the other outside. They are both quite alone. The one inside the ship feels more secure, more in touch with the world. But isn't that an illusion, since he is in a spaceship, very far away from the rest of the world? The me outside feels lonely, yet he is proud of his separateness.

"When I returned from the war, I was the me outside the spaceship. Gradually I am becoming more the me inside. It is better, but I am still far away out in the spacecraft (pp. 146–148).

What Yuval presents is a poignant description of alienation from one's surroundings. Although the mechanism whereby this situation has been produced is described by Yuval as an attempt to escape from pain and fear, the end result seems rather similar to what Laing presents as a sense of engulfment.

A split between one's body and experience, another result of ontological insecurity, is demonstrated by another episode from the same group. Amos, a soldier in the reserves as well as a part-time policeman, reports a recurring fantasy in which he is wounded in his leg during battle, and this imagined event gives him a great amount of pleasure, instead of the more expected reactions of surprise, pain and fear (pp. 151–156).

In the group, while trying to relive the fantasy in detail, the pleasure disappears. Amos allows himself to feel the pain and, reluctantly, to admit his fears. Yet, this therapeutic experience of rapprochement of the body and self is completely forgotten by Amos several weeks after our session. The split is reestablished; it is probably highly necessary for Amos' adaptation to his demanding reality.

Another mode of ontological insecurity which seems to be experienced by members of the groups is petrification, the feeling one has lost one's humanity, emotions and inner life. This is dramatically expressed by Avi, a young psychotherapist who participated in the war as a tank commander in the South about a year before the date of our session. The following is an interview with Avi.

Avi: Since the war I felt as if all my feelings were dead. I see this young girl; she is my patient. As she sits there, weeping, confused, week after week, I feel impatient. I don't accept her feelings; I don't know, actually, what she feels. All I wish to tell her is: For heaven's sake, pull yourself together!

I have this pressure in my chest. I don't feel anything as I am talking. I pick things out of my head, stuff that I have been thinking about for a long time now. Perhaps something is happening to me here and now, yet I am out of touch. I am hot, my legs are heavy, but I don't feel anything.

In the war I went through a very tough situation, lots of people killed and wounded. I had to evacuate a pretty big unit. On my tank were people in different shapes — wounded, burned, dead. I evacuated them, went back to the front, and kept fighting. Then I got wounded myself and arrived at the hospital. As I lay there, at the hospital, my sole preoccupation was evaluating my performance. I wanted to know if I was good, competent or not. I don't feel any of the pain or grief about what I lived through. I tried to . . .

Interviewer: To feel pain?

Avi: Yes, anything. I wanted to feel sorrow or to dream, to have nightmares like the others — I never had one dream about the war. And I ask myself: Can a person like me treat others? Feeling is the main thing in psychotherapy, I think. I'd have quit a long time ago if not for the positive feedback I kept getting. If I were really a block of ice, as I feel now, would I get this feedback from others?

Interviewer: Be a block of ice.

Avi: What do you mean? What do you want from me? I can't add anything to what I told you about the war. This is the actualization of the image of the ice block. There is nothing to add. I talked about my inner freezing to the army psychiatrist at the hospital, and he said it was functional . . . a functional reaction. It is, perhaps, functional for a computer, but I don't want to be a computer (pp. 175–177).

Using fantasy and other techniques, Avi reaches the inner wall inside him, but for a long time he cannot fathom what is on the other side of the wall. People in the group also feel another manifestation of Avi's inner paralysis or death, which reminds us of the need for isolation. One of the members comments:

"My strongest impression . . . is how you refuse to accept anything from us. When we say pleasant things, stroke you, you refuse to accept; and when we criticize you, you call us all a bunch of weaklings . . . . You lack humility, you are so proud and unforgiving, as if you were playing the role of God (p. 121).

After a long session he finally discovers an old, neglected part of his personality. Avi the boy, small and husky, a spoiled little boy. This forgotten boy has, however, the ability to feel, to relax, to enjoy and create music, and Avi asks him: "Give me back the ability to cry." (p. 184)

His inner wall tumbles down.

The ways traversed by Avi and Zoe are similar although each of them starts from the other end: Zoe is totally weak, lacking his protective facade, and gradually he rebuilds a sense of new, moderate strength. Avi starts by identifying with his tough exterior to the point of almost annihilating his inner being, and slowly he reowns his feelings and vulnerability by becoming more human, more real.

In my experience, Avi's problem is more prevalent for Israeli men than is Zoe's. Quite frequently, men used the groups to work on their feeling of inner numbness, their difficulty to admit weakness, to experience and express feelings, and to tolerate them in others. In the next section we will examine the possible sources for this prevalent situation.

ROOTS OF THE PHENOMENON

Sometimes Israelis feel that social norms and pressures demand constant dedication, and repeatedly put the individual in situations which test his strength and require heroic performance. This pressure can produce internalization of the demand and its adoption as a personal value guiding one's life. As observed by Illan: "In those of us who are sabras, who went through primary and secondary schools, with a strong involvement in the youth movements especially, the image of the hero was clearly implanted .... Moreover, if you accept this ideal, you volunteer for a certain kind of army service, as I did .... This was what we felt was socially demanded of us. We wanted to conform with the image .... But I didn't feel any internal conflict" (p. 245).

In some cases, however, the social demand creates a conflict with personal needs and goals, and conforming with the external demand is experienced as due to coercion or as producing a growing alienation between the inner and outer selves.

Right after the Yom Kippur War, Sol developed this theme in one of my workshops. He dramatized the internal conflict by two voices: the one demanding perfect strength and dedication is saying:

"You coward, you little boy, go hide, baby, run to your mama! Don't look away, I am talking to you. You ought to be ashamed of yourself for acting this way! Oh, what a great outstanding hero you are, my boy!"

The other voice answers:

"What do you want? I do my best, I am not a hero and don't want to be one. You have no right to talk to me that way. In the war I did feel afraid, but I am sure not more than the others, and I acted like a man, like a good soldier. No one could complain" (p. 134).

When asked for the source of this demanding part, Sol answers:

"I don't know. Just this country, I guess, being born in Israel and educated this way. We are all born to be heroes, to fulfill all the expectations of generations and generations of Jews out there. I don't know. This is, perhaps, only part of the whole story. Maybe my father gave it to me. He is a tall man, bigger than me, and stronger, too. He fought in the War of Independence, was an officer. I am not, you know. I am doing fine, but my ambitions are not in that direction" (pp. 134–135).

Although while relating his feelings, Sol realizes that his father is not demanding from him any more strength than he actually has, it is apparent that he has lived with the constant feeling that such a demand is directed at him from the outside. Obviously, such a demand may create the facade we are exploring.

The most direct cause for the tough, strong aspects of the Israeli personality is, naturally, fear of death and injury, the basic need for survival under threatening conditions. These conditions, whether real or imagined, make strength a very necessary ingredient for the continuous life in Israel. Indirectly, the threatening life circumstances, with their broad repercussions in daily experience, may produce the psychological phenomenon of ontological insecurity with its resulting "pseudo-strength," which is, according to Laing's approach, not real inner strength but a facade, actually a defense against inner helplessness.

Fear of death, or of life rendered unworthy of living, was demonstrated in some of the cases above. It was one of the central themes in a year long group which was conducted in 1973/74, following the Yom Kippur War. This group has dealt repeatedly with the image of an invalid in a wheelchair — an image which was brought up in a dream of one of the female participants. Edna (pp. 148–151) dreamt about a young man in a wheelchair. Yet she herself, in our work on the dream, could not even in fantasy enact the invalid's role.

"I feel so disgusting when I am an invalid, and completely dependent on other people . . . . It is very important for me to feel strong, to maintain my strength all the time" (p. 149).

Other people identified with the image:

Orna: As you worked I imagined myself as an invalid, without legs in a wheelchair. I felt such despair, everything was gone forever, no more joy in life . . . . never to have intercourse, never to have children (p. 151).

A related process is that of blocking one's feelings of fear, grief and despair since facing them is too threatening and might overwhelm one's self completely. The denial of these feelings may often create a harsh, inflexible exterior, the famous Israeli stereotype. In the groups, this process seemed to exist in women as well as in men.

One of the most outstanding demonstrations of the fear of emotional flooding can be found in the work of Tamar, a war widow (pp. 163–174, 186–192). As many widows and bereaved families in Israel, Tamar has difficulties in the mourning process. Clinging to the role of the heroine, who keeps functioning in spite of her tragedy, she admits:

"The easiest thing for me would be to give up, to sit at home all day, to cry and feel sorry for myself" (p. 170).

A similar reason seemed to underly the apparent emotional indifference of several of the male participants of the groups. When men in the group talked about their actual experiences during combat, they often referred to the mask of efficient apathy which they wore during the severest conditions. Yet, as we saw in Avi's case above, it may be very difficult to unmask it even when the battle is over. Another case in this context is that of Mory (pp. 86–90), who worked in the group immediately after his beloved military commander was killed as his jeep hit a land mine.

Mory: Yesterday, you know, I found out that my commander was killed. Another one in the chain. And today . . . I didn't go to the funeral. I am, how would you say, "functioning". . . . I really can't imagine who am I punishing by blocking myself like that or not letting myself speak

> now. My reaction to the news yesterday was very familiar,
> sort of typical of me. It reinforced my sense of being
> different from everybody else, a feeling I have always had.
> Something is wrong with me. I have always been ashamed,
> have always been trying to hide something from the world.
>
> Interviewer: Ashamed of what?
>
> Mory: Lots and lots of things. Ashamed of not having a father,
> for one. This always made me feel different from the
> other children. I tried to hide it from the children, tried
> to cheat them sometimes (pp. 87–88).

Obviously, Mory is blocking his pain, thus adopting a tough un-
natural front because he is afraid of immersing himself and being
completely flooded by these feelings. Later, Mory reveals that his
fear of feeling has another source: he learned to hide his emotions
from his mother, a holocaust survivor, who cannot feel anything
anymore. Due to his personal background, Mory is afraid that if he
lets himself feel, he will have to feel *all* his parents' pain, the holocaust, all the horrors and atrocities, as if his choice in the emotional
sphere is either all or nothing.

Undoubtedly, the memory of the holocaust, even if not experienced
directly, has a profound effect on emotional life in Israel. To be
different than the holocaust generation means to be strong, the
oppressor rather than the oppressed. This seems to be a sure way to
prevent another holocaust from occurring.

Yoav's work on his nightmare evolves around this theme (pp. 78–
86). He tells the following dream:

"In my dream I am in the Jewish ghetto in my parents' town in
Poland. I see my father, only he looks very old with a white beard,
like pictures I saw of Jews from the old times. My mother is also
there, but I don't see her face. It is nighttime, and I wake up to the
sound of violent knocking at our door. Lots of times I wake up as I
hear the knocking. The next episode is in the morning. There is a
huge square in town, and we are all gathered there. All the Jews.
There are thousands of us, maybe more, and it is unnaturally quiet.
I have a clear picture of the pavement of this square. The stones are
beautiful and very old. So many people have walked on them,
smoothed them over, that they are almost alive. Right now you
don't see the stones. Every inch is occupied by feet, by the standing

people. And the way they stand there somehow looks as if they were in a synagogue for prayers. The older, most respected members of the community stand up front. The women are all in the back. At the edge of the square, and on the roofs and windows of the neighboring houses, stand German soldiers, their machine guns aimed at the crowd. I know we are going to be killed in a moment and am struck by the complete silence, the serenity of the scene. No one moves. Now the inevitable happens. Shots from all directions, and all these Jews fall in silence, as if they were made of rags. I fall, too, but I know I am not dead. I push my head through these very light bodies, maybe rags, and I peep out carefully. That's how far my dream goes. All I know is that I am the sole survivor of this huge crowd."

The dilemma presented in Yoav's dream is fairly obvious: he can be a victim, he can be a murderer. Or, in the terms of the dream, he can be inside or outside the door. To Yoav, both are detestable, and the choice impossible. Yet it is possible that the memory of the holocaust haunts Israeli minds to such an extent that any means are justified for the end of escaping that experience and preventing its possible recurrence. This would again explain why many Israelis have to cling to their strength to the point of denying any flaws or weakness.

Yoav's work on his dream has, however, pointed to a possible solution. It is emotionally grasped by Yoav himself when he says: "I am an Israeli and not a holocaust victim — not a Gestapo officer, either" (p. 86).

Yet it is verbally summarized in the clearest fashion by one of the female participants:

"There was one thing that stood out for me, in your work. Your dilemma is to be strong or helpless, and if you can be both, arrive at some integration. Now I noticed one time when you conveyed strength very clearly. This was at the beginning, when you identified with the Gestapo knocking on the door. Strong and aggressive, strong and immoral. While the weak ones, they had God, religion, and all the human morality on their side, and thus accompanied, they walked into the gas chambers. And I grasped something while you worked, which is true for me and maybe for you, too: I am afraid of our becoming really powerful because then we may also become immoral. I wish you could, I could, be convinced that there exists a combination of being strong and virtuous at the same time" (pp. 85–86).

It seems to me that this kind of strength, "virtuous" strength, would be based more on inner security and conviction, and would not be exhibited by the inflexible tough exterior many Israelis project.

CONCLUDING REMARKS

The clinical material assembled and demonstrated in this paper represents, of course, just one way of looking at a highly complicated phenomenon. Simply put, this viewpoint states that the apparent toughness of Israelis, and of Israeli men in particular, results from excessive social stress on the need for heroism, which is, in turn, produced by multifaceted processes of various historical origins, such as the Zionist revolution against the Jewish Diaspora image, the trauma of the holocaust, and the continuous political and military tension in the Middle East. It is possible to conceptualize the tough front Israelis project to others and to themselves as an overreaction to the demand for strength and/or as a compensation for an inner sense of insecurity. Both interpretations may find support in the data presented above, and as psychological processes they are probably correlated. Whether the continuous stress of life in Israel has also some positive psychological effects was not discussed or demonstrated in the present work.

Gathering instances from the cited material, it is possible to guess at the nature of some of the themes, needs and experiences which lie — more or less dormant, under the mask. Although the external front is quite homogeneous, the implicit processes producing it and its opposite hidden pole vary between individuals. For some, the opposite pole is a feeling man, one who is able to experience and express pain and pleasure; for some it is the fearful, lost and helpless person; it may be a child, playing and relaxed, a dreamer, a poet or a musician, a supportive person able to love and care deeply for others, or just somebody who is satisfied being the way he is, without too many demands and restrictions. All these neglected parts, had they found expression in more individuals more often, would have certainly enriched life in Israel in the personal and social, as well as in the various cultural domains.

What can be done to produce some change in the picture depicted in this paper? First, there must be awareness of the need to change the image. Not everybody agrees, however, that change is good or necessary. Some even think that the tough part of the Israeli personality should be reinforced, or else existence under the current difficult conditions could not be maintained. This is, to my mind, another manifestation of the same "toughness" phenomenon, namely, the rigidity, the inability to see any alternatives to the present situation.

If and when people realize that some change is necessary, I believe that achieving the change would not be a process too long or too difficult. The fact that many men went through this process within the groups provides some support for my claim. Schematically, this is a two-step process. First, one must explore the opposites of "strong," "tough" and "totally competent." These opposite poles may differ for different individuals, and each has to find his own personal polarities, and let himself experience them. Second, one has to search for a way to integrate the opposite ends, to find a viable compromise and allow expression of both poles, the strong and the weak. When this is achieved, people will find out that by shedding the tough facade they will not lose any of their real strength; rather, they will have gained in the process.

REFERENCES

Alon, N., and Omer, H. Treatment of the chronic post-traumatic syndrome. Unpublished manuscript.

Amilianer, A. Aspects of self-suppression as a function of acculturation processes experienced by Moroccan origin parents of Beer-Sheva high school students. Ph.D. thesis, Hebrew University, Jerusalem, 1979.

Fagan, J., and Shepherd, L., (eds.), *Gestalt Therapy Now.* Palo Alto, Calif.: Science and Behavior Books, 1970.

Frankl, E. V. *Man's Search for Meaning.* Boston: Beacon Press, 1959.

Hatcher, C., and Himmelstein, P., (eds.), *The Handbook of Gestalt Therapy.* New York: Jason Aronson, 1976.

Laing, R. D. *The Divided Self.* Baltimore: Penguin, 1959.

Lieblich, A. The motif of mutilated legs in a Gestalt group: One year after a war. *Voices,* Summer, 1975, 54–56.

Lieblich, A. *Tin Soldiers on Jerusalem Beach.* New York: Pantheon, 1978.

Lieblich, A. Living with war in Israel. In: *Stress and Anxiety,* edited by Spielberger, C. D., and Milgram, N. New York: Wiley, 1980.

Perls, F. S. *Ego, Hunger and Aggression: The Beginning of Gestalt Therapy.* New York: Random House, 1969 (a).

Perls, F. S. *Gestalt Therapy Verbatim*. Lafayette, Calif.: Real People Press, 1969 (b).

Perls, F. S. *In and Out the Garbage Pail*. Lafayette, Calif.: Real People Press, 1969 (c).

Perls, F. S. *The Gestalt Approach and Eyewitness to Therapy*. Palo Alto, Calif.: Science and Behavior Books, 1973.

Perls, F. S., Hefferline, R. F., and Goodman, P. *Gestalt Therapy*. New York: Julian Press, 1951.

Polster, E., and Polster, M. *Gestalt Therapy Integrated: Contours of Theory and Practice*. New York: Brunner-Mazel, 1973.

Simkin, S. *Gestalt Therapy Mini-Lectures*. Millbrae, Calif.: Celestial Arts, 1976.

Smith, W., (ed.), *The Growing Edge of Gestalt Therapy*. New York: Brunner-Mazel, 1976.

Stephenson, F. *Gestalt Therapy Primer: Introductory Readings in Gestalt Therapy*. Springfield, Ill.: C. C. Thomas, 1975.

3.
Courage Under Stress[1]

Reuven Gal [2]
Israeli Defense Forces

*"There were giants on the earth in those days; . . . the same
became mighty men which were of old, men of renown."*

Genesis 6:4

Despite abundant professional literature dealing with the psychological aspects of war and the behavior of soldiers in battle, it is
surprising how little research has been conducted on the subject of
battlefield bravery. This may be because many such studies are as
yet classified, or were prepared by military establishments and are
thus unavailable to the general public.

Theoretical and methodological difficulties have also hindered
systematic research in this area. For example, the extensive study
conducted immediately after World War II by the Social Sciences
Research Council of the United States, published under the title,
The American Soldier (Stouffer et al. 1949), has surprisingly little
to say on the subject of heroism. Its index does not contain a single
entry under the headings *Bravery, Courage, Heroism,* or *Valour.*
Only one chapter, "Combat Motivation Among Ground Troups,"
can be considered as vaguely relating to this topic, and even here, the

[1] An early and tentative version of this report was presented at the 2nd International Conference on Psychological Stress and Adjustment in Time of Peace and War, Jerusalem,
June 1978, Israel.
[2] The author wishes to thank Miss Rivka Dinner for her dedicated assistance throughout the
various stages of this study.

emphasis is on motivational factors rather than on specific acts of courage. In addition, the motivations studied were not those which make individuals perform acts of heroism, but rather those which motivate continued battle performance. Clearly it might take as much — if not more — courage to remain day after day in a hazardous combat situation for an extended period of time as to perform single acts of blazing heroism. But the principal motivation reported by the soldiers surveyed (veterans of combat in both the European and Pacific theaters of war) was the singularly unheroic — although eminently reasonable — one of "getting the job over with and going home." Thirty-nine percent of the soldiers surveyed reported that this was their principal motivation for continuing the fight.

The present report focuses on a different class of motivated behavior, that of one-time, unusual heroism. The military Medal of Honor is defined (in the *Encyclopaedia Britannica*), as *a decoration awarded for conspicuous gallantry and interpidity at the risk of life, above and beyond the call of duty, in action with the enemy.* The subjects of the present work were Israeli soldiers who had been decorated with the Medal of Honor for feats of unusual bravery in the course of the 1973 Yom Kippur War.

The State of Israel, during its 33 years of existence, has gone through four wars. Serving in a combat unit, or participating in war activities, is not unusual in the Israeli environment. Yet, a glance into some of the acts of bravery that occurred during these wars raises many questions concerning this extraordinary behavior, whether with specific regard to the Israeli experience, or in more general terms.

Some of the major questions in the field of heroic behavior are: How can feats of bravery be explained? What are the special charac- teristics of the hero? Are there heroes at all, or is a hero born out of a specific situation? A number of researchers (Goodacre, 1953; DeGaugh and Knoll, 1954; Moskos, 1973; Larsen and Giles, 1976; and Shirom, 1976) have come to the conclusion that the dominant motivating factors for acts of courage can be found in the structure of the social relationships within the primary group: the squad, the platoon, or the company. These researchers emphasize factors like morale, group cohesiveness and a sense of mutual responsibility as possible reasons for a combatant to risk his life above and beyond the call of duty in a combat situation. With regard to the personality predispositions of the particular hero, the relevant traits, according to this view, are "social" traits such as sociability, loyalty, etc. (Trites & Sells, 1957).

Another approach relates heroic deeds to cognitive elements rather than to social factors. Thus, Juliard & Juliard (1968), in their attempt to analyze the psychology of the French resistance fighters during World War II, used a cognitive interpretation of heroic deeds: they defined bravery as the willingness to take reasonable risks, as opposed to fearlessness, which was defined as the willingness to take unreasonable risks. Using these terms, heroes are those who take reasonable risks when this is indeed the most appropriate behavior — in a dangerous situation. Their behavior is not lacking cognitive control.

The two studies (Egbert et al. 1957, 1958) concerning the differences between fighters and nonfighters among American soldiers in Korea also seem to support this cognitive approach. One of the differences revealed was a higher average intelligence among the fighters.

Rather than viewing them as the result of certain personality dispositions, acts of bravery can be viewed as products of particular situational constellations. Researchers who have approached the question from this point of view have carried out systematic analyses of situations leading to acts of heroism. Thus, for example, Blake and Butler (1976) examined the circumstances that led 207 American soldiers to earn the Medal of Honor in Vietnam. The various aspects relating to the acts for which the medals were awarded were factor-analyzed into two main categories: (1) life-saving activities, and (2) war-winning activities. While the first category included cases like rescue attempts, unusually aggressive actions and smothering grenades with one's body, the second category was comprised of activities like rear defense, refusal of medical attention and initiation of leadership behavior. Blake and Butler's analysis thus exemplifies an attempt to describe acts of heroism not vis-a-vis personality traits or cognitive factors, but rather by using situational terms to characterize those acts.

In a recent presentation (Gal and IsraelashWili, 1978), it was suggested that under conditions characterized by high levels of stress, the situational approach might explain heroic behavior better than an analysis of the individual's traits. In the present work, an attempt was made to systematically analyze the situational factors that characterize those circumstances under which extreme feats of heroism were carried out by Israeli soldiers.

Subjects and Procedure

Characteristics of heroism were examined in this study by analyzing about three hundred cases of extraordinary heroism that occurred during the Yom Kippur War, and resulted in eligibility for Medal-of-Honor awards. These cases were examined with regard to the *individual* factors that characterized the persons involved, and with regard to the *situational* factors under which the heroic act took place.

The population studied consisted of Israeli soldiers who were awarded Medals of Honor at the conclusion of the Yom Kippur War.

The procedure for determining the allocation of the awards was as follows: A specially appointed committee examined the information available and carried out a preliminary selection of candidates. The candidates (if alive) and eyewitnesses were then interviewed by members of the committee. On the basis of what they read and heard, the members of the committee decided whether the deeds were worthy of decoration, and if so what level of decoration should be awarded. The military authorities defined three types of awards:

1. *Exemplary Award* ("Ott HaMoffett"): awarded for behavior that is an example of excellent soldiery.
2. *Bravery Award* ("Ott Ha'Oz"): awarded for deeds of extreme bravery performed under fire.
3. *Gallantry Award* ("Ott HaGvurah"): awarded for extraordinary acts of heroism performed under fire with extreme risk to one's own life.

A total of 283 medal recipients comprised the final group of subjects (S's) in this study — 194 soldiers who received the Ott HaMoffet (third degree) and 89 soldiers who were decorated with the Ott Ha'Oz (second degree). The sample did not include holders of the highest level decoration, the Ott HaGvurah, since they constituted a too small and too exceptional group.

Preliminary checks on several major variables did not show significant differences between those awarded the Exemplary and those receiving the Bravery awards. Thereafter, both groups were combined for the purposes of this study. Tables 1, 2 and 3 present the following background factors of the medal recipients: type of military service, branch of service at the time of the action, and military rank.

Table 3-1. Distribution of Medal Recipients According to Types of
Military Service.

TYPE OF MILITARY SERVICE	N	%
COMPULSORY SERVICE	80	28.3
PERMANENT FORCE	90	31.8
RESERVE	113	39.9
TOTAL	283	100

Table 3-2. Distribution of Medal Recipients According to Branch of Service.

BRANCH OF SERVICE	N	%
ARMOR	152	53.7
INFANTRY (INCLUDING PARATROOPERS)	51	18.0
AIR FORCE	22	7.8
MEDICAL CORPS	18	6.4
NAVY	7	2.5
ENGINEERING CORPS	6	2.1
ORDNANCE	5	1.8
GENERAL STAFF*	4	1.4
OTHER	18	6.4
TOTAL	283	100

*Officers with the rank of colonel and above.

Table 3-3. Distribution of Medal Recipients According to Military Rank.

MILITARY RANK	N	%
LOWER RANK (Private, Private 1st Class, Corporal)	35	12.4
NONCOMMISSIONED OFFICERS (Sergeant, 1st Sergeant, Regimental Sergeant)	67	23.7
INTERMEDIATE OFFICERS (2nd Lieutenant, Lieutenant, Captain)	106	37.4
SENIOR OFFICERS (Major, Lieutenant Colonel, Colonel)	75	26.5
TOTAL	283	100

INDEPENDENT VARIABLES

Individual Factors

The medal recipients were analyzed with respect to three classes of variables and compared to matched control groups (the information was obtained from computerized personal military history files of the individuals). The three classes of variables were: (1) biographical background variables; (2) military background variables; and (3) personality evaluations.

1. *Biographical background variables:* age, physical fitness level (on a scale of 21–97, where 97 reflects perfect health), place of birth, and origin.
2. *Military background variables:* This group of variables included the following:
   a. General Quality Score (GQS). This is used in the Israeli armed forces as a general selection index and is a composite of four factors: IQ, level of education, level of command of the Hebrew language, and a motivation index. The GQS index has a lower limit of 43 and an upper limit of 56. As a single score, it represents a general indication of the individual's "quality." Nevertheless, the author found it necessary to separate the components of this overall index into two categories: intelligence and motivation. Hence, the following two indexes (the PPR and the MSI) were analyzed independently.
   b. Primary Psychotechnical Rating (PPR). This is simply an intelligence evaluation score ranging from 10 to 90. It is derived from a version of the Raven's Progressive Matrices and an Otis type of verbal test. The PPR comprises about one-third of the General Quality Score.
   c. Motivation-to-Service Index (MSI). This index varies between 8 and 40, and reflects the recruit's motivation to serve in the army, particularly in combat units. The MSI is derived from a semistructured interview administered to all recruits before their enlistment to the army.
   d. Number of Military Courses. The number of courses the subject (S) has completed during his military service.

e. Course Scores. These are the averaged scores obtained in the various military courses. The last two indexes reflect the S's' general level of soldiery.

f. Absences Without Official Leave. The frequency of recorded unauthorized absences, an indicator of possible adjustment problems during military service.

3. *Personality Evaluations.* An attempt was made to analyze and compare personality factors existing in the personal files of some of the subjects. These S's were either commissioned officers or had been candidates for officers school who had gone through the preliminary examinations required for officers' candidacy.

The personality evaluations presented in this study were selected from 77 available files. These evaluations included the following characteristics: leadership, intelligence (an evaluation referring mainly to the *social* intelligence trait of the person), decisiveness, sociability, devotion to duty, perseverance under stress, and emotional stability. Scores on these characteristics were allocated by trained psychologists who had interviewed and otherwise assessed the candidates at the Officers Selection Base. The range of possible scores is 1 to 7 for the decisiveness and leadership characteristics, and 1 to 5 for the other characteristics.

Control Group

The scores achieved by the medal recipients in the Biographical and Military background categories were compared with scores obtained by a control group.

The control group was carefully established. First, only those units in which 3 or more individuals were awarded were identified, and for each Medal-of-Honor recipient a group of matched individuals was selected who resembled the medal recipient in three aspects: served during the war in the same unit, had the same rank, and held an identical position (task). Although the number of matched individuals or, rather, counterparts, varied from 3 to 200 combatants for each medalist, the final control group was comprised of groups of three randomly chosen subjects for each subject in the experimental group.

Thus, the final comparison was made between 51 medal recipients in the experimental group[3] and 153 individuals in the control group. The third group of the individual factors, the personality evaluations, were compared to a set of mean scores drawn from the general population (Atzei-Pri, 1977).

Situational Factors

The situational variables were obtained from descriptions of heroic acts appearing in the files of Oz-award recipients, and from evidence presented to the committee. Only clear-cut instances were included, whereas those that had been based on general behavior during a prolonged battle were not analyzed.

Twelve distinct categories of situational characteristics were obtained by a procedure in which three judges (experienced military psychologists) categorized the details of brave acts according to various situational variables. At the end of a series of reliability and stability tests the following twelve categories and their respective alternatives were established:

1. Type of battle
    What was the nature of the battle conditions under which the act of bravery was carried out?
    a. Offense/attack.
    b. Defense/retreat.
2. A few against many
    Was the act of bravery carried out in the face of severe odds?
    a. Yes.
    b. No.
3. Surrounded by enemy
    Was the brave act carried out while surrounded by the enemy?
    a. Yes.
    b. No.

---

[3] A set of t-tests was administered in order to check the possibility that these 51 cases were not a random sample of the original 283 subjects in the entire experimental group. The tests indicated that such was not the case.

4. Face-to-face battle
   Was the act of bravery carried out in face-to-face or short-range confrontation?
   a. Yes.
   b. No.
5. Original unit
   Was the bravery act carried out within framework of original unit?
   a. Yes.
   b. No.
6. Presence of commander
   Was the commander present while the brave act was carried out?
   a. Commander absent.
   b. Commander present.
7. Commanding position
   Was the brave act performed while the hero was in a commanding position?
   a. Yes, as the official and "original" commander.
   b. Yes, but as a "spontaneous" commander (took command under the circumstances).
   c. No, was not in a commanding position at all.
8. Upon command
   Was the brave act carried out as a result of an explicit command?
   a. As a result of command, or beyond an explicit command.
   b. Without any explicit command.
9. Isolation
   Was the brave act carried out in isolation?
   Was the hero isolated during the event?
   a. Physically isolated.
   b. Psychologically isolated (others were present but inactive).
   c. Not isolated, acted together with others.
10. Saving the wounded
    Did the brave act involve the rescue of wounded?
    a. Yes.
    b. No.
11. Saving the lives of others
    Did the brave act involve saving the lives of others (not wounded)?

    a. Yes.
    b. No.
12. Staying alive
    How did the brave act end, regarding the hero's life?
    a. Death.
    b. Survival.

A total of 72 cases of the Oz award were analyzed vis-a-vis those 12 situational factors so that each case was endorsed by one of the alternatives comprising each factor. Thus, each one of the heroic acts was characterized by a profile combined of 12 scores. These profiles were then analyzed by the Minimal Space Analysis (MSA) technique (Lingoes, 1968) in an attempt to establish a systematic typology of heroic situations. The MSA technique had been previously applied, in a similar way, to several studies within the social and behavioral sciences (e.g., Bloombaum and Milton, 1968; Lieblich and Haran, 1969).

RESULTS

The distribution of age and physical fitness level (or Medical Profile) of the subjects, as well as the distribution of their countries of birth and origin, were obtained for both the experimental and control groups. These distributions are shown in Tables 4, 5 and 6.

Table 3-4. Distribution According to Age Groups of Experimental and Control Groups.

AGE GROUPS	EXPERIMENTAL GROUP		CONTROL GROUP	
19–22	20	39	52	34
23–25	15	28	47	31
26–30	13	25	42	28
31–36	4	8	9	6
37–47	–	–	2	1
TOTAL	52	100	152	100

t-test: t = 0.35; p, N. S.

The mean age of the awards recipients, as well as that of their counterparts, is relatively low, between 24 and 25 years. It should be recalled that more than 70% of the award recipients were reservists (i.e., must be older than 21). There was no significant difference, however, between the age means of the experimental and control groups. The two groups also showed relatively high levels of physical fitness. Although the mean Medical Profile of the award recipients was somewhat higher than that of their matched counterparts ($p < .025$), this difference is not significant in medical terms since both means fall into the highest category of the Medical Profile.

Table 3-5. Distribution According to Physical Fitness Level of Experimental and Control Groups.

PHYSICAL FITNESS LEVEL	EXPERIMENTAL GROUP		CONTROL GROUP	
(MEDICAL PROFILE)	N	%	N	%
45–76	–	–	12	8
82–85	5	10	9	6
89–97	46	90	132	86
TOTAL	51	100	153	100

t-test: $t = 2.35$, $p < .025$.

Table 3-6. Distribution By Countries of Birth and Origin of Experimental and Control Groups (Numbers in Brackets Represent Frequencies).

COUNTRY	BIRTH				ORIGIN			
	EXPERIMENTAL GROUP		CONTROL GROUP		EXPERIMENTAL GROUP		CONTROL GROUP	
ISRAEL	84%	(43)	75%	(114)	14%	(7)	14%	(21)
EUROPE	10%	(5)	12%	(18)	75%	(38)	62%	(91)
ASIA-AFRICA	6%	(3)	13%	(20)	11%	(6)	24%	(36)
TOTAL	100%	(51)	100%	(152)	100%	(51)	100%	(148)
chi^2	chi^2 = 2.35		(N. S.)		chi^2 = 3.83		(N. S.)	

Table 6 shows the distribution of the countries in which the subjects were born as well as their countries of origin. Since Israel is an immigration state for Jews of all origins, it is interesting to look into what differences can be found among various ethnographic groups. Specifically, the comparison between the western (mainly Europe) and the eastern (i.e., Asia and Africa) groups is meaningful. Each of these groups comprises about 50% of the population of Israel.

Table 6 indicates that the great majority (84%) of the award recipients were Israeli-born soldiers, and of European origin (75%). Only 6% of the awarded heroes were born in Eastern countries. A chi^2 test between the distributions of the experimental and control groups did not yield significant differences, not even with regard to country of origin (chi^2 = 3.83).

Military Background Variables

The means of six indexes related to the S's' military background are presented in Table 7.

Table 3-7. Means of Indexes of Military Background.

No. VARIABLE	EXPERIMENTAL GROUP		CONTROL GROUP		t	p
	MEAN	N	MEAN	N		
1 General Quality Score (GQS)	53.97	29	53.20	136	1.33	N.S.
2 Primary Psychotechnical Rating (PPR)	71.81	51	69.23	150	0.94	N.S.
3 Motivation to Service Index (MSI)	29.1	40	28.56	115	0.72	N.S.
4 Number of Military Courses	2.93	44	2.82	127	0.40	N.S.
5 Mean Score of Courses	79.86	44	74.58	127	3.85	0.001
6 AWOL	–	51	0.98	153	2.06	0.041

Although variables 2 and 3 are the subscores that comprise nearly all of variable 1, the General Quality Score, they are presented separately to enable a more detailed investigation. The means of those three variables (shown in Table 3-7) represent very high levels (of general quality, intelligence, and level of motivation, respectively). In comparison to norms derived from the entire military population, the mean GQS of the medalists is in the 93rd percentile; the means of the PPR and the MSI fall in the 86th and 95th percentiles, respectively.

The mean scores of the three "quality" variables were slightly higher in the experimental group, but did not depart significantly from the corresponding means in the control group.

The two groups also did not differ with regard to the number of military courses taken during their prewar military service (a mean frequency close to 3 courses per individual in both groups). However, the level of achievement obtained in these courses was significantly higher ($p < 0.001$) for the Medal-of-Honor recipients ($\bar{x} = 79.9$) than for their matched counterparts ($\bar{x} = 74.6$). A slight difference ($p < 0.05$) in the mean number of days of absence without official leave was also found: while the group of medalists had not a single instance of unofficial absence, the mean number of days of absence in the control group was 0.98.

Personality Evaluations

The examination of personality variables and their relationship to the behavior of war heroes in this study is confined to very general personality evaluations, compared in a very cursory way to similar data. The mean scores of 7 personality characteristics were computed for 77 subjects who had gone through the selection procedure in the Officers Selection Base in the experimental group. Since the corresponding data for the control group was not accessible, these means were compared to data obtained from a random sample of 300 soldiers who had passed the Officers Selection Base examinations in 1975 (Atzei-Pri, 1977). Table 8 includes the mean scores of the subjects by group.

Medal-of-Honor recipients scored higher, in comparison to a comparable (not specifically matched) group, on four personality characteristics: leadership, devotion to duty, decisiveness, and perseverance under stress (all at the level of $p < .001$). No significant differences

Table 3-8. Mean Scores of Personality Evaluations.

PERSONALITY EVALUATIONS	EXPERIMENTAL GROUP		COMPARISON GROUP		t	p
	MEAN	N	MEAN	N		
Sociability	3.94	77	3.96	273	0.57	N.S.
Social Intelligence	4.06	77	3.90	273	0.44	N.S.
Emotional Stability	3.20	77	3.12	273	1.02	N.S.
Leadership	3.31	77	2.34	273	6.13	0.001
Devotion to Duty	4.19	77	4.01	273	4.45	0.001
Decisiveness	3.24	77	2.34	273	12.32	0.001
Perseverance under Stress	2.94	77	2.18	273	11.81	0.001

were found in the other three personality evaluations: sociability, social intelligence, and emotional stability.

Situational Factors

The heroic acts investigated in the present work were also analyzed with regard to their situational components. Using the MSA procedure, spatial distributions were obtained, where each point in the space diagram represented a single case of a heroic act. Figure 3-1 shows an example of such a diagram ("Staying Alive"), with the scattered points representing either a killed or a surviving hero.

Twelve such space diagrams were similarly produced by the MSA technique, each corresponding to one of the twelve situational characteristics defined by the researchers. The separate regions in each diagram divide the given cases into the different alternatives attached to each situational variable. Since the location of each case in the different "maps" is fixed, an analysis of a group of cases located in a given region *across* several "maps" yields certain profiles (comprised of several situational characteristics), each of which represents a distinct type of heroic situation.

Four such types were identified and labeled in a descriptional manner. The first type of heroic situation can be described by the following situational characteristics: A group of soldiers surrounded by the enemy, outnumbered and occupied in a defending or retreating combat. The act of heroism is carried out, in most cases, by the

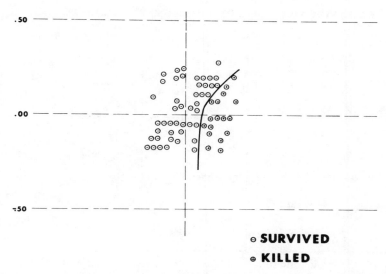

Figure 3-1. A minimal space analysis (MSA) of one situational variable ("staying alive").

formal commanding officer or in his presence, and typically it does not occur in isolation but with the participation of a few others. This type of situation was labeled "the isolated group, fighting with its back to the wall," and it included 20 cases. The following story is an example of this type of heroic situation:

"In the afternoon hours, Lieutenant Y. G., commanding officer of the post, stands and gazes at the border in front of him on the Golan Heights. Suddenly, a heavy artillery barrage lands on the post and the structures within the fortified position collapse. At a distance of approximately five hundred meters from the post, the Syrians deploy a bridge over the tank trap, and hundreds of tanks rush over the bridge, pass near the post, and storm west. In the evening, three Syrian tanks approach the entrance to the post, and when they are hit, the remaining Syrian soldiers jump out of the tanks and disperse. During the night a convoy of armored personnel carriers with infantrymen approaches the position. As the first vehicle reaches the entrance, Y. G. opens fire on it from a distance of approximately thirty meters, followed by the MAG operator standing by him who also opens fire. The second carrier is hit by a bazooka

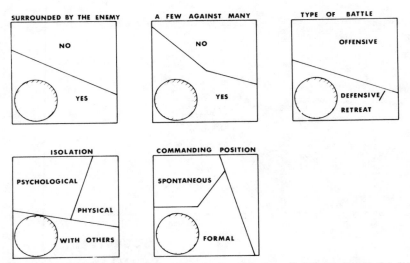

Figure 3-2. Heroic situation I — "The isolated group, fighting with its back to the wall."

shell, and in a short time the convoy is halted. The shelling of the post continues.

"A Syrian recoilless gun arrives opposite the post, and its shells destroy the post and its walls. Under cover of the recoilless gun, five tanks, followed by another three, approach the post, but are forced to withdraw at a distance after our forces' artillery shells land on them. On Sunday afternoon, a Syrian infantry attack begins which approaches and even spills over the post's fence. Since the ammunition supply in the post is rapidly dwindling, Y. G. orders his troops to fire only at a distance of ten meters. The Syrians who climb to the banks of the post are hit by close-range fire and withdraw. In the afternoon hours, Y. G. is wounded by shrapnel, and while receiving blood transfusions he continues, from time to time, to command his troops.

"The next morning the post is shelled with heavy-arms fire, and in the noon hours Syrian soldiers break through to the post and fire frenzily from their weapons in every direction.

"Y. G., who has recovered somewhat, gathers his remaining men, including wounded, and together they break out into the post's courtyard. As they see before them the Syrians, the Israeli soldiers throw their hand grenades and spray the area with their personal weapons, until the Syrian attack is contained. At the same time, Israeli reinforcements reach the ruined gates of the post and extricate the soldiers who held their positions through approximately fifty hours of nonstop fighting.

"During the fighting, Y. G. displayed great courage, resourcefulness and daring, which served as an example for his men."

The second type of situation is characterized by closeness to the enemy during an offensive battle, resulting in a "face-to-face" fight. In most of these cases, there have already been many casualties and wounded to be saved, and the commanding officer himself is injured. Only a score of combatants are left in this situation, and they act in a state of psychological isolation. One individual takes command spontaneously and assumes leadership — ultimately remaining alive.

Thirteen cases were identified in this category, which was eventually labeled "the last remnant and saviour" situation. Here is one account of this type of situation.

"On the morning of Yom Kippur, after Corporal S. A. and his comrades had finished praying in the synagogue of installation El-Al, an alert order reaches them and they hurry to their post on a

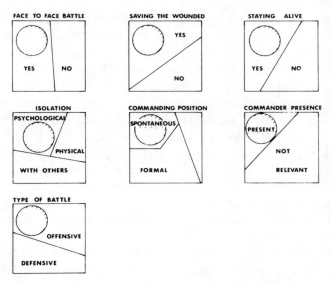

Figure 3-3. Heroic situation II — "The last remnant and saviour."

nearby hill. After four hours of waiting, a heavy artillery barrage lands on the hill, and the men on the post enter the dark bunker. Only with nightfall does the artillery barrage slacken.

"Syrian armor appears on the horizon, stampeding westward and passing by the post. The next day at dawn (Sunday, October 7), the soldiers in the isolated post assume a defensive posture. They open fire with machine guns and Uzi submachine guns at the approaching Syrian infantry. The post commander, M., tries to contact headquarters for artillery support or evacuation. Two half-tracks reach the foot of the hill and are hit, resulting in the death of almost the entire crew. Two soldiers from the third half-track, which succeeds in reaching the hill, join the trapped unit.

"In the afternoon the Syrians are within a distance of approximately two hundred meters from the hill, and the Israeli soldiers in the post hear the order being given to the Syrian infantrymen to attach their bayonets to their rifles. While Corporal S. A. is trying to achieve radio contact for artillery support against the attacking Syrians, a hand grenade is thrown into the bunker and machine-gun fire sprays the area. Immediately afterwards, two additional hand grenades are thrown and the inside of the bunker is sprayed with rounds of machine-gun fire.

"Suddenly, a deep silence falls. Of all the post's men, only Corporal S. A. and another tanker (who joined the unit after Yom Kippur) remained. S. A. passes among the wounded and bandages each one. He fetches a jerrycan from a burnt-out tank outside the bunker, and gives the wounded water to drink, while at the same time encouraging them by saying that they will be rescued soon. At the same time he holds onto two hand grenades with safety pins removed, and at his feet a cocked Uzi — in case the Syrians decide to enter the bunker to check for remaining soldiers. After a period of time that seems forever, the Israeli rescue force arrives and evacuates the wounded. They find that S. A. himself is wounded in the leg and his body has been sprayed with shrapnel.

"S. A. showed great courage, resourcefulness, and loyalty to his fellow soldiers during combat."

The "self-sacrificing" situation is the third one among the four defined situational profiles. This is a situation of a few against many, encircled by the enemy, where it is the hero's regular unit,

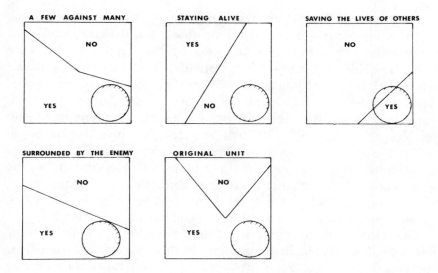

Figure 3-4. Heroic situation III — "Self-sacrificing."

but the assigned commanding officer is not necessarily present. The heroic act is needed to save the lives of the group members, generally resulting with the death of the hero himself.

Seven heroic stories comprise this situational category. Following is the story of the late-lamented Sergeant Y. H.:

"From the beginning of the hostilities, Sergeant Y. H. serves as a tank driver and continues with his tank through two weeks of combat. On Sunday, October 21, his company is fighting against Egyptian units in the Misori region of the central Sinai front.

"In the course of the battle, six Israeli tanks are hit and set aflame, and the crew members who succeeded in extracting themselves climb onto the one remaining mobile tank. When this tank is also hit, the ten tankers jump into a nearby ditch, while holding only two Uzi submachine guns and a number of rounds of ammunition. The Israeli soldiers in the ditch prepare for an all-around defense and soon they see five Egyptian soldiers approaching. Y. H. points his Uzi at the Egyptians and waits until they come within closer range so that he can be certain of killing them. He squeezes the trigger but the Uzi does not fire. He tries to switch from automatic to single-fire and manages to fire individual bullets which do not hit the approaching Egyptians. When they run out of ammunition one of the soldiers runs to one of the nearby crippled tanks in order to bring ammunition, but he is captured by the Egyptians who place him near a half-track and kill him instantly. The first of the Egyptians reaches the ditch and points his weapon at the nine remaining tankers, with his finger already pressing on the trigger. Suddenly, Y. H. jumps out at the Egyptian and with his bare hands attempts to grab the Egyptian's weapon. Although he succeeds in diverting the barrel of the Egyptian's rifle from the direction of his comrades, he himself is wounded from a stray bullet and plunges to the ground. As the eight soldiers leave the ditch with their hands held above their heads, they stand motionless for a brief moment near his body. Y. H. showed great courage, heroic sacrifice, and daring in combat."

The fourth type of heroic situation was entitled "the fight to the last bullet," and it included ten cases. In this situation, a single fighter (or a crew) remains alone in an offensive type of battle (not necessarily a face-to-face battle), acting not upon direct order nor in an attempt to save the lives of others, but in order to fully accomplish the assigned mission. Typically the encounter endures until the hero's death.

The story of the late-lamented Sergeant-Major A. B. is an example of this situational type:

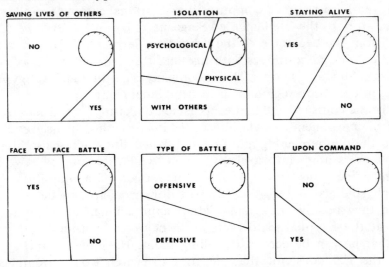

Figure 3-5. Heroic situation IV — "The fight to the last bullet."

"Until Yom Kippur, Sergeant Major A. B.'s unit is in reserve. A. B. is considered to be one of the finest tank commanders in Brigade 7. At ten A.M. his unit is put on high alert status and deployed near Hill Hermonit on the Golan Heights, with his platoon covering the southern side of the unit. With the outbreak of fighting a massive artillery barrage is unleashed by the Syrians, accompanied by aerial bombardment. The Israeli tanks stand in their places, awaiting the Syrian armor.

"At five P.M. Syrian tanks can already be seen moving west of the tank-trap, continuing in a crowded convoy. Due to the distance and dimming light, it is difficult to discern the Syrian tanks until they reach a distance of one thousand to fifteen hundred meters. While A. B.'s platoon is still waiting for the approaching Syrian armor, the platoon commander's tank falls into a pit, followed by the unit commander's tank, which also falls into the pit when trying to rescue the platoon commander. Only three combat-ready tanks remain in A. B.'s platoon, and when the Syrian tanks close to a distance of three hundred meters to the left, he opens with heavy fire on the crowded convoy and "lights up" ten of them, one after another. The distance separating the Syrian tanks grows smaller until they finally pinpoint the source of fire which is wreaking havoc among their tanks, and they aim their guns at his tank. He is aware of the fact that in the end he will be hit by Syrian fire, but he does not withdraw and stands straight in the turret while continuing to hit additional Syrian tanks. Finally he suffers a direct hit and is killed.

"A. B. displayed great courage, resourcefulness and daring in combat."

Thus, four types of heroic situations were identified. Each type was delineated by a unique profile of situational variables, and included several of the heroic cases. The number of cases that fell into each type varied from 7 to 20 (out of the 72 cases). Twenty of the investigated cases, however, were not ascribed to any of the four types, thus demonstrating unique, uncategorized situations in which an extraordinary act of heroism had taken place.

DISCUSSION

One purpose of the present study was to delineate a profile of the Israeli hero in the battlefield. Although the raw data did not include a vast range of background variables, on the basis of the biographical, military, and personality variables that have been gathered, one can conclude that the Israeli Medal-of-Honor recipients (during the Yom Kippur War) do not form an unusual or deviant group, certainly not a group of "supermen."

In terms of their background and military characteristics, it has been shown that about forty percent of the medal recipients were reservists − that is, not "professional" soldiers − ordinary civilians who had been called to fulfill their patriotic duty. It has been frequently stated that the Israeli reservist is practically an all-year regular soldier with eleven months (or sometimes even less) off duty. The high proportion (even in terms of their total proportion within the Israeli Defense Forces) of reserve soldiers among the medal recipients during the Yom Kippur War certainly lends support to this statement. More than half of the decorated soldiers belonged to the armor units, and most of them were either tank commanders or members of tank crews. Being part of a cohesive group is also typical of the infantry units and the paratroopers; they also had a relatively high rate of heroic deeds done.

The distribution of the medals includes the entire scale of military ranks, from privates to colonels. There is a clear overrepresentation, however, of officers (mostly commanding officers) in this list. That about 64% of the medal recipients were officers (much above their representation in the troops) might point to the profound significance of the commanding role in the battlefield in facilitating extraordinarily brave behavior. More specifically in the Israeli Defense Forces, it has been always emphasized that the commander of the unit holds the overall responsibility for the lives of the unit members. This, along with the tradition that the Israeli commanding officer stand always in front of his men, was probably among the main causes for the high proportion of officers and NCOs among the medalists.

On the average the award recipients were relatively young (24–25 years old), and generally in good physical shape. The great majority of them (84%) were Sabras (i.e., Israeli born), or sons of European-born parents (75%). Only a few of them were of eastern origin (i.e., they or their parents immigrated to Israel from Islamic countries). For reliable conclusions about the relationship between socioethno-graphical variables and the combat behavior of Israeli soldiers, one should require a much more detailed analysis of the data. From the present analysis, however, it can be concluded that in the Israeli Defense Force of the seventies, it was much more likely for Israeli-born individuals of European origin to perform an extraordinary act of heroism in the battlefield than it was for any other ethnic group.

The group of medal recipients clearly represent a very large cross section of the Israeli soldiers in terms of their general quality. Their mean General Quality Score, which is based on their levels of intelligence, education and motivation, falls high up in the 93rd percentile of the entire population. The mean score of the motivation index alone was even higher (at the 95th percentile). Their achievements in military training courses also reflect the high level of a "good fighter." The Israeli medalists also demonstrated high (although not extremely high) intellectual ability. This is in accordance with the findings of several authors (Egbert, et al., 1957, 1958), who, after studying American GIs in Korea, claimed that fighters were intellectually superior to nonfighters. The mean score of the intelligence indexes of the medal recipients in the present study is in the 86th percentile of the entire IDF population; it certainly disproves the frequently made claim that only unintelligent people run conspicuously high risks.

In this study, the available data concerning personality characteristics was rather limited and superficial. More careful and systematic research is obviously needed in order to investigate the detailed motives and personality predispositions of war heroes. Nonetheless, in light of the findings of the present study, one can say that the members of the awarded group (more accurately, only those in the group who were officers or had been candidates for officers) were slightly more devoted to their duty, more decisive and more persevering under stress, and showed slightly higher leadership capacity than their peers in the same population. While these findings certainly do not distinguish Israeli medal recipients on the basis of their personality dispositions, they might, nevertheless, indicate that the award recipients represent a large cross section of Israeli soldiers, even in terms of personality characteristics.

The attempt of this study — to further distinguish the award recipients in the Yom Kippur War from their close and immediate counterparts, i.e., individuals of the same rank, identical position, and in the same unit and under the same circumstances — did not yield a clear, distinctive profile of the medalists. While the award recipients received significantly higher grades in their military training courses than their matched peers, one might derive from this that medal recipients were better professional soldiers. But since this was the only significant difference among all the statistical comparisons made between the experimental and control groups, this finding should be weighed with due caution.

Israeli heroes, then, are not a distinct species. Apparently, they are not *born* heroes, they *become* heroes. Based on the results of the present analysis, it seems that there is little chance of predicting *who* among a defined group of individuals, and in a given set of circumstances, will become a hero. The least that can be said, meanwhile, is that perhaps we can distinguish some qualitative categories in which there is a relatively greater probability of discovering potential heroes.

Would it be wiser to look upon situational factors in order to predict the occurrence of an epic action? Several authors (e.g., Gal and IsraelashWili, 1978) suggest that situational variables might, indeed, be more fruitful than personality variables in predicting an individual's behavior, especially under extremely stressful conditions. A variant of such an approach has been adopted in the study of American Medal-of-Honor winners (Blake and Butler, 1976). The present analysis has demonstrated that the situational and circumstantial characteristics of some of the combat situations that occurred during the Yom Kippur War perhaps contributed more than the individuals' personality qualities in explaining the variety of the gallant and courageous behavior manifested under exceptional circumstances.

The situational analysis that had been applied in the present study, using Guttman's MSA method, revealed four specific types of situations, each characterized by a combination of several variables. It has been shown that these characteristic variables can be systematically categorized and reconstructed. The four typical situations were, after some thought, labeled in an epic manner as follows:

1. "The isolated group, fighting with its back to the wall"
2. "The last remnant and saviour"
3. "Self-sacrifice"
4. "The fight to the last bullet"

Thus, for example, each of the combat arenas that were empirically categorized under the first heading had five distinct situational characteristics in common: It was a retreat/defense battle, the group was surrounded by the enemy and outnumbered, the soldiers were still functioning as a group, and the commanding officer was present. This specific combination of characteristics accounted for 20 feats of heroism out of the 72 cases that were investigated. Other combinations yielded similar number of extreme acts of bravery.

It can be said, then, that when in a given battle a certain combination of conditions forms, there is a high probability that one or more feats of gallantry will occur.

The situational prediction is, of course, far from being precise, nor can it point at the specific individual that will actually carry out the gallant action, if any. Obviously, a person X situation interactional approach is still required in order to best predict the behavior of certain individuals under certain conditions. The present results, however, are in accordance with the general proposition made by Gal and IsraelashWili (1978) that as a situation becomes more stressful and threatening, there will be more situationally related factors than person-related factors that will account for the observed behavior.

In many of the interviews held with combat heroes after the Yom Kippur War, the awarded heroes used to express their doubts as to whether they had been more worthy of the Medal of Honor than some of their peers in the same unit. The question: "Why *me* in particular?" was often presented, not necessarily as a token of humility. In the light of the present study, it seems that in many of the given cases it was indeed the specific constellation of the situational circumstances that evoked the exceptional behavior, while the determination of the particular individual who accomplished this behavior was almost a mere chance.

While Blake and Butler's (1976) factor analysis resulted in two categories of heroic acts, the space analysis applied in the present study yielded four main categories. A more careful examination of the characteristics of the Israeli cases reveals the predominance of the "social" element in the behavior of these heroes. In three out of four situational categories the awarded acts were carried out not while the hero was alone, but in the presence of others, most frequently his unit members. Almost half of the cases involved the risk of one's life for the sake of the survival of others. In many instances, the heroes said in later interviews, "I did it for my friends because I was convinced that they would have done the same for me." It seems then, that group morale and cohesiveness, as well as the sense of commitment to one's unit and friends, play a major role in instances of combat gallantry in general (cf. Goodacre, 1953; DeGaugh and Knoll, 1954; Moskos, 1973; Trites and Sells, 1957), and in the Israeli instance in particular.

REFERENCES

Atzei-Pri, M. Response frequencies in Officers selection base's Files. *Research Report*, Classification Branch, Israeli Defense Forces, Israel, 1977.

Blake, J. A., and Butler, S. The Medal-of-Honor, combat orientation and latent role structure in the United States military. *Sociological Quarterly*, 1976, *17*(4), 461–567.

Bloombaum, M., and Milton, C. The conditions underlying riots as portrayed by Multidimensional Scalogram Analysis. *American Sociological Review*, 1968, *33*, 76–91.

DeGaugh, R. A., and Knoll, D. V. Attitudes relevant to bomber crew performance in combat. *U.S. Air Force Personnel Training Research Center Bulletin*, No. 54–18, Randolph Air Force Base, Texas, USAFPRIC, 1954.

Egbert, R. L., et al. Fighter I: An analysis of combat fighters and non-fighters. *A Humrro Technical Report*. Washington, Human Relations Research Office, 1957.

Egbert, R. L., et al. Fighter I: A study of effective and ineffective combat performers. *A Humrro Special Report* No. 13. Washington, Humrro, 1958.

Gal, R., and IsraelashWili, M. Personality traits versus situational factors as determinants of individual coping with stress: a theoretical model. Paper presented at the *International Conference on Psychological Stress and Adjustment in Time of War and Peace*. Jerusalem, Israel, 1978.

Goodacre, D. M. Group characteristics of good and poor performing combat units. *Sociometry*, 1953, *16*, 168–179.

Juliard, A. L., and Juliard, A. S. A psychological analysis of resistance fighters during World War II. *Journal of Psychology*, 1968, *68*(2), 267–280.

Larsen, K. S. and Giles, H. Survival or courage as human motivations: the development of an attitude scale. *Psychological Reports*, 1976, *39*, 299–302.

Lieblich, A. and Haran, S. Personal styles of reaction to the frustration of others, as portrayed by Multidimensional Analysis. *Multivariate Behavioral Research*, 1969, *4*, 211–222.

Lingoes, C. The multivariate analysis of qualitative data. *Multivariate Behavioral Research*, 1968, *3*, 61–94.

Moskos, C. C. The American combat soldier in Vietnam. *Journal of Social Issues*, 1973, *31*(4), 25–37.

Shirom, A. On some correlates of combat performance. *Administrative Science Quarterly*, 1976, *21*(3), 419–432.

Stouffer, S. A., DeVinney, L. C., Star, S. A., and Williams, R. M. *The American Soldier, Volume II.* Princeton, N.J.: Princeton University Press, 1949.

Trites, D. K., and Sells, S. B. Combat performance: measurement and prediction. *Journal of Applied Psychology,* 1957, *41,* 121–130.

Part II
Stress as a
Social Phenomenon

4.
Structure, Interrelations and Solidarity of Elites, and Reactions to Stress

(Some reflections on the Israeli experience)
Shmuel N. Eisenstadt
Hebrew University, Jerusalem

Israel provides a very good illustration of a society under stress — and hence the opportunity to analyze the impact of such stress on social organization and behavior. Above all, however, it allows the analysis of the question whether it is the objective situation of stress that is the determinant of such specific patterns of organization and behavior, or rather the subjective perception that can be the crucial factor.

On the one hand, there is little doubt that Israel has indeed been, from the very moment of its emergence as a state, under continuous stress, as is evident in its being under a continuous state of seige manifested by the hostility of its neighbors, the five wars — the War of Independence (1948-9), the Sinai campaign (1956), the Six Day War (1967), the War of Attrition (1970–1), and the Yom Kippur War (1973) — all giving rise to the predominance of security problems in the political and social life of the country.

This predominance has been evident in many aspects of Israeli life. Among the most important are the heavy burden of the defense budget on the total national expenditure, the important place of the

95

security establishment (like the air industries) in the economic development of the country, the universality of military service and reserve duty up till the age of 55, the development of a security-military and security ethos, the relatively high prestige — at least up to the Yom Kippur War — of the military (especially its upper echelons), and the concentration of almost all prime ministers on the problems of war, the military, and security in general. This predominance was also evident in the centrality of security problems in the public consciousness and in the self-awareness of Israeli society. This could be seen not only in manifold literary expressions, but also in the fact that three of the most important of the wars — the War of Independence (1948), the Six Day War (1967), and the Yom Kippur War (1973) — played a prominent role in the development of Israeli society, the creation of a national self-image, the crystallization of Israel's problems, and the growth of awareness of such problems.

The stress, or feeling of stress, was probably also intensified by the manifold internal problems that developed in Israel: the absorption of new immigrants, the problems of economic development, modernization, and the like.

What then was the Israeli reaction to stress? Israeli society has developed a high level of ability to cope with its problems. This is evident from its emerging victorious — albeit with many scars — from all the wars, and in its success in absorbing immigrants into the framework of a democratic process and a relatively modern economy. This could not be achieved without problems and partial failures. But in the very process of coping with such problems, we can identify some paradoxical patterns of organization and behavior that in themselves may be seen, and have often been so presented in public discourse in Israel, as reaction to stress.

The most important of these paradoxical features are organizational expansion and flexibility. These can be seen in the organization of the army, the expansion of educational and social services, and in economic frameworks. This expression is, however, combined with relatively little creative institutional imagination, unlike in the former pre-State (Yishuv) period that saw the creation of institutional innovations such as the kibbutz, the moshav, the Histadruth, and the revival of the Hebrew language.

Unlike in the former period there developed a very strong tendency to define the problems of the society in relatively static terms. The external and internal environments of the society were defined as given to be adapted to, actively if possible, but not by restructuring them through the creation of new institutional and cultural patterns.

The clue to the development of this paradoxical situation lies in the fact that the great organizational expansion of the basic institutional frameworks has been shaped in a mode that can be designated *dynamic conservatism.* While dynamic conservatism is to some degree common to many postrevolutionary societies, in Israel it has acquired some specific characteristics.

The principal identifying characteristic of this type of conservatism is the readiness to give up vested interests by openly taking on new problems and coopting new groups into organizational frameworks, as opposed to being tied to the narrow interests of existing groups and organizations. At the same time, however, the attempts to solve new problems are made within the existing cognitive conceptual frameworks and institutional frameworks. This, by necessity, preserves the existing relationships between centers of power and organizational frameworks, but, significantly enough, changes the relationship between these frameworks and the ideological premises and value orientations from which they were established and for which they functioned. One of the most important examples of this approach was the absorption of immigrants into moshavim built according to the principles of the first pioneering groups, and the extension of the Histadruth and of party activities to many of their areas, which helped assure these people of their status in Israel's political scene.

Thus there developed a situation characterized by high levels of dynamism in all spheres of life, and by the mobility of the institutional frameworks developed in the initial phase of nationhood.

This situation, which in certain aspects was widely recognized and to some degree deplored in public discourse, was often attributed to the predominance of security considerations. The necessity of devoting most of the nation's energies to security and military problems and to coping with many new social problems was perceived as the main factor determining Israel's social development. Some behavioral characteristics that developed among Israelis, such as irritability and the continuous oscillation between expressions of solidarity and lack of civility, were also attributed to the same factor.

And yet, this conclusion is a rather superficial one. It takes the amount of stress, as it were, as an objective given directly influencing the emergence of social behavior and organizational pattern. This apaproach assumes that the definition of stress within a society is just a reflection of objective degrees of stress.

Indeed, on the whole, from the fifties on, there developed within Israeli society a high level of self-perception of being under stress. The society defined its own situation as one of being under stress, and there developed a tendency to explain many of its weaknesses, like those mentioned above, as attributable to stress. And yet, the very definition of such a situation is something that has to be explained. While, of course, it is obvious that to some degree these perceptions and definitions have developed in response to the objective condition of stress, it need not be assumed that the relative centrality of this perception, which has developed in Israel from the fifties on and has strongly intensified from the sixties on, is the only possible reaction to this situation. Neither is it obvious that the importance of this self-perception is attributable only to the intensity of stress, just as it need not be assumed that the specific organizational and behavioral patterns that have developed in Israel were the natural responses to situations of stress.

It is not at all clear that this stress was necessarily objectively greater than that under which the Yishuv existed, or, for that matter, greater than that of some other societies in difficult situations.

It seems to us that to some degree at least, both the self-perception and definition, as well as the specific patterns of responses analyzed above, cannot be understood except when related to some important internal processes that developed in Israeli society. From the fifties on, a very complicated feedback process has developed between the objective situation of stress and its perception by Israeli society.

Many parts of Israeli society have defined their own solidarity and identity in terms of such stress, and hence we have to look for the explanation of this situation in some of the processes that have influenced the reshaping of this identity. Only by analyzing these processes is it possible to understand the specific Israeli response to stress — and above all its self-understanding in terms of stress — especially as compared with other periods in its development and possibly with other societies.

The most important of these processes have been those of revolutionary societies undergoing transformation. Israeli society has shared many transformation processes and their related problems with other postrevolutionary societies such as the USSR, Mexico, many of the newly formed nations, and perhaps even early nineteenth-century U.S.A. Prominent among these processes is the transformation of revolutionary groups from sociopolitical movements into rulers of states, and the concomitant institutionalization of the revolutionary vision in a modern state apparatus. Furthermore, economic expansion and modernization have implied growing social differentiation and the absorption, within the framework of economic expansion, of relatively underdeveloped sectors of the population.

But the concrete contours of these processes, the problems they engender as well as the mode of response to them, have differed greatly in Israel as compared to other postrevolutionary societies. The key to understanding the specific characteristics of the Israeli response to the transformation processes lies — as in all such societies — beyond the specific facets of these processes; it is found in the nature of the transformation of the revolutionary elite, in the attempt of the elite to direct postrevolutionary development, and in its attempt to find support and legitimization for such direction.

The most crucial aspects of Israeli development were the strong commitment of most of the revolutionary elite to a democratic pluralistic setting and a tutelary/paternalistic orientation to the broader groups of the society. These aspects are seen in the attempts of the central political elite to free itself from both the limitations and obligations of the movement, from sectarianism as well as from routinization. The political elite attempted to base its power on a more direct appeal to the broader strata, while at the same time trying to control — within a democratic, pluralistic framework — the autonomous political expression of these strata.

The above transformation has been connected, first of all, with the transformation of the basic societal ethos and, second, with the transformation of the structure, internal cohesion, and interrelations of the major elite groups in general, and of the political elite in particular. It also implied access to the centers of political power that developed from the early fifties, and culminated with the 1977 elections.

Two of the main components of the transformation of the basic revolutionary ethos were: (1) explaining the legitimacy of the system in terms of its being a constitutional pluralistic democracy instead of in terms of the ethos of national renaissance and social ideology; and (2) the egalitarian application of the elite revolutionary ethos, with a smaller emphasis on equality of commitment and obligations.

The transformation of the dominant ethos was closely related to the two above-mentioned processes. From the late forties and early fifties there took place in Israel, contrary to the basic ideological premises and institutional model that was prevalent in the earlier period, and to some degree also contrary to that concrete situation that existed in the period of the Yishuv, a continuous process of differentiation and mutual segregation of "specialized" elites. This included the economic, military, academic, and political elites in particular. Each elite was granted maximum autonomy and benefits within its special institutional framework. At the same time, these elites became separated from the centers of political decisions, from power and parties, with the concomitant weakening of the internal solidarity of the various elites in general, and the political elite in particular. This inevitable outcome was the result of the gradual atrophization of the political elite and of the political process in general.

While some of these changes were, in a sense, the natural results of economic expansion and development and of the establishment of the State, their intensity and character can be understood only by taking into account the transformations that took place in the political legitimation process and, above all, in the attempts of the central political elites in general, and of Ben-Gurion in particular, to free themselves from the limitations of the former movement.

The segregation process was reinforced by several structural processes related to the mode of expansion of the major institutional frameworks analyzed above, especially the educational system and the army. The development of the educational system has reinforced the segregation of the elites and fractured their internal solidarity. The educational system has tended to unify and "academize." It has had a growing orientation to quantify attainments, and has weakened the most distinct elite nuclei and orientations.

The army inadvertently reinforced the segregationist tendencies of elites. Primarily, during the period of military service, it weakened the nuclei of solidarity formed in the schools and youth movements. Only formations like the Nahal could be maintained, but even here only marginally.

The other side of all these processes was, as has been indicated above, the atrophization of the process of selecting the political elites of all the parties, the atrophization of internal party/political process, and the weakening of the internal solidarity of the political formations. This weakening became clearly evident in attempts to broaden the political parties by coopting new leadership elements, particularly from the army, without undergoing long periods of political socialization. This led to growing tensions between the new elements and many of the already existing elements in the parties.

The Israeli pattern of responses to stress, the definition of the basic situation of the society and the components of its identity and solidarity in terms of stress, the tendency to an adaptive-static definition of environment, and the organizational and behavioral patterns analyzed above can be fully understood only through the "mediation" of the processes of transformation of elites, their internal solidarity, and their relationship with the broader sectors of Israeli society.

5.
Dynamics of Three Varieties of Morale: The Case of Israel

Louis Guttman and Shlomit Levy
The Hebrew University of Jerusalem and
The Israeli Institute of Applied Social Research

It was in the midst of the Israeli War of Independence. The Israel Defense Forces (IDF) had grown rapidly from a disciplined underground group — the Hagana — into a large, formally structured organization in which many of the personnel lacked training for such a new enterprise. Based on experience with the American army during World War II, the social research unit of the IDF attempted to prepare educational material for the quickly learning officers, on how to help their men and themselves to cope with the various stressful situations on the front lines and in the rear. Fear in battle had been a recurring theme in many researches conducted abroad. Above all, there was a focus on the concept of morale.

An illustrated brochure surveying the problems of morale — with suggestions on how to cope with them — was prepared by the Research Unit and submitted to the Chief of Staff, General Yaakov Dori. He immediately approved it for publication, and ordered it to be distributed under his own signature to the six thousand officers of all ranks. But with one proviso. The (Hebrew) title had to be changed from "On morale depends the victory" to "On the spirit of the Army depends the victory."

General Dori did not want to use a foreign word like *morale*. In the absence of a literal equivalent of the term in Hebrew, he suggested the Hebrew word for *spirit* to be about as close a translation as possible. Actually, researches on morale face a more fundamental problem than that of translation. The term does not appear to be sharply defined in any language.

Toward the outbreak of World War II, a Morale Division was set up within the American army. Its mission was to study and improve the morale of soldiers. Various aspects of morale were studied, from complaints about food to willingness to fight the enemy. While it was tacitly agreed that such varieties of behavior were kinds of morale, no formal definition for *morale* emerged, even in the postwar volumes published on this work (Stouffer, *et al.*, 1949). The senior author of the present paper had drafted a chapter for those volumes on this issue. Among other things, that chapter presented a matrix of correlation coefficients between some thirty varieties of morale behaviors of the soldiers. These coefficients varied in size from low to high, and in a manner that negated the hypothesis that there is a single common factor for morale. This draft chapter was omitted from the volumes, and remains unpublished. However, the message about the multivariate and multidimensional nature of morale was carried over to the work done in the Israel Defense Army. It was amplified in the subsequent continuing survey of the civilian population, which has been conducting periodic and cumulative studies, and which is the source of the data to be presented and analyzed here.

The present paper is devoted to a study of changes in the Israel population over time, with respect to three varieties of morale: mood, feeling of ability to cope, and assessment of Israel's situation. An attempt will be made to arrive at generalizations on how these changes are related to stressful events of various kinds.

The data is taken from the continuing survey, which is conducted jointly by the Israel Institute of Applied Social Research and Hebrew University's Communications Institute. This survey was initiated just before the outbreak of the Six Day War, in June 1967 (Guttman, 1971). It was conducted in the field during the week of the war and during each of the two weeks following. It was then conducted every four months until the outbreak of the Yom Kippur War of October 1973. During that October, the survey was conducted in the field virtually daily. Beginning with November, these became weekly surveys, and then continued with spacings of two to three weeks until today.

The rich data gathered on all these surveys give a unique opportunity to study in detail the dynamics of the reactions of a population in periods of relative stress and of relative peace. These are the only systematic data of their kind known to us, and will serve as the basis for the present analysis. The populations surveyed have usually been comprised of Jewish residents of the larger cities (Jerusalem, Tel Aviv, Haifa, and Beer Sheva) and their suburbs. Occasionally, surveys of smaller municipalities have also been taken. These surveys show little difference, if any, on most of the issues studied. The three particular morale items on which the present paper focuses were studied repeatedly in the continuing survey, generating an empirical time series that is portrayed in Figure 5-1. The rest of this paper is to give a conceptual framework for, and an analysis of, the phenomena portrayed in Figure 5-1.

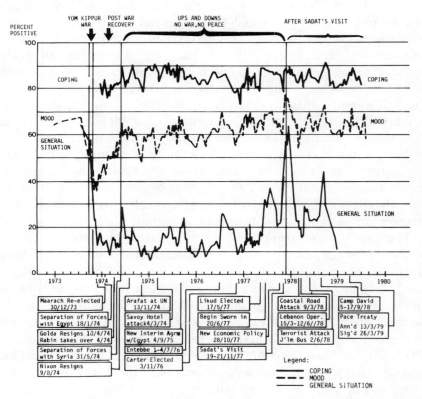

Figure 5-1. Coping, compared with mood and general situation: 1973-1979.

DISTINCTION AMONG VARIETIES OF MORALE

Israel is often depicted by journalists — and by many social scientists who also make pronouncements without systematic data — as a country that lives under stress. They give the impression that Israelis behave as if under the constant threat of war, and possess either a "holocaust" complex or a "Masada" complex or both. The actual data show that there is no siege mentality, nor are any supposedly related complexes prevalent among Jewish Israelis. To the contrary, foreign policy and security problems have little correlation with the everyday behaviors of Israelis, apart from increasing their sense of solidarity and readiness for economic belt tightening. Little correlation holds between assessments of the country's problems and an individual's personal situation. Personal situations are consistently regarded as not so bad by most of the population, even when the vast majority assess the country's situation to be very serious. In terms of morale, the Yom Kippur War was *not* a psychological earthquake.

Proper perspective on such matters cannot be attained without a sharp distinction between at least three varieties of morale: cognitive, affective, and instrumental. This threefold classification holds for all behavior and not for morale alone, and can be further divided into many other facets. As indicated above, the present research exploits only one representative of each of these three varieties.

Cognitive behavior is exemplified here by the survey item of assessment of Israel's general situation. The wording (originally in Hebrew) is as follows:

In your opinion, what is the general situation of Israel like today?
Answer categories: Very good, Good, Not so good, Not good, Not good at all.

The affective item selected is *mood*, with the wording:

How is your mood these days?
Answer categories: Very good almost all of the time (or all the time), Good most of the time, Sometimes good, sometimes not good, Not good most of the time, Not good almost all of the time.

The instrumental variety of morale studied is the *ability to cope,* with the wording:

Do you think you can adjust to the present situation?

Answer categories: I can definitely adjust, I think I can adjust, I think I cannot adjust, I definitely cannot adjust.

CORRELATIONS OVER A POPULATION
VERSUS CORRELATIONS OVER TIME

An extensive and detailed analysis of a score of varieties of adjustive behavior (including the three above), with emphasis on their inter-correlations at a given point of time, is given in Levy and Guttman (1975; 1978). As pointed out in their analysis, while assessments concerning one's reference group (like one's country) ostensibly refer to an object other than one's self, the referent and self can still be regarded as aspects of a single object, namely, one's greater self. Thus, at a single point in time, all such adjustive behaviors should obey the First Law of Attitude (cf. Gratch, 1973; Shye, 1978), and have positive or zero intercorrelations.

The correlation between two variables over *individual responses* at a given point in time for a population is quite different from the correlation between the variations in that population's *averages* for those two variables over many points in time. The time series refers to such averages in terms of a percent positive response.

Two theoretical problems attend such time series. First, what percentage constitutes "good" or "normal" morale for each variable? Second, what kinds of stress situations induce changes in the positive response of the population? It would be desirable, of course, to have answers to these questions in terms that are invariant across cultures. Examining Israeli data may yield clues — for future research — as to what should be included in cross-cultural studies. As of now, we know of no data from other countries with which Israeli results can be compared.

THE CONCEPT OF "NORMAL" MORALE BEHAVIOR

If "normal" is defined to be the percent positive response that is typical of periods relatively free of disturbing events that affect the country as a whole, then two of the three varieties of morale in Figure 1 have a rather clear base percentage for this. In periods of relative tranquility, 55 to 65 percent of Israelis express a "positive" mood. Fluctuations go above and below this, depending on events.

The base percentage for coping is higher, being perhaps around 80 percent. This difference in level may reflect the relative importance of these variables for survival. One cannot survive without coping, but one can cope despite a negative mood. Both these variables are of a personal nature, so each may have a universal baseline for individual survival.

In contrast, assessment of the situation of the country is not only cognitive, but refers to one's environment rather than to one's self. It does not seem plausible that there should be a "normal" baseline for assessing one's environment. Environment may sometimes be objectively better and sometimes objectively worse, without any necessary implications for one's own survival. And indeed, Figure 5-1 shows the dramatic change in the assessment of the general situation of Israel from before to after the Yom Kippur War, without a correspondingly large change in personal assessments.

AFFECTIVE CHANGES WITH TIME: MOOD

The highest moods recorded for the population (during the course of the Continuing Survey) occurred at two separate periods: two weeks after the Six Day War and three days after Sadat's dramatic appearance in Jerusalem. On each of these occasions, mood rose *after* the event, it apparently taking time for the positive import of the event to sink in. Similarly, the three next highest peaks followed the Entebbe rescue, the Camp David conference, and the signing of peace treaty with Egypt.

These changes were observable for mood since the time series on that item goes back to before the Six Day War, as shown in Figure 5-2. In the period between the Six Day War and the Yom Kippur War, the continuing survey was in the field only about three times a year, so that the information for this period is not as detailed as for the years following the Yom Kippur War. The lowest point of mood was recorded on November 7, 1973, with only 36 percent responding positively. This was the day before the national day of mourning declared for the war dead. Mood rose, but very slowly for the next month. Another six months passed before mood returned to "normal."

Another dip in November 1974, occurred in the days preceding Arafat's scheduled first appearance before the United Nations

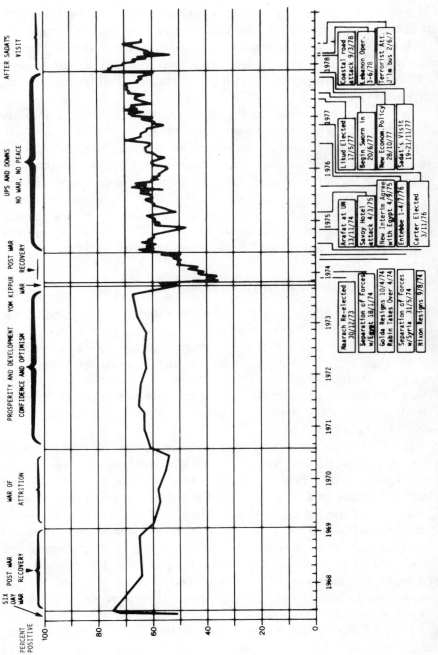

Figure 5-2. Mood of Israelis 1967–1979.

Assembly in New York. Mood quickly bounced back immediately after the appearance. The Savoy Hotel terrorist attack led to another dip, but not so great, again with almost immediate recovery. No later terrorist activities had such effect as this first one, the public becoming somewhat saddened by each, but returning to "normal" within days afterwards.

If one were to seek generalizations about the effect of national stressing events on mood on the basis of the time series of Figure 5-2, a major one might be that *anticipation* of a negative event reduces mood more strongly than does the event itself. This was true for both the preliminary and the final announcements of the casualties of the Yom Kippur War, and for the Arafat UN debut. Uncertainty can have a negative effect on mood. Sad events, of course, also affect mood, but not as drastically. A further important finding is the relative ineffectiveness of repeated terrorist activities.

Conversely — as already indicated — strong positive national events make their impact on mood most apparent some days *after* the event. The decline from high peaks of mood is usually more gradual than is the recovery from anticipation of negative events.

COGNITIVE CHANGES WITH TIME: ASSESSMENT OF ISRAEL'S SITUATION

As already remarked, a concept of a "normal" level for cognitive behavior does not seem relevant for morale. In particular, such a concept does not seem to be relevant to our particular example of cognition: assessment of the general situation of Israel. The extent of "normality" of behavior with regard to such a perception variable might be more appropriately defined in terms of the discrepancy between the perception and the "reality." If the "real" situation changes, then the perception of it should change accordingly.

With regard to the general situation in Israel, we have no objective assessment of the "real" situation. In particular, we have no criterion for ascertaining whether or not the "real" situation changed from before to after the Yom Kippur War. However, the time series in Figure 5-1 shows a dramatic drop in the Israeli perception of this situation from before to after October 1973. In contrast to mood, the negative postwar assessment never returned to the prewar level, with the temporary exception that occurred during the few days following Sadat's appearance in Jerusalem.

Apart from the sudden gross change in level, the perception of Israel's general situation does not seem to stabilize very much. In some respects, it behaves like mood in local ups and downs following events affecting the country as a whole, but the swings are larger than for mood and do not always return to the previous level. In a sense, the Israelis may be said to be "realistic" in their reactions to objective events. However, the correlation at any given point of time between this "realism" and other varieties of morale is not very great although it exists. Monotonicity coefficients are typically between 0.35 and 0.45. In the first week of the Yom Kippur War and in the third week thereafter the situation-mood correlation reached its lowest value: 0.24.

It would indeed be considered unhealthy morale were mood, coping, and other behaviors dependent largely on the assessment of the situation. "The battle is lost but we have only begun to fight" is a popular phrasing of this point of view. Not to recognize the reality of a lost battle is not considered to be good adjustive behavior.

INSTRUMENTAL CHANGES WITH TIME: COPING

The least variation over time occurs for the third of our varieties of morale variables: coping. According to Figure 5-1, the level of coping behavior remains consistently high, regardless of events. Its variations are also relatively small about the constant "normal" level. These variations sometimes go together with the variations of mood and sometimes not.

One popular conception of morale is that of the ability to "hold fast." Of our three varieties the closest to this is coping. Great events are needed to make a drastic change in some varieties of morale behavior. But even the greatest of the events that have occurred during the course of the Continuing Survey may not have any basic impact on the ability to hold fast.

BACKGROUND TRAITS AND MORALE

It is of interest to know whether different sectors of the population react differently to stressing events of a national character. Our general conclusion can be stated very simply. As in many other problems of human behavior, when expressed in terms of actual correlation coefficients, static background traits, such as age, education, income and sex, rarely have a substantial relationship with morale behaviors. Such correlation coefficients are rarely above 0.30, and are usually much below this. By and large, different sectors of the population behave similarly with respect to the varieties of morale under study.

Such population homogeneity is certainly true with respect to the cognitive and coping varieties of morale. As for the affective variety, there is an exceptional relationship of mood with sex, and also to a certain extent with education, as shown in Table 5-1.

Usually men report somewhat better mood than women, the monotonicity correlation coefficients ranging from 0.20 to 0.30.

Table 5-1. Changes in Correlations Between Mood and the Background Traits of Sex and Education, 1967-1978.

SURVEY PERIOD	SEX (MEN, WOMEN)	EDUCATION (FROM LOW TO HIGH)
Six Day War		
(4–9) . 6 . 1967	0.49	
(11–16) . 6 . 1967	0.42	
February, 1968	0.27	0.28
November, 1968	0.30	0.33
February, 1969	0.32	0.31
June, 1969	0.33	0.31
Peak of Attrition War		
February, 1970	0.42	0.28
April, 1971	0.33	0.40
March-April, 1973	0.08	0.37
Yom Kippur War		
(7–15) . 10 . 1973	0.44	0.33
(16,17,19) . 10 . 1973	0.54	0.27
(21–22) . 10 . 1973	0.46	0.24
(25–29) . 10 . 1973	0.46	0.23
January–March 1974	0.26	0.23
April, 1974	0.19	0.27
After Sadat's visit to Jerusalem		
(11–18) . 12 . 1977	0.07	0.50
(3–5) . 7 . 1978	0.19	0.25

But this difference becomes sharper (monotonicity coefficients reaching 0.54) under stressing national events — especially war. Conversely, the correlation with sex almost disappears in periods of relative peace and prosperity (monotonicity coefficients 0.07).

During the Six Day War, during the peak of the War of Attrition with Egypt (February 1970), and during the whole month of October 1973 (Yom Kippur War), women expressed much lower mood than did men (coefficients of correlation being from 0.42 to 0.54). These differences diminished in the periods following each of these three events, but still men reported higher mood than women. However, as already mentioned, in periods of relative prosperity and higher prospects for peace, as at the beginning of 1973 and shortly after Sadat's visit to Jerusalem in autumn 1977, women and men expressed the same level of mood.

Men and women do not differ in their behaviors with regard to the two remaining varieties of morale, cognitive and instrumental. Both sexes are similar in perception of the situation and in feeling able to cope with it instrumentally, despite their differences in affective response.

As to the correlations of mood with education, a more stable pattern was observed over time. Usually, the lesser-educated report somewhat lower mood than do the better-educated, with monotonicity coefficients being about 0.30 and reaching even higher levels (over 0.40), especially during relatively calm periods.

Even for static background traits, the three varieties of morale react somewhat differently. The differences are even more marked in relation to dynamic variables. The three particular varieties examined over time in the present paper give but a glimpse of the richness of the multivariate system of varieties of morale behaviors in response to stressing events.

REFERENCES

Gratch, H. (ed.), *Twenty-Five Years of Social Research in Israel*. Jerusalem: Jerusalem Academic Press, 1973.

Guttman, L. Social problem indicators. *Annals of the American Academy of Political and Social Science*, 1971, 393:40–46.

Levy, S., and Guttman, L. On the multivariate structure of wellbeing. *Social Indicators Research*, 1975, 2:361–388.

Levy, S., and Guttman, L. The conical structure of adjustive behavior. Paper presented at the Ninth International Sociological Congress in Uppsala, Sweden, August 14–19, 1978.

Shye, S. (ed.), *Theory Construction and Data Analysis in the Behavioral Sciences.* San Francisco: Jossey-Bass, 1978.

Stouffer, S. A., et al., *Volumes I and II. The American Soldier: Studies in Social Psychology in World War II.* Princeton: Univ. Princeton Press, 1949.

6.
Emotional Response to Stress in Israel: A Psychoanalytic Perspective

Raphael Moses
Israeli Institute of Psychoanalysis

The nonmedical layman will expect from the psychiatrist's contribution certain unequivocal and perhaps unassailable facts that indicate
either the existence of behavioral or medical manifestations as a
response to stress or their absence or mitigation. Unfortunately, the
present status of research in this area is such that the reader who
comes with these expectations will be seriously disappointed.

An external stressor, mediated by the host's response (due to a
variety of factors that I will discuss later on), elicits a stress response from the individual. The individual's stress reaction may,
if one proceeds systematically, be manifested in the following
different areas: physical, intrapsychic, or interpersonal.   In the
physical area, we look for the epidemiological studies indicating
average or increased incidence and prevalence of physical illness and
different types of accidents.   In the intrapsychic area, we look for
the statistical evidence on incidence and prevalence of emotional
disorders and suicide and attempted suicide.   And finally, in the
interpersonal area, we look for that kind of emotional disorder
that results in interpersonal behavioral manifestations, manifestations of delinquency, and other antisocial behavioral acts.

In other words, I am tempted to present you with epidemiological medical data about somatic, psychosomatic, and psychiatric illnesses, and about crime and delinquency, accidents and suicide. From all those, I would then deduce, and demonstrate, that in Israel there is, or is not, evidence to show that the state's population reacts to stressor factors more than that of other countries. This utopian medical model does not work. Therefore, we shall not be able to answer the global question of whether there is, in the Israeli population, more or less or the same amount of stress reaction as in other populations.

I shall present data from two of these areas, the psychosomatic and the psychiatric, to show that our question cannot be answered in this way. In the psychosomatic area, there is a general consensus that external stressor factors, be they single or recurring events, or continuous ongoing conditions, do lead to, or at least are positively correlated with, most psychosomatic illnesses. One of the most striking findings with regard to one of the most researched psychosomatic illnesses, myocardial infarction or heart attack, has shown that Yemenite immigrants to Israel show a remarkably low incidence of this disease; but after twenty years in Israel, these immigrants had almost reached the much higher incidence and prevalence of the dominant Israeli population. This dramatic finding leads researchers to look for the reasons. Do they lie in the stresses of civilization, in the acculturation patterns, in the change in diet, in the changed climate, the changed patterns of physical activity, or in the stresses of living in a country beset by wars? It appears that the stresses of civilization and, somewhat less so, dietary factors influence this remarkable change. Yet it is very hard to define exactly what are the stressor influences of civilization, i.e., Western civilization, or what are the effects of industrialization and urbanization.

In New Guinea, there have been unusually rapid changes from a bush-type to a modern city-type life between 1965 and 1978. The report of a learned physician (Burton-Bradley, 1979) shows that cultural change is a significant variable in the appearance of psychosomatic and psychiatric illnesses. Though some individuals suffer as a result of this process, the doctor found, surprisingly, that others thrive on it! Two Finnish researchers (Mattila and Salokangas, 1979) similarly conclude that "the association often found between life changes and subsequent illnesses hardly justifies the conclusions of a direct causal relationship, due, among other reasons, to the lack of an adequate distinction in the methodological and conceptual framework between the inner and outer world of the individual." Their study shows that stress caused by life changes has a differential effect on different groups of individuals, depending on the individual's general adaptive capacity, his specific vulnerabilities, and on whether the social environment functions supportively or as an additional stressor. A study of Filipino-Americans in Hawaii (Brown, 1979) discerns two strategies of urban adaptation. One strategy emphasizes isolation from the urban culture, while the other emphasizes maximal involvement. Both strategies reduce stress levels in individuals as measured by physiological variables, but people who utilize neither strategy have higher stress levels. A study from Iran (Bash, 1979) shows a quite different variable: Here the poor migrants showed significantly more psychiatric illness than the nonpoor migrants, yet no psychosomatic illnesses. Similarly, the urban poor showed significantly more psychopathological phenomena and less psychosomatic disorders than the nonpoor.

Clearly, we must look to more sophisticated and refined studies to learn more about the problem. One such study can be found in the combination of a widely researched illness, myocardial infarction, with a sophisticated methodological tool, twin research. E. Kringlen (1979) extracted from 10,000 identified hospital patients in the age group 40–69 78 twin pairs where both were still living and one was healthy. His main unequivocal finding was that a pressing and tension-creating work situation is the one identifiable predisposing factor for coronary heart disease in both identical and nonidentical twins. Russeck (1965), Russeck and Russeck (1976), Theorell and Floderus (1977), Hinkle (1974), Rahe et al. (1973), and Marmot and Syme (1976), all address these same questions. They make it quite clear that the questions to be asked are more specific and more differential ones. We must thus ask: Which population groups will be more prone to certain diseases at certain strategic points in their life? How can such groups at risk be identified, in order to consider preventive measures? The question of whether the apparently increased amount of stress in Israel leads to more pathological reactions does not, however, produce unequivocal results in the area of psychosomatic illnesses.

The same is true for psychiatric illnesses. A critical assessment by Levav (1977) makes this clear. The study of treated cases, as we know, is biased information because there is much untreated illness, and the researchable treated cases reflect illness in the lower rather than the higher social classes. True prevalence studies, i.e., systematic studies of a given total segment of a population, are also plagued by methodological problems (Aviram and Levav, 1975). The findings that emerge from these studies are again quite specific ones and in line with what we would expect through common-sense psychodynamic knowledge: The "partnerless" are a population more at risk.   Or, in line with the results of studies presented above: low-educated respondents had higher rates of emotional disorders. Foreign-born Israelis had higher rates of emotional disorder than native-born Israelis; yet, when controlling for education, no such difference was found (Abramson, 1966).   The lower the class, the higher the rate of emotional disorder; and African-born men and European-born women had higher rates of such disorders (Polliack, 1971, and Polliack, 1976).   Higher rates of recognized emotional disorders were found in immigrants from Europe and America, than in immigrants from Asian and African countries (Hoek, Moses, and Terespolsky, 1969). These, then, are the findings as regards psychiatric illness. There is a similar dearth of useful findings regarding delinquency, suicide, and accidents.   Only the number of traffic accidents is unequivocally high in Israel.

Where does this leave us? What, if anything, can we say about the emotional responses to the seemingly so markedly increased stressor factors that have been existing in Israel even before it became a state?   I believe that we must look in greater detail at two areas in addition to the external stressor factor.   First, we must analyze the population and check whether we can identify certain characteristics, somatic or psychological, that are part of the health status of the individual.   As such, they may be precursors of disease, and are therefore of much interest and relevance to those who practice preventive and public health (Kark and Mainemer, 1977).   But not only must the individual be examined in more microscopic ways to determine where he stands between health and illness, the community or society, too, must be viewed in more detail, and this in two respects.   On the one hand, it is important to locate social foci of disorganization or unrest, which may serve to foster individual foci of less than good functioning in the members of the community or society.   Secondly, we must look for social manifestations that

are themselves an indication of borderline functioning or malfunc-
tioning of the group and of its individuals.

PSYCHOANALYTIC PERSPECTIVE

A German romantic poet of the eighteenth century, Novalis, said:
"Theories are nets; only he who casts will catch." Otherwise, we
might add, there is a danger that the fish will stay in the sea. The
theory that I am using to analyze the reactions of Israeli society,
the Israeli nation-state and its member-individuals, is the psychoanalytic one, which is used as a general psychological theory. In
recent years it has become more acceptable to look at political
persons and political phenomena through lenses that look below the
surface of the consciousness and take unconscious factors into
account. Sometimes this is called psychohistory. But just as the
early settlers of the kibbutzim in Israel practiced a misunderstood
psychoanalysis (for example, by explaining that having the children
living away from their parents, in the children's house, helps avoid
the trauma of the primal scene, or the bad influences of the oedipus
complex), so psychohistory at times seemed to practice a misunderstood depth psychology. A good example of psychohistorical
biography at its best is a biography of T. E. Lawrence that won the
Pulitzer prize and in fact deals also with our part of the world (Mack,
1976). Mack makes use of psychiatric and psychoanalytic knowledge
not in order to diagnose conventional psychopathological entities,
but to understand how special qualities were developed by Lawrence
that enabled him to achieve what he set out to do or become, how
areas of conflict seemed to collaborate with special abilities and
shape the direction of later accomplishments or intensified the
motive for achievement (pp. xxvi and xxvii, *ibid*).

A first attempt at a psychoanalytic history of two ethnic groups in
conflict was recently published about Cyprus (Volkan, 1979).
Volkan, who was born in Cyprus, describes insights into his own
psychological defenses and adaptive manuevers and his ways of
stereotyping in Cyprus. He describes how his ethnic group distorts
and how it tests reality, and he uses a personal dream to highlight
problems of his community. Through all these, the view of the
Turkish Cypriots and their interactions with their Greek neighbors
and enemies attains a depth and perspective that are unusual. People

thus come alive in a greater sense than is usual in scientific essays, more akin, in fact, to the creative depth found in literary and other artistic presentations.

It is by the use of this particular net, that of psychoanalytic theory at its present stage, that I propose to catch some pertinent data about Israeli reactions to the stress of the state of hostilities and tension interrupted by five wars in the last forty years. It is the outsiders who come to Israel who are immediately struck by phenomena that the Israeli citizen, involved and engaged in them day by day, does not seem to notice. To him, perhaps, they become evident when he leaves Israel to go to another country, or when he returns — when, in short, he gains some perspective.

The two phenomena that have the greatest impact upon outsiders are the intensity with which aggression is expressed in daily life: people push in queues, passions are inflamed by drivers who each feel the other is criminally negligent of traffic laws. Visitors to Israel are quite unsurprised by the inordinately high number of traffic accidents, fatalities, and injuries. What else would you expect, they ask, with people driving the way they do on the roads?

The other impression is perceived only by the more sophisticated observers: "How can you live in daily danger," they say, "and not constantly feel fear, concern and worry, for yourselves and your loved ones?" Those Israelis who have heard comments like this many times often reply in a routine way: "You are safer on the streets of Jerusalem at night than you are in New York!" Or, they will point out knowingly that acts of violence always look much worse from afar. "The bomb in Soho frightens people outside of England much more than the Londoners," they will say. The phenomenon I am describing here is technically known in psychoanalytic terminology as the psychological defense mechanism of denial.

One of the few thorough and methodologically sophisticated studies of psychological responses to stress is that of Irving Janis (1958). Janis combines three approaches in studying the reactions of people who are to undergo major surgery when the operation is viewed as a dangerous situation. An example of the first approach is the psychoanalytic case study of a surgical patient who had been in psychoanalytic treatment four times a week for several years. In the second approach, 23 surgical patients were intensively interviewed and observed both before and after undergoing a major operation. Finally, a lengthy questionnaire about reactions to surgical experiences was administered to about 250 men. Thus, Janis combines the intensive with the extensive study of subjects.

On the basis of these three approaches, Janis formulated both descriptive generalizations about patterns of overt stress behavior and theoretical formulations specifying psychodynamic processes that help to explain the descriptive generalizations (p. 8, ibid). Among the hypotheses derived and tested, there are some that seem directly relevant to the two phenomena I have described, the overt expression of hostility and aggression in daily life, and the denial of external threats and dangers to oneself and to one's loved ones.

EXPRESSION OF HOSTILITY

As regards aggression, Janis states that exposure to the threat of bodily harm tends to sensitize the individual to unacceptable hostile and destructive tendencies in his own aggressive behavior. Normally tolerated, they are now — consciously or unconsciously — felt to violate inner superego (conscience) standards. Even though consciously appraised as an event that cannot be influenced by one's own behavior, the objective threat will unconsciously be assimilated to childhood threats of parental punishment for bad behavior (Hypotheses IA and IB, abbreviated). Furthermore, Janis hypothesizes that "given a stress episode of unexpectedly high victimization (i.e., when the perceived victimization was greater than expected), the probability that disappointment reactions will take the form of externalized rage toward danger-control authorities, or toward other parent-surrogates, will be increased by the presence of external cues which tend to reactivate similar childhood experiences . . . . Such effective cues include action or inaction on the part of danger-control authority, which is perceived as deficient behavior; as such it resembles the apparent deficiencies of one's parents when unfair, excessive or undeserved punishment was inflicted" (p. 205).

If we apply the generalizations derived from the stress situation of an impending operation to the Israeli citizen, we should expect that his being exposed to a threat of bodily harm would have the same results: an increased tendency to awareness of hostile and destructive tendencies within himself that are deemed unacceptable by his conscience. Both of these responses could be conscious or unconscious. In addition, we would expect him to react to the external threat in the same way, unconsciously, as if the threat was perceived as a childhood threat and as punishment for bad behavior. This would result mainly in two kinds of reactions: increased guilt feelings, increased anger, or both. Do such reactions occur?

My answer to this question is an unequivocal yes. The statistics for road accidents are higher than almost anywhere else in the world. The readiness to express aggression in the streets is also noticed by the Israelis: the pushiness in queues, the readiness to pounce on the other for apparent injustices, discriminations, or other seemingly unfair or undeserved behavior. The intensity of rivalries among the various professional groups seems evident. In Israel these rivalries are called the "wars of the Jews," to differentiate them from the more "acceptable" wars, of the Jews against their enemies. A variety of reasons or rationalizations are advanced to explain away some of these manifestations, for example, that in Israel there are less positions available, leading to more intense competition. It seems that the average Israeli is more critical of his colleagues than the American, the English, the French, or even the Swiss, although in their countries the number of available positions is also quite limited.

And yet a case can be made that there are other countries where similar behavior is noticeable. The Mediterranean peoples always make much noise and argue loudly and aggressively; the New Yorkers, too, lash each other with their tongues, and more, they have a higher rate of violent crimes than the Israelis. So how are we to understand what is happening in Israel? I believe that there is indeed an increased expression of aggression in daily life, that this is not totally different from what happens in other countries, yet that it does serve as one of several mechanisms that allow for the dissipation of aggression and hostility generated by the continuous state of political tension and hostilities.

In addition, there would be one other way in which aggressive reactions could be triggered or increased through external stress. If the stress episode leads to a perceived victimization higher than expected — here I would include threat to one's loved ones as well as to oneself as a source of feeling victimized — the disappointment felt toward the danger-control authorities would be increased and would tend to increase externalized rage toward authority figures.

As will be pointed out later, the Arab-Israeli conflict provides an unusual opportunity for the citizens of the states involved to externalize their aggressions on the enemy rather than on the authority figures in their countries. When the behavior of the danger-control authority is perceived as deficient, it will be felt to resemble similar deficient behavior of one's parents when unfair, excessive or undeserved punishment was inflicted. Particularly cruel and senseless terrorist raids provide good examples of this behavior, for instance, Ma'alot, or the Coastal Road Massacre. A remarkably strong reaction of conscious assessment of this deficiency occurred after the Yom Kippur War. When, however, the external threat is directed not at one individual or several but at a whole population, one can assume that there is a strengthening of the disappointment and rage, which is reinforced by all and perhaps even by the mass media, and a mitigation of the guilt reactions, which tend to be more prominent in the individual.

DENIAL

But Janis' study and his hypotheses deal not only with the generation of aggression in response to the threat of bodily harm, but also with the mechanism of denial used in such a situation. Hypothesis 3A of his report states that "the closer an anticipated threat of body damage is perceived to be in space or time, the greater will be the individual's motivation to ward off anticipatory fears by minimizing the potential danger and by intellectually denying that he will be seriously affected by it." Hypothesis 4 states that "under conditions where a person is strongly motivated to deny an impending danger, he will tend to rationalize his self-perceptions of residual emotional tension by mislabeling his affective state and attributing it to other, less fear-arousing circumstances." Among the unconscious modes of defense used to ward off anticipatory fear of external dangers is the aggressive fantasy, which can occur either as a reaction formation against passive tendencies or as the mechanism of identification with the aggressor.

Other hypotheses deal with the reactivation of childhood fears of abandonment and the revival of disturbing childhood memories. After experiencing moderate fear before the event — usually helped by realistic appraisal of the external dangers — the individual will react with relative emotional equanimity to the event itself. A highly fearful response before will usually lead to excessive fear after the stress; a relatively unfearful response prior to the stress will usually result in excessive anger after the stressful event.

Applied to the Israeli scene, these hypotheses would lead us to expect a minimization or denial of the threat and of one's being affected by it. The more one is motivated to deny the external danger, the more one will seek extraneous reasons to explain the reactions that do exist, or to mislabel them, i.e., distort one's affective reactions and attribute them to others, to externalize or project them. Unconscious mobilized modes of defense will include unconscious fantasies of one's own aggression, in part to overcome one's passive tendencies in the face of a threat, and the use of identification with the aggressor, which is seen in the child who acts out on his doll the pain inflicted on him by his doctor or dentist. Now it is he who can do to others what before he had to endure passively.

Indeed, these mechanisms, if used, would be important determinants of individual or, at times, national, behavior. National is used here in the sense that the group of individuals that makes up the nation can react as does one individual, and can mutually support and enhance each other's reactions. We are here encountering the methodological problem of inferring from the reactions of the individual those of the group. Much has been said and written about this theme (Mack, 1978; Lifton, 1979; Lifton, 1978). We cannot deal with it adequately here, but will bear in mind that a group consists of individuals.

The last hypothesis of Janis', that a realistic appraisal of the threat leads to moderate fear before the dangerous event and to a relatively adequate response to the event itself, is in line with what is known about reactions to war and to disasters generally (Moses, 1978). The extremes — the highly fearful and the unusually fearless response to danger, but of which are based on a relatively unrealistic evaluation of the danger — will result in a deviant and nonadaptive response after the event, either excessive fear or excessive anger.

It is therefore reasonable to expect, on the basis of our knowledge of psychological responses, comprising both the conscious and the unconscious, that the threat of external danger will lead to denial of the existence of this danger. Furthermore, the more realistic the assessment of the danger, the more adaptive the response will be

(Moses, 1978). This knowledge has been used in military psychiatry since World War II.

It is also important to realize that the threats of external danger mobilize in all of us childhood fears of abandonment, and tend to revive disturbing childhood memories. Since these are usually unconscious, our tendency to keep them is easily reinforced. Once thus reinforced, we tend to focus on the external event rather than on the unpleasant fears and memories it evokes. We push these fears and memories from our conscious mind, whether they result from actual fears and memories, childhood experiences or the external threat that reactivates them.

Blatant denial of external dangers has been described in disaster reactions. It seems here to be a psychologically adaptive state to deny an impending danger in the first phase, that is, the "threat" or "impending danger" phase. Those whose subsequent reactions are adaptive will, however, cease their denial of the danger during the impact phase, when the chances of escaping intact depend in part upon protective behavior. Yet, denial sometimes continues in the face of a seemingly undeniable event, at a very high cost to property and life. In the United States, 90% of a population sample estimated that there was a real danger of war, while only 2% did something about it (Fritz, 1961). At times, people who become aware of an impending danger do not pass on such information, partly because they do not quite want to believe it, and partly because they fear it would cause panic. This is what happens in natural disasters like tornadoes (Wolfenstein, 1957), and also when an enemy attack is imminent. This refusal to acknowledge reality was seen in Pearl Harbor in 1941 and in the Yom Kippur War in 1973. Even after the impact itself, danger is sometimes still denied, or logical connections are not made. This is very much akin to what happens in the denial of fatal disease (Wiseman, 1972; Hertz, 1975; Feifel, 1977; Becker, 1973; De Vries and Carmi, 1979).

When the atomic bomb was dropped on Hiroshima, a man whose house was hit was convinced that this was a local disaster affecting his house alone. A man in the U.S. woke up after a tornado warning in the middle of the night when the flood had reached his house. He decided that it was just rain, went back to sleep, woke again, and wanted to light a cigarette. His hand encountered the water, which had by then reached the height of his bed. In another tornado area where a warning had been given, two elders were sitting together. When they heard the very loud sounds of the tornado approaching closely, the woman said to her husband: "Do you hear the train over there?" He answered: "No, I don't hear anything" (Marks, 1954).

Denial can best be demonstrated by the Israeli situation before the Six Day War. For example, when Jerusalemites went about their daily activities, apparently oblivious to the threats that lurked at the borders of the divided city: the occasional snipings, the terrorist acts, the reprisals by the Israeli army, which sometimes became so predictable that units were decimated by those against whom they were sent. What was denied were the dangers to daily living, the dangers to one's dear and loved ones, especially those in the army, and the danger to the existence of the state itself. Later on, once the intensely perceived dangers of the Six Day War had abated, and the war had ended with a totally unexpected victory, other psychological mechanisms emerged. There was an inflation of the national ego, a narcissistic overevaluation, a tendency to believe in our omnipotence vis-a-vis our neighbors and enemies. Here, too, there were occasional knocks and pushes in the direction of a more realistic evaluation, for example, the War of Attrition and the sacrifice of human life involved. Yet at the time, there was also much denial of physical danger in everyday life — denial of the danger that the newly existing rockets posed for Israeli cities, denial of the need to have a working and efficient civil defense service — as well as an increased overt concern by parents of sons serving in the Israeli Defense Army. These fears, however, were often kept by the mother to herself; she would grapple with them alone at night. The fathers tended more towards denial. After all, they too had served in the army and had survived. The young men themselves began to evolve jocular references to their not quite hidden fears. Taking leave of each other at the end of school, before going into the army, they would say: "See you under the grass."

This widespread denial culminated in the denial to see the reality of the imminent attack of the Yom Kippur War. There was an arrogant and superior attitude, a belief in an omnipotence that did not allow for the idea of a successful thrust by the enemy; therefore a threat did not exist. After the Yom Kippur War came a deflation, a depression not only in response to the death of near and dear ones, but also because of the required change in self-image. This change made for more realism. The Arab enemies were now seen in a more realistic light. Within Israel, there was much anger and blaming of the leaders — the danger-control authorities, in Janis' terminology. Along with that came the growing belief that Israel was a country that was not only good to die for, but also to live for. This represented quite a change in the ideology that had been so stringent and severe ever since the days of the Yishuv, the Jewish community in Palestine (Moses and Kligler, 1966). This community, which lacked the instruments of authority, predated the State of Israel, and had to rely on the dictates of the individual's conscience to enforce the community's demands on the individual. I am hinting here at a change also in the severity of the conscience of the nation, a change that parallels that of the adolescent who needs to mitigate his conscience, a conscience still so severe because it was built up at a time when it was needed to combat wishes and desires of seemingly enormous intensity. Yet the adolescent's conscience needs to be adapted to the reality of the adult that he is about to become, an adult who is permitted to give expression to wishes and desires that were taboo for the child. And so, perhaps, it is with societies and nations. Once a nation has its own enforcement authorities, it is not necessary for the consciences of its citizens to be as severe as before.

As a result of these changes, denial of external threats and dangers was muted. The more realistic appraisal of Israel in its relations to the Arab world led to the peace negotiations and the peace treaty with Egypt as part of an ongoing peace process. Yet it is important to remember that most of the mechanisms described are still at work, are still being used, and may — and do — become more widely or more intensely used at certain stages of the peace process as the ebb and flow of denial and realistic appraisal are brought into play by different parts of the Israeli community. Thus, for example, it is easy for a hawkish pundit or publicist to warn the public not to trust the peace, and prove conclusively that the enemy is bad, utterly untrustworthy, and only out to plan Israel's destruction under the guise of making peace. Such a maneuver is essentially an attempt to reenlist the projections and polarizations of old, the notion that the enemies are all bad and we are all good, and that to trust in peace is only to be outwitted by the enemy rather than being beaten by him on the field of battle.

Leftist doves, on the other hand, seem to use a reversal of this mechanism, a reaction formation against it: they tend to push aside and deny the bad in those others, to see them as the "good guys," whereas all the critical faculties are directed against our own side.

PROJECTION

Another widely used mechanism is that of externalization or projection. It is most convenient to have an external enemy who can be seen as personifying all that is bad, violent, cruel, barbaric, threatening, against whom it is self-evident and natural, indeed necessary, that one defend oneself and one's family. It is indeed easy to fall into the polarization of good and bad, as we have been as used to seeing it depicted in politics as in the Western movies of old. Yet it becomes more and more difficult to hold on to such views, especially as a result of increased contact with "the enemy." I refer here to the fairly extensive contact between the Israeli and Arab population in the West Bank and in the Gaza Strip. The temptation to stereotype the other is reduced in times of more contact, and grows as soon as violent acts are committed, as tempers flare, hostilities begin, and each side pulls back into its own limited orbit. It is in times of war that the projections are most widely used. The expected cruelty of the Jordanians who threatened Jerusalem at its borders on the eve of the Six Day War was matched only by the actual cruelty of the Syrians during the Yom Kippur War. But the horror stories of barbarities, tortures, unimaginable cruelties committed by the enemy were legion. Similar acts committed by our side were not talked or written about. It was only relatively recently that the Israeli public has been forced to become aware of similar acts committed by its own members.

The forcing onto the public of such a retraction of its projection is, in psychological terms, a most useful and necessary — though very painful — happening. We are required to acknowledge that we, too, have "bad" aspects in us. Just as the individual who is helped through psychological treatment to gradually become aware that it is he who harbors angry and destructive wishes and fantasies, not only the enemy, so does it help a group, community, or nation to become more mature when it need not see all the bad outside in order to see only good inside. This is so because it is only when one recognizes one's bad side that one can begin to deal with it more appropriately. In terms of Janis' studies (1958), the more realistically the situation is perceived, the more adaptive, i.e., adequate rather than deviant, is the response. When one needs to remain unaware of one's own aggression, it must perforce find other ways of expression. The classically paranoid person, who sees aggression only in the other, finally comes to the point where he must kill the enemy to avoid being killed by him, so he rationalizes. Nations tend to act likewise when they perceive their existence as threatened and must therefore go to war to erase the threat. Thus, projection of aggression onto the other fosters aggressive acts, while the ability to be aware of one's own aggression increases the chances of containment and constructive usage. This is true both for the individual and for the nation.

RESISTANCE TO CHANGE

In many ways, then, it is most useful for the psychic economy of a nation to have an enemy, and to hold on to him. There will be many forces at work against the giving up of old patterns, of old ways of behaving and relating, and many difficulties in the way of change. We learn from psychological forms of treatment how much resistance there is in the human psyche against change of any kind — in the individual, in a couple, in a family unit, and in any social system, large or small.

To phrase it differently, having lived for forty years or so in a state of tension and hostility with its Arab neighbors, the Jewish community of Palestine and later the State of Israel, has formed certain basic, rigid patterns of behavior that its citizens have become used to. It is easier to hold on to them, to cling to the safety of the familiar, of the known, than to risk the unknown. Again, we can draw on the analogy of psychological treatment: Change arouses fear, even if it is change from a state of suffering, of pain, and of symptoms that were a past way of living with conflicts. This is so because we do not know whether the new and different will be better. It seems to us, on the contrary, that we must give up a sure foothold for a dangerous and uncertain hope that may well turn out to be an illusion. And so it is with the tension of the Arab-Israeli conflict in Israel. Though logically and rationally it seems worthwhile and desirable to move toward peace, there is much in us that balks at forward movement.

The fear of change and the holding on to past patterns — a very general phenomenon in psychic life — is here part of an ambivalence. We consciously allow ourselves to know that we want peace, but we dare not quite admit to ourselves the other side of the coin: the fears, the wish to stay as we are, the reluctance to move forward. Here, as in all psychic areas, lack of awareness means to remain in a rut. Only when we allow ourselves to know consciously that we want to go forward to more peace will we be able to deal with the negative side of our ambivalence, our fears, and our resistances.

A further aspect of adapting to change of any kind requires of us what in psychoanalytic terminology is called the work of mourning. We mourn a loved one who is no longer with us by a process that leads us to think of him or her, to work the relationship over in our thoughts, to reminisce and remember, and thereby gradually, bit by bit so to speak, to detach ourselves from the love object that is gone. Such a process is painful and long. Only when it is adequately carried out and worked through are we free to go on to new relationships. And so it is with many other things in life. We mourn a limb or an eye that has been lost in a similar fashion. Only when the mourning process has been completed can we adapt successfully to the loss that has become part of us. And so it is with loss of functions, whether through ageing or accidents. The same happens also with every transition from one stage of life to another: from childhood to adolescence, or from adolescence to adulthood. We are required to give up patterns of the past, rights and benefits that we have enjoyed but must give up in order to be more grown-up and enjoy different privileges and have different obligations that go with the new privileges.

Much the same process is occurring in the peace process in which Israel is now engaged. Here, too, there is a need to mourn a stage we are about to leave behind us. We must work through the loss of that which we shall leave behind, discovering what it meant to us, what makes it hard to leave — all this in order to gradually be able to turn toward the new and different state of affairs that awaits us as we go on with the peace process. As with an important relationship that has ended or a stage of life that is about to pass to another, so too it is for the community of individuals that make up a nation. It is for this reason that it is so important that the public be appraised of what is to happen and when, that it be informed by its government of the two sides of the coin, the advantages and the risks, the good and the bad that may await it as it moves forward.

HISTORICAL ANALYSIS

I have undertaken to write a chapter on the emotional response to stress in Israel, and here I am describing obstacles and other phenomena which form a part of the peace process. Is that appropriate? Does it make sense? Do the two hang together? I believe they do.

They hang together inseparably because the tensions and hostilities that have made up the fabric of daily life in Israel for at least forty years have now reached a different psychological point. Until the Six Day War, the stress generated by the political situation and its effect on daily life were faced by both the individual and the state. Between the Six Day War and the Yom Kippur War, the psychological situation had changed markedly in one way: After the threatened destruction of the small state, three and a half fearful and anxious weeks of waiting for war to be unleashed were followed by a victory as unexpected as it was dramatic. The armies of three neighboring states were shatteringly defeated. The territory in which Israelis were free to move grew three times in size. A sudden and unexpected inflation in both the size of the country and self-esteem easily led to feelings of grandiosity. The Israel Defense Army became the main object of self-aggrandizement and of narcissistic omnipotence. This had previously existed to some extent but then grew to inordinate proportions, and could be, yet more easily than before, claimed to be based on reality. The group self of the State of Israel (cf Kohut, 1976) was inflated similarly to what is seen in the individual narcissistic disturbances. As happens with individuals, such narcissistic inflation leads to a distorted view of both the self and of reality. Gradually, Israel began to show some of the "splendid isolation" in the political field that Kernberg (1977) describes for narcissistic personalities in their grandiosity and inappropriate self-reliance. It is by now evident to all that feelings of grandiosity and omnipotence precluded appropriate reality testing and critical self-evaluation at the time the Yom Kippur War began. It is perhaps idle speculation to wonder — if an Israeli government less overwhelmed by its own success had attempted to utilize the remarkable military victory in 1967 to try to reach an early settlement — whether such an offer would still have been refused by the Arabs because of their intense narcissistic humiliation. As we know, Israeli governments by and large have thought they could afford to wait it out, that militarily nothing could happen to Israel, while her Arab neighbors and enemies have declared their renewed refusal to deal or talk with Israel.

The third phase of the development of psychological reactions to the specific stresses of the Arab-Israeli conflict and its vagaries and vicissitudes came after the Yom Kippur War. The inflated balloon of Israeli grandiosity was painfully and saddeningly punctured. As in the Six Day War, there was utter surprise, although quite a different one. It is of interest to learn retrospectively that the Egyptian Army General Staff was unaware that the attack had been planned for the Jewish Day of Atonement. Every Israeli at the time was convinced that this was a cunningly planned strategy, showing thereby how utterly outwitted and overwhelmed they had felt. The depressive reaction that set in was only partially a reaction to the loss of life, the injuries, and the number of soldiers taken prisoner. It was more a response to the seemingly incredible fact that the Israeli army could have been taken by surprise and overwhelmed, that the Barlev line, thought impregnable, could have been broken, and that in this way the narcissistic grandiosity and omnipotence of the Israeli army, and therefore of the state, shared so widely by so many of its citizens, was painfully shattered and suddenly deflated. Feelings of grandiosity and of omnipotence were replaced by those of vulnerability, helplessness, shame and humiliation.

While the period between the Six Day War and the Yom Kippur War had been dominated by the group equivalent of pathological narcissism, after the Yom Kippur War there was a painful coming to terms with a previously denied reality. In this third period, psychological reappraisal and critical self-evaluation followed upon a scapegoating of the danger-control authorities who had failed miserably. It was at this time, when there was a more realistic appraisal of Israel's situation and its future within the region, that President Sadat of Egypt made his dramatic visit to Jerusalem. He spoke of "a psychological barrier, a barrier of fear, of deception, a barrier of hallucinations without any action, deed or decision . . . . A barrier of distorted and eroded interruptions of every event and statement. It is this psychological barrier which I described . . . as constituting seventy percent of the whole problem."

It is reasonable to assume that Sadat had his own reasons for assigning such a large share of the difficulties of the Arab-Israeli conflict to the psychological area. I believe that these reasons are related to the narcissistic gratification he was willing to offer his erstwhile enemy: unexpected and dramatic recognition performed on the public stage that followed a long period where nonrecognition was used as a weapon of narcissistic shaming and humiliation, mainly by the Arabs against Israel, but also to some extent in the reverse direction. As a reward for such a dramatic psychological gesture of recognition and even respect, President Sadat hoped to gain in return everything that would, in its turn, heal the narcissistic injuries of the Arabs: the return of all the lost territories.

But whatever reasons President Sadat may have had, it is clear that he, more than other leaders, recognized that a psychological problem was indeed part of the Arab-Israeli conflict. Such a recognition seems still quite far from the minds of Israeli leaders. I have spelled out elsewhere (Moses and Kligler, 1966) why in Israel psychological and introspective thinking has been widely denigrated. Israeli ideology emphasized the needs of the collective at the expense of those of the individual. For reasons that are only partly related to the pressures of the external needs and dangers, but predominantly to a reaction against and continuation of the values and way of life in the *shtetl,* the East European Jewish town community, Israelis were not allowed the luxury of feeling or recognizing their feelings. Many years ago, Yael Dayan (1961) wrote a book called *Envy the Frightened,* telling the story of a boy who envied those who were able and permitted to feel frightened. Introspection or recognition of the needs of the individual — those of the new immigrants, the holocaust survivors, or, indeed, of those who had to absorb the new immigrants — were just not sanctioned in the Yishuv or its successor, the State of Israel. Indeed, to this day, one cabinet minister can publicly slander another by saying: "He needs to see a psychiatrist." This remains so, although there are today many people seeking psychological treatment, different forms of psychotherapy or psycho-analysis, but most would naturally not have it known that they do.

The lack of psychological awareness and readiness to see psycho-logical motivations in oneself or other is thus an integral part of the

Israeli way of life. No wonder, then, that externalization, projection, and denial fit well with such a psychological economy. Yet here, too, there have been clear signs of a trend for change, slow as it may be. I have indicated the existence of these trends toward more emphasis on the individual and his needs, and more introspection in a paper some years ago (Moses, 1966). That this trend has been maintained can be seen in the increased discussion of psychological problems both on television and, to a lesser extent, in the daily newspapers.

THE PROCESS OF MOURNING

One area where the process of mourning and its absence can be clearly perceived is in the mourning over territories to be given up. A man who loses a limb must mourn this part of himself — before and after its loss if the loss is expected, and afterward if it comes unexpectedly — by dealing with the limb and its loss in a way very similar to that in which an individual mourns a lost loved person. He will reminisce about it, how it used to be, how it would function, how it would feel, and thus gradually detach himself from that which is no more. In the same way, we Israelis need to mourn the territories that we are to give up. Following the Six Day War we became accustomed to regarding these territories as part of Israel, as part of ourselves, and we must now give them up within ourselves so that we can emotionally relinquish them, in addition to doing so physically. This process, as all mourning, is slow and painful, and requires us to come to terms with a new reality. An individual who loses a limb will suffer from what is called "phantom limb," he will feel pain in the leg or arm that is there no longer if he does not adequately mourn the limb. It is only after such mourning has been more or less completed that the pains of "phantom limb" disappear.

When mourning does not take place in its appropriate and full form, as is sometimes seen in mothers who mourn their fallen sons or in husbands and wives who mourn the spouse they lost, then the individual holds on to the past and is unable to free himself for the tasks of the present or the opportunities of the future. Pathological mourning of this kind does not allow a person to engage fully in activities that demand his attention. He is continuously glued to the memories of the dead person, he cannot move away from them, neither for daily activities nor for new relationships. Such clinging to past patterns is a phenomenon found in psychic life in general. It comes up in every psychological treatment, including all those professionals who enter treatment mainly in order to gain awareness of their own unconscious life to be able more effectively to help others with their conflicts. In other words, clinging to past patterns is a universal phenomenon of individual man.

There is one particular form of clinging to past patterns that is more extreme than most others. After encountering a psychic trauma, which overwhelms us, we will be totally engaged in dealing with the traumatic event. We will think about it during the day, dream about it at night, and will have room for little else in our psychic activity. This unusual psychic activity is understood to be an attempt at belated mastery, as has been described many years ago (Freud, 1932; Fenichel, 1950; Moses, 1978). Sometimes it happens that persons who have been traumatized, seek out — strange as this may seem — exactly the type of trauma that they have been exposed to. This is in line with that persistent repetition of past patterns that seems to be characteristic of mankind, which in psychoanalytic terminology is called the repetition-compulsion. It is, as the term implies, a compulsion to repeat past patterns, however painful they may have been then and may still be. It is a repeated reenactment of past relationships and hurts, which does not allow the person to learn from experience, but forces him to repeat the same mistakes. Most of us manage to hide this self-destructive way of behaving behind a facade of seeming adaptation to the society we live in. Only occasionally do we ourselves obtain a glimpse that perhaps this is what we are still doing. It is easier to recognize this phenomenon in others. Often many of us are determined not to be like a parent who showed behavior that we found particularly offensive, and yet we end up at times finding out, much to our chagrin, that we indeed are like that parent in some central respect that we wished painstakingly to avoid.

I believe that there is a danger that the Jewish people may be reenacting a type of relationship that will repeat the many traumas of the past, particularly the many persecutions that have characterized the fate of the Jewish people, certainly ever since the Middle Ages. The danger is that having experienced passively the active persecution

by others, we may tend to perpetuate the role of victim for ourselves, possibly to the extreme of seeking it out. We see hints of such
behavior when the Arab foes of today are viewed as though they
were like the Nazis of the holocaust, or, at times, as though they
indeed *are* the Nazis today. At times, we also encounter in ourselves,
in some of us, the utter conviction that our Jewish fate will repeat
itself, in that we will again be attacked or slaughtered or destroyed.
The danger of such expectations is that they often tend to influence
the events. The person who totally expects to be victimized indeed
brings about this self-fulfilling prophecy. Such a danger can only be
averted by increased awareness of the patterns that we enact in our
life.

For us Jews, for the Jewish people, for the Israeli nation, such
awareness is, I believe, essential to allow us to be certain that we
shall not compulsively repeat patterns of the past, that we shall
not expect to be persecuted and attacked, and thereby — worst
result of all — bring about that which we feared most.

The one means of combating the enormous power of unconscious
motivation as it influences outward behavior is *awareness*. It is
awareness that is slowly, gradually, painfully acquired in the long
and tedious process of psychological treatment. We have little experience about how such awareness can be acquired by larger groups.
We do know quite a bit about the forces operating both for and
against such awareness in small groups. We know something about
the forces operating in large groups, yet not enough (Bion, 1961).
Social systems that, in size, lie between the family or small groups
and large groups such as communities or nations, have at times
sought the professional help that psychiatrists, psychologists, or
psychoanalysts can offer (Sofer, 1961; Rice, 1965). Nations have
not so far sought out such help, nor do we know whether they
will.

Yet this much is clear: Increased awareness is the only effective
tool against unconsciously motivated behavior against which we
are otherwise powerless. And such awareness can be acquired
by bringing matters out into the open, by open discussion and
argument, be it in books, in articles, in newspapers or on television,
or in different kinds of social groups that tackle these different
subjects.

REFERENCES

Abramson, J. H. Emotional disorder, status inconsistency and migration. A health questionnaire in Israel. *Milbank Memorial Fund Quarterly*, 1966, *44*, 23–48.

Aviram, U., and Levav, I. Psychiatric epidemiology in Israel – An analysis of five community studies. *Acta Scandinavica*, 1975, *52*, 295–311.

Bash, K. W., and Bash-Liechti, J. Rural-urban migration, psychopathology and psychosomatic disorders in Central Iran. *Proceedings of the 5th World Congress of the International College of Psychosomatic Medicine*. Jerusalem, 1979.

Becker, E. *The Denial of Death*. New York: Free Press, 1973.

Bion, W. R. *Experiences in Groups*. London: Tavistock, 1961.

Brown, D. E. General stress in a group of Filipino-Americans in Hawaii. *Proceedings of the 5th World Congress of the International College of Psychosomatic Medicine*. Jerusalem, 1979.

Burton-Bradley, B. G. Rapid Culture Change, stress and anomie in Papua, New Guinea. *Proceedings of the 5th World Congress of the International College of Psychosomatic Medicine*. Jerusalem, 1979.

Dayan, Y. *Envy the Frightened*. Jerusalem: Steimatzky, 1963.

De Vries, A., and Carmi, A. (eds.), *The Dying Human*. Tel Aviv: Turtledove Publications, 1979.

Dohrenwend, B. P., and Dohrenwend, B. S. (eds.), *Stressful Life Events*. New York: Wiley, 1974.

Feifel, H. *New Meanings of Death*. New York: McGraw-Hill, Blackistone, 1977.

Fenichel, O. *The Psychoanalytic Theory of Neurosis*. New York: Free Press MacMillan, 1950.

Freud, S. *New Introductory Lectures, Vol. 22*, Standard edition. London: The Hogarth Press, 1964.

Fritz, C. E. Disaster. *In,* Merton, R. K., and Nisbett, R. A. (eds.), *Contemporary Social Problems*. New York: Harcourt, 1961.

Group for the Advancement of Psychiatry. Self-involvement in the Middle East conflict, Oct. 1978.

Hertz, D. G. Confrontation with death. *Dynamic Psychiatry*, 1975, *8*, 197–215.

Hinkle, E. L. The effects of exposure to culture change, social change and changes in inter-personal relations on health. *In,* Dohrenwend, B. P., and Dohrenwend, B. S. (eds.), *Stressful Life Events*. New York: Wiley, 1974.

Hoek, A., Moses, R., and Terespolsky, L. Emotional disorders in an Israeli immigrant community. *In,* Kiev, A. (ed.), *Social Psychiatry, Vol. 1.* 183–196. New York: Science House, 1969.

Janis, I. L. *Psychological Stress*. New York: Wiley, 1958.

Kark, S. L., and Mainemer, N. Integrating psychiatry into community health and care: Epidemiologic foundations. *Israel Annals of Psychiatry*, 1977, *15*, 181–198.

Kernberg, O. *Borderline Conditions and Pathological Narcissism*. New York: Jason Aronson, 1977.

Kohut, H.   Creativeness, charisma, group psychology: Reflections on the self-analysis of Freud. *Psychological Issues,* 1976, *9,* 379–425.

Kringlen, E.   Personality, stress and coronary heart disease: A twin study. *Proceedings of the 5th World Congress of the International College of Psychosomatic Medicine.* Jerusalem, 1979.

Levav, I.   Target groups in community psychiatry: An epidemiological approach. *Israel Annals of Psychiatry,* 1977, *15,* 199–212.

Lifton, R. G.   *The Broken Connection.* New York: Simon and Schuster, 1979.

Mack, J.   *A Prince of Our Disorder: The Life of T. E. Lawrence.* New York: Little Brown, & London: Weidenfeld Nicholson, 1976.

Marks, E. S. et al., Human reactions in disaster situations. Unpublished report, National Research Center, University of Chicago, *Vols. 1, 2, 3,* 1954.

Marmot, M., and Syme, L.   Acculturation and coronary heart disease in Japanese Americans. *American Journal of Epidemiology,* 1976, *104,* 225–247.

Mattila, V. G., and Salokangas, R. K. B.   Stress caused by life changes and its idiosyncratic effect as a factor predisposing to illness. *Proceedings of the 5th World Congress of the International College of Psychosomatic Medicine.* Jerusalem, 1979.

Moses, R.   Adult psychic trauma: The question of early predisposition and some detailed mechanisms. *International Journal of Psychoanalysis,* 1978, *59,* 353–364.

Moses, R.   Community psychiatry in times of emergency. *Israel Annals of Psychiatry,* 1977, *15,* 277–288.

Moses, R., and Kligler, D.   The institutionalization of mental health values in Israel and the United States: A comparison. *Israel Annals of Psychiatry,* 1966, *4,* 148–161.

Polliack, M. R., and Shavitt, N.   Psychoneurosis and mental disorders in the community. *Family Physician,* 1976, *5,* 17–25 (Hebrew).

Polliack, M. R.   The relationship between the Cornell Medial Index scores and attendance rates. *J. Royal Coll. Gen. Pract.,* 1971, *21,* 453.

Rahe, R. H., Bennett, L. K., Romon, N. M.   Subjects' recent life changes and coronary heart disease in Finland. *American Journal of Psychology,* 1973, *130,* 1222–1226.

Rice, A. K. *Learning for leadership.* London: Tavistock Publications, 1965.

Russeck, H. I.   Stress, Tobacco and coronary disease in North American Professional Groups. *Journal of American Medical Association,* 1965, *192,* 189–194.

Russeck, H. I., and Russeck, L. G.   Is emotional stress an etiologic factor in coronary heart disease? *Psychosomatics,* 1976, *17,* 63–67.

Sofer, C. *The organization from within.* London: Tavistock Publication, 1961.

Theorell, T., and Floderus, M. B. Workload, a risk of myocardial infarctions: A prospective psychosocial analysis. *Journal of Epidemiology, 1977, 6,* 17–21.

Volkan, V. D. *Cyprus – War and Adaptation.* Charlottesville: University Press of Virginia, 1979.

Wiseman, A. D. *On Dying and Denying.* New York: Behavior Publications, 1972.

Wolfenstein, M. *Disaster – A Psychological Essay.* Glencoe, Ill: Free Press, 1957.

7.
Children Under Stress

Amiram Raviv

Tel Aviv University

Avigdor Klingman

University of Haifa

Ever since its birth in 1948, the State of Israel has been in a state of war with its neighboring Arab states, and thus its short history has been paved with enough stress-arousing incidents and crisis conditions to cause unrest in states much bigger than Israel. While the adults living in Israel are exposed to a continuously threatening situation, their children are exposed to the effects of the incidents and to the threatening communications, in addition to the reactions of the adults themselves. In this chapter we will discuss the specific characteristics of the stressful situation that children in Israel face, summarize the major research done on the effects of these stresses on children in different conditions, present an interpretation of the research findings and the clinical observations, and describe a number of applied projects based on these interpretations within the framework of the educational system.

CHILDREN IN STRESSFUL SITUATIONS:
A VIEW OF THE SITUATION IN ISRAEL

The typical Israeli child is aware, from a young age, of his country being in a state of war, and of the various dangers awaiting him, his family, and those around him. In spite of the peace agreement reached between Israel and Egypt, the stressful situation has not disappeared. Even as these lines are being written, there are Israeli settlements that are being shelled, and children in these settlements must at times sleep in bomb shelters. Tangible and concrete factors contribute to the feeling of stress in children. For many years Israeli citizens have been the victims of indiscriminate destruction caused by terrorist attacks. While the attacks have fortunately been curbed, between the years 1974 and 1980 there were fourteen terrorist attacks in which hostages were taken. In eleven of these incidents, children were directly involved in the terrorists' actions. A tragic event in which many children were hurt and that frighteningly demonstrates an extremely stressful situation is the massacre at Ma'alot.

On May 15, 1974, close to midnight, three terrorists infiltrated Ma'alot, a small town on the northern border, near Lebanon. They seized control of an apartment in one of the buildings, wounded the head of the family, entered another apartment and killed the mother, the father, and their four-year-old son, and fatally wounded their five-year-old daughter. Afterward they broke into the school building in which high school pupils on a field trip were asleep for the night. Seventeen pupils and teachers escaped from the building, while eighty-six pupils and the school nurse were held hostage for sixteen hours. As the terrorists' ultimatum ended, the armed forces broke in, killed the terrorists, and took over the building. Twenty-two pupils were killed and sixty wounded.

A treatment team that was sent to assist the surviving children held individual and group discussions with them. The following topics were brought up in these discussions.

The pupils repeatedly mentioned the terrible fright that they experienced in the situation, and the fear of being thrown again into a similar situation. There were expressions of pain over the loss of close friends, guilt feelings over their own behavior during the incident, and loss of faith in the teachers who fled instead of taking the responsibility upon themselves. There were complaints of tiredness and inability to concentrate that were due to a great extent to insomnia and nocturnal fears. The pupils mentioned difficulties in returning to their routine framework. In a follow-up study carried out two years after the incident, it was found that 75% of the survivors suffered from insomnia, nightmares, and psychosomatic complaints, 60% reported fearing the trauma would recur, 30% suffered from depression and complained of "a heavy feeling in the chest area," 20% experienced bedwetting, general distress and fear of people ("something terrible will happen to me"). A small percentage were reported to have personality disturbances, regression, and overt aggressive behavior. One girl attempted to commit suicide. But beyond the effects on those who were directly involved in the incident and on their relatives, there were severe functional problems in the educational institution from which the children came. Pupils were absent frequently and groups of pupils — among those that were directly assaulted, and also those that were not — would come together in the hallways and schoolyard, ceaselessly discussing the massacre. The motivation of the pupils, the majority having come from deprived families, was low before the massacre and was then further reduced. This view of the situation was exacerbated by the reactions of the adults: men refused to leave their houses even to go to work, fearing to leave their wives and children at home alone; mothers wandered the streets in shock and didn't even bother to change from their nightgowns and robes into other clothing; teachers found it hard to understand why the pupils were shocked and behaved irregularly and failed to adjust their attitude to the situation. Children who returned from hospitals added to the level of fright with outbursts of crying, tales of their nightmares, and their claim that they felt safer in the well-protected hospital than in their homes (Yanoov, 1975).

The above is not the only incident in which Israeli children served as targets and victims of terrorist attacks. Many children were directly assaulted, were face-to-face with the terrorists, or witnessed severe harm done to their parents as a result of explosives. In 1978, for example, there were 63 incidents in which 21 people were killed and 290 wounded. In 1977, there were 124 incidents and attacks by terrorists in which 40 people were killed and 300 wounded (Government Yearbook, 1979).

Observations of schoolchildren's reactions to war and to terrorist attacks raise the possibility that war is not necessarily the most stressful situation for children. In wartime, children are far from the front, and in the absence of knowledge of the objective dangers they can experience relative security. By contrast, attacks on the civilian rear during relatively tranquil times produce severely stressful situations, particularly when children are directly involved. It seems that the more a child feels that the threat is aimed at him personally, the greater the stress. The degree of stress that each child feels depends undoubtedly on many variables, such as age, sex, personality traits, and environmental and family factors. At the same time, the distance of the child from the site of the incident has a major influence: a child who lives in a border town that is attacked is often under more pressure than a child who lives far from the border (Klingman and Wiesner, 1981). There is also a subjective psychological distance (Benyamini, 1976), which is a result of the degree of personal resemblance to the victim, causing identification. Identifying with characteristics similar to those of the victims explains the high levels of fear found among Israelis of the same age groups and social strata as the victims, even though they are removed from areas attacked by terrorists.

The media in general, and television in particular, contribute their part to the reduction of distances because such attacks are often over-reported. Children in Israel are very much exposed to the news, particularly television news (Adoni, Cohen, 1979), and by absorbing a great deal of information they are indirectly exposed to many stressors.

Examination of the life-style of the normal child, even when he isn't directly exposed to danger, brings to light many potential causes of stress. Even though some of them, such as repeated warnings not to touch suspicious objects, are meant to protect the child, at the same time they make him aware of the constant danger around him.

The theme of suspicious objects that may be bombs is frequently discussed on television. A short propoganda filmstrip warning people to be aware of suspicious objects and describing the appropriate behavior in case one is discovered is shown almost daily. In just about every school in Israel parents have guard duty, checking every person that enters the school. These security measures have become a routine formality at the entrance to all movie theaters and other public places. A few times every year schoolchildren practice civil defense measures: they enter shelters, test the alarms, practice first aid, and in the higher grades train emergency procedures in preparation for war.

The schools in Israel devote a great deal of attention to the topics of heroism and the fighters in Israeli wars. Every year, the day before Yom Ha'Atzmaut (Israeli Independence Day), everything comes to a standstill, a memorial siren is sounded, and the nation unites with its heroes. Thus, the army and the price of victory occupy a child's attention at a young age. Many children have firsthand experience of the absence of their fathers, who have military service in the reserves. Many fathers don military uniforms and serve in the army at least one month each year. Soldiers in active service or in the reserves are often seen on the streets while on leave. These daily sights intensify the awareness of Israelis and their children of the real pressures in their everyday life. It must also be pointed out that almost every boy in Israel is drafted into the army at the end of high school. The end of childhood in Israel is marked by compulsory conscription for a period of three years. The youngsters leave their home and enter a strict and spartan framework in which the elements of danger and potential harm are intensified. This transition often causes tension and unrest among many young men and women.

In addition to a description of the objective stressors, a few additional facts about Israel may provide a wider and more meaningful perspective of our main theme.

In Israel there are about three million Jewish inhabitants, one million of whom are children in various educational frameworks. The limited size of the population intensifies personal involvement and stress (Breznitz, 1980). There is a feeling of a shared fate. Thus the personal distance is reduced and everyone feels threatened. The official educational policy encourages this feeling of involvement and shared fate. The communications media also contribute to this atmosphere so that even a child removed from the sight of the attack may experience some of its impact.

Israel is a country of immigrants. Alongside immigrants from Europe, most of them from families that survived the holocaust, came hundreds of thousands of immigrants who escaped from Arabic countries. The educational and cultural gaps between the various subpopulations have not yet been bridged, and contribute to the high degree of sensitivity and unrest.

In a typical classroom in Israel there are pupils whose parents came from different countries of origin, and the socioeconomic backgrounds of their families are heterogeneous. Even though most of the schoolchildren in Israel are native born, according to data from 1978, only 12.5% of them have native-born parents. The melting pot of various cultures is another relevant factor that must be taken into account when examining the stress situations that children of immigrants must face.

The Yom Kippur War, like an earthquake, shook all facets of life in Israel. Suddenly, the relative sense of security achieved in the Six Day War was shattered. It is important to note that the joy of victory in 1967 was particularly great and was accompanied by a sense of great relief because it came after a period of anticipation character-ized by high levels of anxiety and fear of casualities. Thus the surprise and the shock that came in 1973 because of the lack of preparedness and the intensity of the trauma due to the high rate of Israeli casualties (2,500 killed and 10,000 wounded). The war itself lasted only three weeks, but the impact on the population can be seen as a trauma whose effects are continuous (Kaffman, 1977).

The stresses of the war were acute because they evoked the latent fear of genocide and memories of the holocaust. It should be remem-bered that many Israelis are themselves survivors of the holocaust, or the children or grandchildren of survivors. The children in Israel are made aware of the holocaust and its implications to the nation from reading, studies in school, and the mass media. There exists in Israel a formal policy of rememberance of the holocaust as a per-manent facet in the national consciousness. In schools a certain amount of time is specifically allocated for the teaching of this topic. Year by year there is a memorial day during which the events of the holocaust are described again and again. Israeli children also attain a great amount of information from literature describing the suffering of Jews during the war, particularly the deaths of the more than one million children who were killed in concentration camps. Thus, when discussing the stress that Israeli children experience, one should not forget the existence of the shadow of the holocaust that is continuously in the background of all actual stressors.

So far we have tried to describe the situation with particular em-phasis on the child in Israel and the specific stressors to which he is exposed. These should be added to the stressors that, while not specific to Israel, are yet very important. Diseases and various crises in the life of a child and his family are recurring factors that produce personal stress in children as individuals. It is enough to recall that during the years 1977–1979, more than 10,000 children were harmed in car accidents. Most of them were only superficially wounded, but some were killed and quite many were seriously wounded.

Once again it is important to recall the small number of citizens in Israel to understand the implications of the impact of these accidents. They not only affect the accident victims and their families, but also all their friends and classmates. The high rate of solidarity and involvement characteristic of Israeli society substantially increase the amount of stress that various crisis situations produce. This phenomenon can also be seen in relation to personal crises and family problems. In addition to increasing the stress, there is acute sensitivity and awareness of pain and a great deal of support from the social support systems to which a child belongs. There are, of course, social units in which the support is particularly strong like in the kibbutzim (Kaffman, 1977). But in other echelons of the society as well, one can identify phenomena of social support that are activated during crises (Halpern, 1980). In this, perhaps lies the strength of Israeli society.

In order to introduce the reader to a comprehensive and systematic picture concerning children and adolescents under stress in Israel, we shall refer to the literature and results of research conducted in this area.

COMPARATIVE AND LONGITUDINAL STUDIES

Unfortunately, Israel is a natural laboratory for the study of war stress, especially since the Yom Kippur War (Milgram, 1978). Studying an Israeli population experiencing war stresses and situational crises, scholars and professionals from the behavioral sciences have been able to document and systematize certain stress-related phenomena and ways of treating people under stress.

Two international congresses dealing with stress were hosted by Israel in 1975 and 1978. In each one of them many works were presented with the theme of children under stress. Not all the presentations were based on empirical research, and some of them described various phenomena that could not be easily measured and quantified. Often one deals with a population that is particularly sensitive or with themes that are almost impossible to measure. Problems of professional ethics and technical difficulties as well as difficulties related to personal involvement of the researcher often make it difficult to promote research in this area. And yet, some of the work that was done in Israel concerning reactions of children to stress throw interesting light on the topic.

We shall now review the most critical works that exemplify the problems and characteristics of the research on children under stress in Israel.

Death of a Parent

The death of a parent is a major trauma and causes one of the heaviest stressors in the life of a child. Many soldiers who fell during the Israeli wars left children as orphans. Traffic accidents and disease also leave many children orphaned from father or mother. The suffering of the orphans and their sorrow as well as their adjustment to the new situation raised many critical questions. Some of the research by Israeli scholars attempted to test children who became orphans. The common aim of these studies was to describe the difficulties characteristic of these children in order to provide a rationale for help.

Elizur (1978) made a systematic survey in an attempt to define the typical responses of coping with the trauma and compare them with responses that inhibit adjustment. In order to test the responses of normal children whose fathers died during the war, the mothers and teachers of 24 orphans that were raised on a kibbutz were interviewed 2 to 6 months after the death of the father. Following 18 to 20 months after the death of the father, the same mothers and teachers were interviewed again. As a comparison group, 24 mothers of orphans who lived in the city and who had characteristics similar to the mothers of the kibbutz were also interviewed.

The orphans under consideration were one to ten years old. The findings of the survey clearly indicate the extent to which the death of the father in war is a particularly stressful situation for the small child. The disturbance of the equilibrium that is brought about by the father's death and the resulting changes in the family create major obstacles to the ability of the child to cope (Kaffman and Elizur, 1977). The children exhibited disturbances in their day-to-day functioning and in their interpersonal relations. Various symptoms and behavioral problems appeared close to the time of the disaster, but also persisted one and a half years after the event. Most of the responses of the children could be divided into two categories: (1) Responses of mourning typical of young children, which include various defensive reactions such as denial, repression, and emotional release through crying and extreme moods, memory recall and the search for a father surrogate. (2) Behavioral problems and symptoms that appeared or intensified after the disaster. Eighty-six percent of the children demonstrated responses like crying, moodiness, sadness, and depression for one to six months following the death of the father. The other symptoms included a particularly intensified dependence on the mother or on the educator, intensified aggression and expressions of anger, restlessness, and various fears. Nocturnal fears, especially those related to the disaster, appeared in 50% of the children. It seems that the feeling of helplessness of the child vis-a-vis the trauma increases the level of anxiety, reduces the basic confidence, and increases the dependency needs of the child (Kaffman and Elizur, 1979). Fifty percent of the children exhibited serious mourning responses and adjustment disturbances, even one and a half years later (Elizur, 1978).

Kaffman and Elizur point out that there is actually no typical psychological syndrome that can be seen as the normal mourning response. The specific combination of various symptoms, the duration of the responses and their intensity, are different from child to child. After taking those differences into account, however, it was possible to see some responses that were typical of most of the children. Chief among them was the immediate reaction of the child to the stress involved in the death of the father in terms of his emotional reactions. The above results do not confirm the findings of other scholars that tend to decrease the importance of the emotional reaction in the mourning of children (Fleming and Altchul, 1963; Nagera, 1970; Wolfenstein, 1966). Most of the children expressed their suffering openly and intensely. It is conceivable that the different results are due to the differences in the methods used. While the data are often based on clinical reports that are given retrospectively, in the Israeli study they were based on reports by mothers who observed the emotional responses of their children closely and recently. There were differences between the reports of the teachers and those of the mothers, indicating that even the teachers were quite unaware of the children's expressions of sorrow since these were more latent in school than at home.

Forty-five additional children who lost their fathers in the Yom Kippur War were tested in order to evaluate the impact of the loss on a short-term basis (three to six months). Lifshitz (1974) was particularly interested in the social organizational context of the child. She found specific behavioral patterns characteristic to orphans. They exhibited reduced interest in the teacher and in the school materials, as well as less interest in their peers. The teachers tended to describe the orphans as a group that is different, and they see them as "too mature" or "too childish."

Another Israeli study (Smilansky and Diksal, 1977) tested the adjustment of orphans in the educational, social, and emotional spheres. These were all orphans of either the father or the mother, and no distinction was made between the causes of death. The research was conducted about two years before the Yom Kippur War and included 281 children that were orphans for various periods of time. The subjects in this study were compared to peers from their own class and it was found that their scholastic performance is below average. Evaluation of their cognitive functioning, as given by the teacher, was also found lower than those of nonorphans. A sociometric test revealed that the orphans are more often rejected as compared with the control group. This result is quite surprising because it is often thought that other children in the same class will understand through their parents and teacher that orphans should not be rejected even if they are not highly liked. It appears, however, that the teachers were totally unaware of this rejection.

It is conceivable that the main reason for this rejection lies in the children's response to death. This subject causes inhibition and rejection of intimate relations with children who lost one of their parents. It was found that the orphans have reduced self-confidence, are more given to moodiness, and give up easily when confronted with obstacles. The expression of the above behaviors can be added to the other factors leading to rejection by the nonorphans, who are at a loss when facing these behavioral manifestations.

Another aspect of the adjustment of orphans concerned the age of the children. According to Smilansky and Diksal (1977), the adjustment of the orphan does not depend on the age during which the death occurred or on the number of years that have since passed, but primarily on the age at the time of the evaluation. The critical variable, according to them, is the perception the orphans have of the concept of death and its various aspects, and to what extent they are able to apply this conception to the dead parent. In the absence of a clear understanding of the concept of death, so they argue, the child will be more disturbed and unable to concentrate in studies.

Lifshitz and her associates (1977) also did not find differences in the amount of adjustment of orphans of different ages. On the other hand, in a study (Lifshitz, 1974) that was conducted before the Yom Kippur War, it was found that orphaned children below the age of seven were defined by their teachers as having more difficulties than those that lost their parent at a later age. Fifty-seven percent of the orphaned children below the age of seven were described as having internal problems, as compared with fourteen percent of children that had both parents. No such significant difference was found among children that were orphaned after the age of seven.

Lifshitz and her associates (1977) tried to explain this contradiction by pointing out that the teachers' evaluations of adjustment in children shortly after the disaster do not indicate differences in behavior. The findings of Elizur and Kaffman (1979) do not, however, support this explanation. On the basis of evaluations made close to the time of the death, they point out certain expressions of sorrow in kindergarten children that are different than those of school children. It should be recalled, however, that this study employed a different methodology, which concentrated on different aspects and different criteria of behavior, and therefore there is a problem in comparing the two researches. It was found that young children were more deeply involved in talking about the deceased and in recalling memories. Kindergarten children also denied the finality of death more often than school children. This last phenomenon fits well with Smilansky's 1980 finding concerning the development of the concept of death by children. In the last year of kindergarten and the first grade, about 75% of the children showed understanding of the various aspects of the finality of death, whereas in second grade more than 90% were able to completely demonstrate the finality aspect of death. This may also be one of the reasons for the difficulty exhibited by older orphans in discussing the death of their father or mother. Other differences included more expressions of dependency, difficulty in taking leave, and nocturnal fears in the younger children.

Since the problem of adjustment is a multidimensional one, it is difficult to take a simple position on this problem. It is reasonable to assume that there are many additional variables that influence the outcome of the loss of a parent. In this context it is worthwhile to mention the position of Elizur and Kaffman (1979). Their investigation of the reactions of sorrow by brothers and sisters of different ages within the same family indicates that they are very much influenced by the example given by the remaining parent, whereas behavioral problems are more often determined by developmental, personality, and environmental causes.

It seems that acquisition of the concept of death is one of the developmental factors that greatly contribute to the adjustment of the small child. In other studies Smilansky (1980, 1981) tested the stages in the evolvement of the conceptualization of death by orphans and normal children. It appears that children in Israel are relatively advanced in the acquisition of a mature concept of death as compared with children that were tested in the United States and Europe. Salience of the theme of death in the life of the child is clearly a facilitating factor. Smilansky (1980) quotes a work by Cana'ani that compared the extent of development of the concept of death in children that live in an air force base with those that live in the city. The ages of the children were four and a half to five and a half years old. The intimacy of the residence and involvement in the life of the community, particularly following a tragedy in the lives of a pilot's family, contributed to the awareness of death and caused the children of the pilots to acquire a higher score on conceptualization of death than those who lived in the city.

Following the Yom Kippur War it appeared that the theme of death was more familiar to the children than before. They talked about it freely and frequently. While there was no significant difference in the level of conceptualization of death before and after the Yom Kippur War (Smilansky, 1980), if the analysis was made separately for underdeveloped and developed children it could be seen that the former gained in conceptualization of death after the war, whereas the latter did not change. It thus seems that the additional information due to the war itself helped the conceptualization of those children who could yet develop.

Along with descriptions of orphan-adjustment problems, scholars have tried to investigate factors that can increase the chances of coping in those children. Various kinds of social support are seen as variables that are particularly important in this context. According to Lifshitz et al. (1977), the adjustment of the orphan depends to a great extent on his family functioning as a cooperative and responsible group. The orphans in kibbutzim were found to adjust better than those of the cities or the moshavim. This can to some extent be accounted for by the greater amount of social support that children in the kibbutz have access to. It is also possible that the sensitivity of kibbutz educators and specific professional advice frequently given to kibbutz mothers are also influential factors. Kaffman and Elizur (1980) found that while bereavement is a major stressor to children everywhere, there were some systematic differences between kibbutz and city children. These differences, according to the authors, could be partly attributed to the higher level of social support in the kibbutz. It was found that city orphans are on the whole more anxious and less secure, exhibit higher levels of behavioral problems such as insomnia and nocturnal fears, are more dependent on adults, and are to a greater extent looking for a "father surrogate."

The conceptualization proposed by Caplan (1974) concerning support systems and their value in reducing the stress in crisis situations serves Halpern (1981) in her analysis of the factors contributing to the adjustment of orphans. The behavior of orphans who were invited for a vacation by the military unit to which their fathers belonged before they were killed demonstrated that they developed a kind of mutual help network. Their relationships with each other were very similar to the relationships of adults who create self-help networks (Halpern, 1980). The interviews with those children clearly indicated that these meetings were very satisfying to them because they were allowed to be with children like themselves. They felt that mutual entertainment with brothers of the same fate was a reward for the negative stigma of orphanhood that they shared. At the same time, however, it must be pointed out that classmates can also serve as a support group for the orphans. This was found in a study by Halpern (1981) conducted nine months after the Yom Kippur War. Peer support systems were particularly strong in classes that studied in groups rather than those using frontal lectures. The results also indicated that the extent of social support is a direct function of the amount of stress to which the child is subjected. Halpern believes that the conditions of stress actually serve as the causes for the instigation of social support.

Anxiety in Children

Milgram and Milgram (1976) investigated the impact of war on children who were not directly hurt. They compared the levels of anxiety of eighty-five children before the Yom Kippur War and after it. No correlation could be found between the two levels of anxiety. Children that had low levels of anxiety before the war increased their anxiety after it, but there were no visible differences among those that were already high on anxiety before the war started. The authors argue that children that saw the world as quite safe before the war were shaken by the experience, and their level of anxiety consequently went up, while those who saw the world as threatening and anxiety-provoking did not change their levels of anxiety. Girls of low socioeconomic status who had particularly high levels of anxiety before the war actually decreased their level of anxiety after it. It is possible that by finding a focus for their worries they could reduce their diffuse anxiety. Another sort of stress, although obviously much smaller than war itself, is the prolonged absence of a father due to military service in the reserves. Many fathers take part in this service and even in tranquil periods are absent for a few weeks every year. During the Yom Kippur War many men were mobilized for periods as long as six to nine months with the exception of a few brief vacations. Thus, many families experienced long periods of anxiety and worry even after the active war was over. It should also be recalled that the period directly after the Yom Kippur War was far from quiet and there were many casualties.

Ziv et al., (1974) compared the drawings of a hundred children whose fathers were on active duty with those of a hundred children whose fathers were not absent. It appeared that the absence of the father preoccupies the child, and this is expressed in the way he draws the family. Children of absent fathers drew the family with the father left out more often than those who had their fathers at home. This was particularly visible in the drawings of girls. In addition, boys of absent fathers drew various weapons more often than boys whose fathers were at home. At the same time, however, no significant differences in the general level of anxiety could be seen. The authors believe that the drawings reflect attempts to *cope* with the anxiety rather than the anxiety itself.

Another clue to the effects of mobilization on children could be seen in the work of Kaffman and Elizur (1977) that dealt with bedwetting in kibbutz children. One of the factors that was found to be related to bedwetting was the long absence of the father due to reserve service.

A study compared the attitudes of children living in areas that were subjected to shelling with the attitudes of children of similar social strata living in areas that were not shelled. It was found that children in the shelled areas demonstrated stronger attachment to their homes (Ziv et al., 1974). The researchers believe that this is indicative of a defense mechanism against anxiety that increases the need for affiliation. The teachers in these areas also reported greater solidarity in school during periods of shelling. An interesting finding concerning aggression towards the enemy was found in this study. No difference in the amount of expression of overt aggression against the enemy was found between children living in the shelled areas and those that were safely distant.

When analyzing unconscious aggression as measured by projective techniques, it was found that children who were living in shelled areas exhibited greater amounts of aggression. This probably reflects the importance of socialization on the behavior of the children. The consistent and strong policies of Israel have always put emphasis on the wish for peace, and this is transmitted to the children through many agents of socialization, both formal and informal. The educational system in particular reinforces this attitude of refraining from animosity against the enemy. A similar finding concerning wishes of peace and the absence of aggression against the enemy was found in another study by Ziv and Nebenhaus (1973), and lends support to the above explanation. A similar picture could be seen among high school children as well (Rofe and Lewin, 1980). High school children living in areas that are subjected to shelling indicate less hawkish attitudes than their counterparts living in the center of the country.

Another study of anxiety in children by Ziv and Israeli (1973) was conducted before the Yom Kippur War. The anxiety level of 103 children of seven different kibbutzim that were frequently shelled was compared to that of a control group of 90 children living in kibbutzim that were not under fire. Contrary to the hypothesis that shelling causes a higher level of anxiety, this was not found. The authors tried to account for their finding by postulating that continuous adaptation and habituation to a stress causes it to become less threatening. Another explanation is related again to social support, which is perhaps higher in a kibbutz that is directly subjected to danger.

In a recent study (Klingman and Wiesner, 1981) an attempt was made to investigate the relationship between the proximity to areas of tension and the level of fear in children between the ages 11 and 13. Using an Israeli version of FSS by Wolpe and Lanz (1964), translated by Goldberg et al. (1975), it was found that children who are closer to areas of tension reported higher levels of anxiety. It was also found that children living in places with small populations are more afraid than those living in towns with large populations.

The influence of living in an area characterized by active warfare on personality dimension repression/sensitization, daydreaming, and nocturnal dreaming in adolescence was investigated by Rofe and Lewin (1980, 1981). They compared high school children from a township near the border to those living in the center of the country. The results indicate that those who live in the high-tension areas are more repressive, and they have fewer daydreams and fewer nocturnal dreams as well. Content analysis of their dreams revealed that they contained fewer elements of aggression and anxiety. The authors believe that living under the constant threat of war increases the need to use repressive mechanisms both on the personality level and as a general method of coping with everyday life stressors.

Zuckerman-Bareli (1979) studied the fears and anxieties of a town that was often exposed to shelling. Thirty-eight percent of those interviewed claimed they forbade their children to play outside immediately following terrorist acts, while 9% claimed the same following shelling. In one of the terrorist acts in that town, 18 people were killed, 8 of them children. This increased the tension of the children immensely. Ophir (1980) tried to help the children to cope with their anxiety by devising a special simulation game. He found that as a result of playing the simulation game, the estimated probabilities to be hurt, which were exaggerated before the game, were significantly reduced, and thus contributed to the reduction of state anxiety.

Professional Intervention During and Following The Yom Kippur War

With the reduction in active warfare, professionals and paraprofessionals found the opportunity to document their experiences during the hectic period of the war itself. Various descriptions appeared in professional journals, most of them in Hebrew, and they could serve as a systematic attempt toward the planning of a rationale for subsequent intervention.

It appears that the intensity of alarm reactions depends on the physical and psychological involvement of the school population in the traumatic events. Thus, variables such as the number of pupils and teachers that had casualties, missing in action, or wounded in their families can influence the amount of negative expressions in a particular school.

The way a school responds to an emergency of this magnitude depends on the quality of its leadership and its level of organization. This characteristic was well documented, particularly in view of the fact that many members of the faculty were mobilized for long periods of time and the system was thus tested in suboptimal conditions (Benyamini, 1976).

A common educational-institution reaction to the outbreak of the Yom Kippur War was the initial shock of the surprise, which led to various degrees of paralysis during the first week of the war. According to Danieli (1974), Nir (1974), and others, the war produced a sense of bewilderment, worry, and anxiety in the educational institutions. This could be seen in diffuse behavior, increased tension, and change in the ordinary routine. The psychological services themselves suffered from similar problems. Toward the second week, most of the services were organized to an extent that allowed meaningful intervention, which increased throughout the war and the months immediately after. During this period many citizens were depressed and anxious, and in many families the tension and worry concerning the father were maintained for as long as he was actively mobilized. Many children reacted with worry and restlessness, particularly in the postwar period.

The counseling and psychological service of schools dealt with a variety of populations. It seems that very little help was given to the children directly. There was a salient tendency to refrain from having a professional who is not part of the child's immediate environment interfere in the life of the child. This prevented unnecessary stigmatization.

Interestingly, at first there were very few extreme symptoms of psychopathology in children. The school population, particularly the very young children, when compared with the adult population, adapted more quickly to the new situation. In the first phase the general tension increased the children's concentration and their attachment to the existing frameworks. There were fewer cases of deviant behavior. Nir (1974) claims that the children reacted in a more mature and responsible way to what was happening around them.

In cases where parents were offered an open-door policy of counseling for children's problems the response was quite minimal (Danieli, 1974; Nir, 1974). However, when the psychological services initiated group meetings for parents, many came. It seems that the collective meeting of parents served many needs, such as exchange of information, tension reduction, and affiliation. An important conclusion from the above is that in tension situations one should not wait for the parents to ask for help but rather the educational system and the mental health services should be the initiators. Group meetings reduce the stigmatization of psychological help and allow mutual support. In this way many latent themes are brought into consciousness and increase the chances of effective coping.

The rationale for counseling parents about the anxieties of their children lies in the behavior of the parents themselves (Benyamini, 1976). Since parents are models for their children, those that succeed in maintaining their tranquility and coping effectively help protect their children from fears and worries. Thus, counseling intervention ought to be directed specifically toward the parents themselves. Spielman (1974) stressed the need to counsel teachers to deal with the classroom situation in addition to using the regular materials that also deal with problems that are related to the war and its consequences. She is confident that the most effective way to help the children is through their teachers. While this model of counseling teachers is accepted in Israel today (Raviv, 1979), it is less frequent during routine times, and the psychologists devote most of their time to examining and treating individual children (Ziv, 1980; Raviv, Wiesner, and Bar-Tal, 1981). This state of affairs makes the transition during emergencies from child-oriented to teacher-oriented counseling particularly dramatic.

Needless to say, during times of distress the teachers themselves can gain from contact with a professional counselor. Thus, the support of teachers served two different goals:

1. To help the teacher cope with her tensions and anxieties by encouraging their expressions.

2. To guide the teachers in their attempts to cope with the children's problems, such as death, orphanhood, and diffuse anxiety (Abraham, 1976).

While some psychologists emphasized the first goal (Abraham, 1976, 1980), that is, the counseling model in which the psychologist contributed his knowledge of the sensitive area of death (Ilan et al., 1974; Klingman, 1980), having discussions with children about the central issues of the war, discipline problems, concentration, etc., was the one more frequently emphasized by the psychologists (Avnon, 1974; Amir, 1974; Schwartz, 1974). Nir (1974) distinguished between two types of teachers who were in need of counseling, those who emphasized the immediate problems too much and got carried away without any framework, thus contributing to the increase in tension and disciplinary problems, and those who emphasized the routine to an extent that did not allow any discussion of other highly relevant problems. The latter, by their avoidance of the issues, often caused restlessness among their pupils. It appears that the need for empathy towards the child, expressions of interest by the teacher, and other basic psychohygienic principles that are good for every day are also the best basis for effective help during times of emergency.

Those schools that were well integrated and had supportive faculty members during peaceful times functioned and coped effectively during the war. Schools that developed psychological services during peaceful times knew how to make good use of them in emergency. To some extent, however, other schools, once they found themselves in trouble, responded positively to the offer of help and confirmed Caplan's (1964) claim that in a crisis there is greater willingness to accept help.

Practical Implications

The Yom Kippur War and the emergencies that followed it demonstrated the need to prepare the educational system for possible future crises. The various studies in this area indicate that the impact of the various stressors was to a great extent modified by the effectiveness of the schools as such. In order to increase the chance of coping effectively in future emergencies, it was thought worthwhile to invest in actively preparing the various components of the educational system.

Such preparation, however, produces problems of its own due to defensive avoidance. Thus, the various attempts to produce "stress inoculation" had to use indirect methods, such as intervention on the community level or role simulations (Klingman, 1977; Ayalon, 1980; Klingman and Ayalon, 1980). Through role simulation it is sometimes possible to penetrate the defensive avoidance of the teachers and bring about attitude change. Klingman and Ninio (1980) simulated an explosion in an ammunition factory. Setting off an actual explosion made the simulation more realistic and helped the participants to reconstruct their feelings and fantasies associated with such catastrophies. At the same time, the rareness of such an event makes it easier for the participants to maintain some of their defense mechanisms.

Kubovy (1970, 1980) developed techniques conducive to counseling and psychological treatment through the direct use of the teaching materials. By taking advantage of classes and exercises in literature and biblical studies for the development of psychological sensitivity of the pupils, the teacher, according to Kubovy, can indirectly promote mental health. While during "normal" days it is thought that fears and anxieties cause more damage if they do not find expression, the actual practice of the above ideas during the war demonstrated that there is a need to control the amount of such expressions. The experience with this method during the war (Kubovy, 1974, 1980), following a terrorist attack (Aharanstan and Wolf, 1975), showed that it helped the teachers to find the balance between the uncontrolled expression of emotions and strict, inflexible routine.

Klingman (1980) suggests that stories from the readers be used by the class, particularly if they relate to the themes of death and separation. Through literature the child has the opportunity to release tensions, to map his feelings, to reach insight, and at the same time the stories serve as a distancing factor that allows the disciplining of emotions. At any time the teachers can return to the content of a story to avoid some of its implications if they become too threatening to the children.

Another technique that can be used is creative writing. There is an assumption that the children's fantasies and stories can play a healing role. Gal (1980) points out that by giving an appropriate stimulus, the teacher can induce the child to freely vent his feelings and conflicts through expressive writing. The same point is made by Klingman (1980), who emphasizes the self-initiated catharsis of creative writing, and by McKinney (1976), who emphasizes its particular advantages to inhibited children. An emergency kit containing a sample of lesson plans to be used in situations of stress was developed by Ayalon (1980) and includes creative writing, movement, nonverbal communication, simulation games, and so forth.

While all professionals see the teacher as the central figure in any attempt to prepare the educational system for emergencies, there are occasions when the teacher is unable to fulfill a positive role. Two main categories of difficulty exist in this context:

1. *Lack of knowledge.* Even an experienced teacher need not necessarily be an expert in psychology and mental health.
2. *Anxiety.* Even the most experienced teacher can sometimes react to a difficult situation with anxiety, which leads to inadequate behavior. When confronted with the problems of a child, she may react with her own defenses (Caplan, 1970; Raviv, Klingman, and Horowitz, 1980).

During emergencies, a third factor emerges, namely, the problems and anxieties of the teacher herself. She, like other women, may have a husband or a son on the front. In Israel, more than 75% of the teachers are women, and during a war the entire educational system relies on women. Thus, psychologists and counselors in schools have to support teachers dealing with their own difficulties (Abraham, 1976, 1980).

In spite of the peace treaty between Israel and Egypt, the dangers and tensions remained very much the same. When observing children playing outside, one is struck by the lack of visible signs indicating the strain to which they are subjected. Life is stronger than the stressful reality, and in spite of their sensitivity, children are sufficiently flexible to adapt. The central question remains, however, what is the psychological cost of this remarkable adjustment, and what is the best way to reduce it?

REFERENCES

Abraham, A. Supportive groups for teachers in time of war. *Studies in Education,* 1976, *12,* 27–36 (in Hebrew).

Abraham, A. Women teachers in time of war. *In*, A. Raviv, A. Klingman, and M. Horowitz (eds.), *Children under Stress and in Crisis.* Tel Aviv: "Otsar-Hamoreh" Publishing House of the Teachers' Union, 1980, 280–290 (in Hebrew).

Adoni, H., and Cohen, A. Children's responses to televised war news films. *Megamot Behavioral Sciences Quarterly,* 1979, *25,* 49–64 (in Hebrew).

Aharanstan, S., and Wolf, O. Kiryat Shimona project. *Israeli Journal of Psychology and Counseling in Education,* 1975, *5,* 14–18 (in Hebrew).

Amir, O. Psycho-educational clinic in war time. *Israeli Journal of Psychology and Counseling in Education,* 1974, *4,* 41–43 (in Hebrew).

Avnon, M. Group work with teachers in Haifa and the Northern regions. *Israeli Journal of Psychology and Counseling in Education,* 1974, *4,* 51–55 (in Hebrew).

Ayalon, O. *Emergency kit.* Haifa University, Hahevra Leisum, 1980 (in Hebrew).

Benyamini, K. School psychological emergency interventions: Proposal for guidelines based on recent Israeli experience. *Mental Health and Society,* 1976, *3,* 22–32.

Breznitz, S. Stress in Israel. *In*, H. Selye (ed.), *Selye's Guide to Stress Research (Vol. 1),* New York: Van Nostrand Reinhold Co., 1980.

Caplan, G. *Principles of Preventive Psychiatry.* New York: Basic Books, 1964.

Caplan, G. *The Theory and Practice of Mental Health Consultation.* New York: Basic Books, 1970.

Caplan, G. *Support Systems and Community Health: Lectures in Concept Development.* New York: Behavioral Publications, 1974.

Danieli, A. A small clinic operation in emergency. *Israeli Journal of Psychology and Counseling in Education,* 1974, *4,* 32–35 (in Hebrew).

Elizur, E. Children's reactions to the death of father in battle. *Israeli Journal of Psychology and Counseling in Education,* 1978, *9,* 27–34 (in Hebrew).

Fleming, J., and Altchul, S. Activation of mourning and growth by psychoanalysis. *International Journal of Psychoanalysis,* 1963, *44,* 419–432.

Gal, I. Creative writing as a therapeutic tool. *In*, A. Raviv, A. Klingman, and M. Horowitz (eds.), *Children under Stress and in Crisis.* Tel Aviv: "Otsar-Hamoreh" Publishing House of the Teachers' Union in Israel, 1980, 232–250 (in Hebrew).

Goldberg, J., Yinon, Y., and Cohen, A. A cross-cultural comparison between the Israeli and American Fear Survey Inventory. *Journal of Social Psychology,* 1975, *97,* 131–132.

Halpern, E. Children's support systems in coping with orphanhood: Child helps child in a natural setting. *In*, N. Milgram, C. D. Spielberger, and I. G. Sarason (eds.), *Stress and Anxiety, Vol. 8.* New York: Hemisphere Publishers John Wiley & Sons, 1981.

Halpern, E. Children in crisis and support system: Some thoughts on mutual aid networks and helping children. *In*, J. Williamson (ed.), *World Mental Health Monograph on Self Help and Mutual Help,* 1980.

Ilan, E., and Aner, N. Children in mourning: A guide to psychologists, school counselors, nurses and educators. *Israeli Journal of Psychology and Counseling in Education,* 1974, *4,* 32–33 (in Hebrew).

Israel Government Yearbook, 1979.

Kaffman, M. Kibbutz civilian population under war stress. *British Journal of Psychiatry*, 1977, *130*, 489–494.

Kaffman, M., and Elizur, E. Infants who become enuretics: A longitudinal study of 161 kibbutz children. *Monographs of the Society for Research in Child Development*. Chicago, Illinois: University of Chicago Press, 1977, *42*, 170.

Kaffman, M., and Elizur, E. Children's reactions to the death of father: The early month of bereavement. *International Journal of Family Therapy*, 1979, *1*, 203–229.

Kaffman, M., and Elizur, E. Bereavement responses of kibbutz and non-kibbutz children following death of father. Unpublished manuscript, 1980.

Klingman, A. Death education through literature: A preventive approach. *Death Education*, 1980, *4*, 271–279.

Klingman, A., and Ayalon, O. Anticipatory intervention: A model of coping in stress situation within the school. *In*, A. Raviv, A. Klingman and M. Horowitz (eds.), *Children under Stress and in Crisis*. Tel Aviv: "Otsar-Hamoreh" Publishing House of the Teachers' Union in Israel, 1980, 192–211 (in Hebrew).

Klingman, A., and Ben-Eli, Z. A school community in disaster: The application of primary and secondary prevention in situational crisis. *Professional Psychology* (in press).

Klingman, A., and Ninio, J. *Simulation: A school in emergency*. Jerusalem: The Psychological and Counseling Service, Ministry of Education, 1980.

Klingman, A., and Wiesner, E. The relationship of proximity to tension areas and size of settlement of residence to fear level of Israeli children. Research report, Jerusalem: Psychological and Counseling Service, Ministry of Education, 1981.

Kubovy, D. Teaching-contents as a means for improving mental health. Jerusalem: School of Education of the Hebrew University, 1970 (in Hebrew).

Kubovy, D. The application of therapeutic teaching methods in an emergency situation. *Studies in Education*, 1974, *2*, 167–174 (in Hebrew).

Kubovy, D. Therapeutic teaching and its application in emergencies. *In*, A. Raviv, A. Klingman, and M. Horowitz (eds.), *Children under Stress and in Crisis*. Tel Aviv: "Otsar-Hamoreh" Publishing House of the Teachers' Union in Israel, 1980, 212–231 (in Hebrew).

Lifshitz, M. The effect of fatherlessness upon the perceptual differentiation and integration of preadolescents. *Megamot Behavioral Sciences Quarterly*, 1974, *20*, 347–372 (in Hebrew).

Lifshitz, M., Berman, D., Gilad, D., and Galili, A. Bereaved children: The effect of mothers' perception and social organization on their adjustment. *Megamot Behavioral Sciences Quarterly*, 1977, *23*, 129–142 (in Hebrew).

McKinney, F. Free writing as therapy. *Psychotherapy: Theory, Research and Practice*, 1976, *13*, 183–187.

Milgram, N. A. Psychological stress and adjustment in time of war and peace: The Israeli experience as presented in two conferences. *The Israel Annals of Psychiatry and Related Disciplines*, 1978, *16*, 327–338.

Milgram, R. M., and Milgram, N. A. The effect of the Yom Kippur War on anxiety level in Israeli children. *The Journal of Psychology*, 1976, *94*, 107–113.

Nagera, H. Children's reactions to the death of important objects: A developmental approach. *The Psychoanalytic Study of the Child*, 1970, *25*, 360–400.

Nir, A. Adaptation and preparation: Guidelines for operation of the school psychological services in Tel Aviv in the Yom Kippur War. *Israeli Journal of Psychology and Counseling in Education*, 1974, *4*, 44–50 (in Hebrew).

Ophir, M. Simulation game as a therapeutic method for state-anxiety. *In*, A. Raviv, A. Klingman, and M. Horowitz (eds.), *Children under Stress and in Crisis*. Tel Aviv: "Otsar-Hamoreh" Publishing House of the Teachers' Union in Israel, 1980, 274–279 (in Hebrew).

Raviv, A. Reflections on the role of the school psychologist in Israel. *Professional Psychology*, 1979, *10*, 820–826.

Raviv, A., A. Klingman, and M. Horowitz (eds.), *Children under Stress and in Crises*. Tel Aviv: "Otsar-Hamoreh" Publishing House of the Teachers' Union in Israel, 1980 (in Hebrew).

Raviv, A., Wiesner, E., and Bar-Tal, D. National survey of school psychologists' perceptions and attitudes. Research report, Jerusalem: Psychological and Counseling Service, Ministry of Education, 1981.

Rofe, Y., and Lewin, I. Attitudes toward an enemy and personality in a war environment. *International Journal of Intercultural Relations*, 1980, *4*, 97–106.

Rofe, Y., and Lewin, I. The effect of war environment on dreams and sleep habits. *In*, N. Milgram, C. D. Spielberger, and I. G. Sarason (eds.), *Stress and Anxiety, Vol. 8*, New York: Hemisphere Publishing, 1981.

Schwartz, Y. The school in a time of emergency. *Studies in Education*, 1974, *2*, 157–166 (in Hebrew).

Smilansky, S. The concept of death of Israeli children. *In*, A. Raviv, A. Klingman, and M. Horowitz (eds.), *Children under Stress and in Crisis*. Tel Aviv: "Otsar-Hamoreh" Publishing House of the Teachers' Union in Israel, 1980, 102–140 (in Hebrew).

Smilansky, S., and Diksal, T. School adjustment of fatherless orphans of primary level. *Megamot Behavioral Sciences Quarterly*, 1977, *23*, 141–156 (in Hebrew).

Spielman, M. Psycho-educational clinic service in war time. *Israeli Journal of Psychology and Counseling in Education*, 1974, *4*, 36–40 (in Hebrew).

Wolfenstein, M. How is mourning possible? *The Psychoanalytic Study of the Child*, 1966, *21*, 93–125.

Wolpe, J., and Lanz, P. F. A fear survey schedule for use in behavior therapy. *Behavior Research and Therapy*, 1964, *2*, 27–30.

Yanoov, B. Short-term intervention: A model of emergency services for times of community crisis. *Social Security*, 1975, *9–10*, 5–19 (in Hebrew).

Ziv, A. The school psychologist at work. *Israeli Journal of Psychology and Counseling in Education*, 1980, *12*, 25–33 (in Hebrew).

Ziv, A., and Israeli, R. Effects of bombardment on the manifest anxiety level of children living in kibbutzim. *Journal of Consulting and Clinical Psychology*, 1973, *40*, 287–291.

Ziv, A., and Nebenhaus, S. Frequency of wishes for peace of children during different periods of war intensity. *Megamot Behavioral Sciences Quarterly,* 1973, *19,* 423–427 (in Hebrew).

Ziv, A., Kruglanski, A. W., and Schulman, S. Children's psychological reactions to wartime stress. *Journal of Personality and Social Psychology,* 1974, *30,* 24–30.

Zukerman-Bareli, C. The effects of border tensions on the residents of an Israeli border town. *Megamot Behavioral Sciences Quarterly,* 1979, *25,* 198–213 (in Hebrew).

Part III
Israel as a Stress Laboratory

8.
On War and Crime

Gideon Fishman*
University of Haifa

Stress seems to occur "whenever there is a departure from optimum conditions which the organism is unable, or not easily able to correct" (Welford, 1974, p. 1). To suggest that certain social situations may provoke stress in certain individuals is almost as trivial as saying that everything is relative, or that no two people are alike.

The definition of stress as a consequence of poor tension management (McGrath, 1970; Antonovsky, 1974) poses a problem for a macro-level analysis, since it focuses on the personality level. When the issue of stress is discussed on a societal level, one must still refer back to the individual, for it is only the human organism, only its psychological make-up, which may become subject to stress. Attributing stress to society as a whole would simply be a careless reification. Society may indeed be stress-producing, and in that case the relevant issue for study is the effect of stressful situations. This effect may legitimately be studied on the macro level through the examination of increases or decreases in various social pathologies, all of which are the result of individual stress and its manifestations.

While a variety of situations to which a person is exposed may produce anxiety, it is possible to visualize a continuum, at one end of which are situations that have stressful connotations for a limited number of individuals, and at the other end of the continuum, situations

*The author wishes to thank Dr. Eugene Weiner and Dr. Vered Kraus for their helpful comments and advice.

that are likely to produce stress in most people (Basowitz et al., 1955, p. 54). Situations that are assumed to be universally stressful will here be referred to as generalized stress situations, as opposed to individual stressful events, those which evoke stress among only a few individuals as a consequence of personal idiosyncracies.

Wars and periods of general mobilization in anticipation of the outbreak of hostilities may be considered examples of a generalized stress situation that "due to its intensity and its explicit threat to vital functions is likely to overload the capacity of most organisms" (Ibid.). Such situations are expected to have some impact upon other social facts. Teele (1970) points out that social stress situations are associated with various manifestations of social pathology or, as others (Lemert, 1948; Becker, 1963) prefer to call it, deviance.

Our study will not engage in delineating the psychological processes of stress and its emergence, but rather will attempt to analyze a stressful event — war — and examine its effect on an aggregative change in deviant behavior, especially acts of violence. Such changes are assumed to be indicative of the response of the plurality of individuals to a stressful situation.

Among the most serious and alarming forms of deviance are undoubtedly the acts of homicide and attempted homicide. The two are considered by criminologists to be identical forms of behavior, except for the outcome. The difference in outcome is due only to luck, i.e., in the case of attempted homicide, the clumsiness of the perpetrator, or poor choice (or unavailability) of weapon. We shall examine the effect of war on violent antisocial behavior and compare it with other common forms of deviance, such as crime against property and theft.

The measurement of deviance, as specified above, requires some comment. The most readily available data are accumulated in annual police reports, especially in the less serious crime categories. Although the data on homicide can be assumed to properly represent the relevant crime volume, this claim cannot be made regarding theft of various kinds, fraud, etc. Furthermore, if a longitudinal study of several crime categories is attempted, police reporting may be inconsistent over time. Policy changes in reporting and changes in legal definitions of various offenses may reduce the reliability as well as the comparability of such data. The data on homicide and attempted homicide are considered to be among the most consistent and reliable over time, and have not been affected by definitional changes. Hence their attraction for the researcher. In the category of crime against property, both the reliability of reporting to the police and the consistency of some definitions of specific offenses are dubious. For these reasons, reference should be made to the aggregative level of this category, rather than to the specific crimes it includes. Theft is also one of the specific crimes for which there is a systematic record, although the known volume is assumed to be the result of underreporting at an estimated ratio of about 1:3 (Ennis, 1967). A very useful model for our study of the effect of stress on deviant behavior is proposed by Cobb in his chapter "A model for life events and their consequences" (1974). This model suggests that in stressful situations an interplay occurs between personal characteristics such as psychological defense mechanisms, psychological needs, abilities, and genetic predisposition, and social situation factors such as current life situation and social support. We shall concentrate only on the social situation factors, specifically the social support variable, and assume that the personality factors remain, to a large extent, constant.

According to established sociological theories (Durkheim, 1968), an increase in social support is expected when a threat is posed to society. War was defined above as a situation of this type. The generalized stress evoked by such situations brings about an increase in social cohesion, i.e., social support. It is hypothesized that a general reduction in social pathology will occur in time of war, owing to the fact that the stress generated by the war is managed not only by the psychological coping mechanisms and other personal predispositions, but also by the strong social support the individual gains as a victim of the generalized stress. However, this social support is not constant; it tends to change over time. We assume that the strong support and tight cohesion that are responses to generalized stress will prevail for only a limited time. This is analogous with the physiological view (Selye, 1956) that adaptation to stress always requires a special concentration of effort that, when prolonged, produces a state of exhaustion.

Furthermore, we expect that social support will be stronger and more effective when generalized stress exists, and that it will weaken when the stress diffuses and becomes individualized, namely, when the event is differentially perceived by different individuals.

Following these proposed relationships, it is suggested that social pathologies will become more frequent as time passes from the onset of stress. We should thus find more social deviance after the war than during its course and, if the war is relatively prolonged, more deviance at the end than during the initial stages of the war. This response to stress is due to both the reduction of social support and the individualization of stress over time. In the case of a short war, as the wars in Israel have been, social support is weakened by the elimination of the generalized stressor, and does not tend to reemerge when individualized stress occurs. It might be said that in time of war, one problem is common to all individuals, whereas, at a later stage, what is common to all individuals is that very few share the problems of the others.

HISTORICAL PERSPECTIVE

The study of war and crime dates back to social philosophers such as Erasmus, Sir Thomas More and Machiavelli, who speculated that wars left a legacy of increased crime and lawlessness (Abbott, 1918; 1927; Hamon, 1918). Modern scholarly research on the issue has been concentrated around two major wars, the First and the Second World Wars, and not surprisingly so. Studies of the impact of war on the crime situation were conducted in Austria (Exner, 1927), France (Calbariac, 1928), Italy (Levi, 1929), Czechoslovakia (Solnar, 1929), Germany (Leipman, 1930), the United States (Engelbrecht, 1937; Sutherland, 1943), and England (Mannheim, 1941; 1955). While there is a consensus among researchers that, in comparison with the war period, the postwar era is characterized by an increase in crime rates, there is disagreement about the reasons. While one view (Exner, 1927) attributes crime increases to economic problems after the war, another suggests that higher crime rates are a result of "general cheapening of all values, loosening of family ties and weakened respect for the law, human life and property" (Mannheim, 1955, p. 112). Sellin (1926), who has conducted by far the best study of that period, compared changes in postwar homicide rates in five belligerent nations in World War I with those in four nonbelligerent nations. He concluded that in the belligerent nations crime rates did increase, but the differences between these nations and the nonbelligerent nations were not uniform.

The impact of war on crime became a relevant issue again due to World War II. Several studies were conducted during the war itself. Reckless studied the effect of war on delinquency, crime, and prostitution (1942). Glueck (1942) studied its effect on juvenile delinquency, and Bromberg (1943) investigated the impact on crime in general. After the war Von Hentig (1947) tried to trace the causes of crime, and the war was examined as a possible cause. Lunden (1963; 1967) examined postwar changes in crime patterns in five countries by comparing the raw number of crimes committed after the war with the number of crimes committed during a single year prior to the outbreak of war. The postwar increases revealed by his study were attributed to social changes brought about by the war, including social disorganization, increased mobility, and the disruption of community life.

More recent studies of crime changes during wars are very scarce. Tanter (1969) referred to the impact of the Vietnam War, and he noted an increase in crimes of violence *during* the war years. This he tried to explain by suggesting that "as the war continues, it facilitates a state of 'normlessness' in which traditional structures against criminal acts lose their effectiveness" (Tanter, 1969, p. 436). In their comprehensive study, Archer and Gartner (1967) found that combatant nations in the world wars were more likely to experience higher homicide rates than the nations in the control group, i.e., nations not participating in a given war. Among noncombatant nations, homicide rate changes were evenly distributed: in some nations the rate decreased, in others it increased, and in some it remained unchanged. However, for the 25 war nations studied, postwar increases outnumbered decreases by 19 to 6. Of the 19 nations, some experienced a very large increase, such as Italy after World War II, where crimes increased by 133 percent, more than double the prewar rate. On the other hand, in Belgium after World War I the increase reached only 25 percent. Archer and Gartner (1967) also discovered that in other instances the rates decreased. Such was the case in Finland and Northern Ireland after World War II, and in Israel after the 1956 Sinai campaign.

It seems from most of the studies that the general pattern has been a sharp drop in crime during the initial year or years of war, followed by a return to the prewar level (Mannheim, 1965; Lunden, 1963). There is some evidence, as well as theoretical arguments to be discussed below, that would lead us to expect an increase in the level of some crimes in the postwar period.

THEORETICAL CONSIDERATIONS

Previous research findings that suggest that crime rates tend to decrease during the first stages of the war and increase afterward inevitably raise the question why this should be so.

The stress approach discussed previously may be suggestive, especially when merged with social variables such as cohesion, solidarity, or social support. This framework proposes that war, being a generalized stressor, produces social support (at least in its initial stages) that enables the individual to cope better with his stress, and that consequently lowers the rate of social pathology. Thus, crime rates will be relatively low. Sumner (1906, p. 12) suggested that wars increase discipline and the strength of the law, and Mannheim pointed out that in times of war the criminal, like the law-abiding citizen, is impressed by the war conditions that "make it every man's duty to give as little trouble as possible" (1941, p. 108). However, the decrease in crime cannot be assumed to result solely from social cohesion. Other factors have to be taken into account, such as the reduced efficiency of law enforcement, and an overall leniency (Sutherland, 1956) that diminishes the number of crimes reported. Furthermore, the fact that a large proportion of the young male population is mobilized for the war effort reduces actual crime during such time (Bennett, 1953).

After the war the men are demobilized and law enforcement returns to normal functioning. We would therefore expect the crime rate to rise. As the war ends, or is prolonged beyond a certain point, social solidarity is reduced and social support mechanisms are no longer readily available to deal with individual problems that become sources of stress. This also contributes to the rise in social pathologies in general, and crime in particular, after the war.

The major task for theoretical consideration at this point is to specify which crimes are expected to increase during the wave of social pathology generated after the war (or after its initial stages). The patterns of criminal behavior are expected to be influenced both physically and normatively by the war's impact.

Among the most striking characteristics of the war, besides the assumed solidarity during its initial stages and disorganization when it drags on or ends, include other factors that may be relevant to our inquiry. Wars are characterized by a death toll that can be measured as the ratio of soldiers killed out of the total population. Another characteristic is the increase in the amount of weapons held by the civilian population immediately after the war. Finally, perhaps the most important factor is the effect of the war on the value system. It is suggested that the legitimization of killing during the war brings about a change in attitude toward life and its sanctity. Hence it is hypothesized that after a war people will be less inhibited in their expression of aggression.

One would expect the behavioral manifestations of stress to be channeled through the perceived opportunities created by the new situation. While there is hardly any reason to expect an increase in crimes against property as a result of war, crime against person is expected to rise due to the normative depreciation of human life and the availability of weapons. The theoretical analysis is presented schematically in Figure 8-1.

Archer and Gartner (1967), having assembled a comparative file of domestic data for 110 nations, tried to determine whether postwar homicide increases occur and why. They established that most of the combatant nations in the study experienced substantial postwar increases in their homicide rates. They concluded that the duration

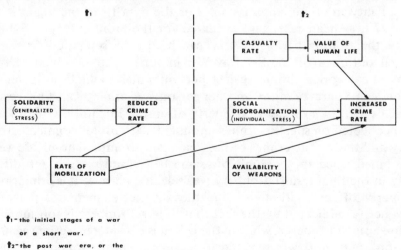

t_1 - the initial stages of a war or a short war.
t_2 - the post war era, or the latter stage of a prolonged war.

Figure 8-1. Impact of war on crime in two time periods.

of the war, its outcome (winning or losing), and the postwar economic situation were not significant in causing any variation in crime rates. Postwar increases in violence were most frequent among nations with a high death toll in combat. This implies that, far from providing a catharsis for violence, wars serve to legitimize further violence. On the basis of this conclusion, it may be hypothesized that the higher the casualty rate during the war, the stronger will be the residual effect on the level of violence in the postwar period.

In the following section, the impact of war on crime in Israel will be examined. We shall try to provide a reasonable account for differential crime rates before and after the war, as well as for the disparity in the rates of specific crimes within the same time period.

THE ISRAELI CASE

The impact of war on crime in Israel will be examined with regard to two wars: the Six Day War (June, 1967) and the Yom Kippur War (October, 1973).

Monthly data from the Israel Bureau of Statistics were obtained for the month in which the war occurred, for the three years prior to each war, for the year of the war itself, and for the next three years. These are the most refined data available and at least control for seasonality in crime commission. For the data from the years 1964 to 1970, a mean rate was calculated for the months May and June since the waiting period in May can hardly be separated from the actual outbreak of the Six Day War in June. The data include two general categories: crime against person, which includes all offenses intended to harm or injure another person, and crime against property, which includes a variety of property offenses. In addition, data were also collected on specific crimes: homicide, attempted homicide, robbery and theft. The crimes of homicide and attempted homicide were combined since they exhibit the same behavioral pattern and differ only in the final result. Robbery was selected because it is primarily a property offense, although it includes distinct elements of personal violence (as indicated by the fact that in Israel robbery is considered a crime against property, while in the U.S. it is considered a crime against person), and theft was selected to represent a pure property offense.

Table 8-1 presents the relevant crime rates per 100,000. It is obvious that all crimes reach their lowest rate during the war. This

Table 8-1. Distribution of Various Crime Rates Before and After the Wars.

MONTH (MAY AND JUNE)	CRIME AGAINST PERSON	CRIME AGAINST PROPERTY	HOMICIDE AND ATTEMPTED HOMICIDE	ROBBERY	THEFT
1944	31.9	228.6	0.24	0.20	150.0
1965	39.0	240.0	0.25	0.13	100.0
1966	35.0	260.0	0.26	0.26	100.0
1967	20.0	230.0	0.18	0.14	100.0
1968	27.2	263.7	0.21	0.21	164.8
1969	28.4	267.5	0.31	0.32	169.2
1970	26.8	326.5	0.16	0.42	209.0
OCTOBER					
1970	24.3	356.8	0.13	0.67	215.6
1971	28.2	354.7	0.13	0.46	206.5
1972	30.9	320.5	0.18	0.72	194.2
1973	16.4	195.1	0.12	0.33	124.9
1974	30.4	298.7	0.35	0.38	185.4
1975	440.0	344.8	0.52	0.81	190.0
1976	420.8	355.2	0.37	0.82	188.3

Table 8-2. Mean Crime Rates Before and After the Wars.

	CRIME AGAINST PERSON		CRIME AGAINST PROPERTY		HOMICIDE AND ATTEMPTED HOMICIDE		ROBBERY		THEFT	
	1967	1973	1967	1973	1967	1973	1967	1973	1967	1973
BEFORE	35.3	34.7	242.9	344.0	0.25	0.15	0.20	0.62	116.6	205.4
AFTER	27.5	297.9	285.9	332.9	0.26	0.41	0.32	0.67	181.0	187.9
t	3.29	118.9	4.06	N.S.	N.S.	13.0	N.S.	N.S.	3.34	N.S.
p	$p < 0.05$	$p < 0.001$	$p < 0.01$			$p < 0.001$			$p < 0.05$	

finding is valid for both wars. The apparent trend is an increase after the war. However, not all offenses return to their prewar level after each war. A comparison of the mean rates for the same months for three years before and after each war (Table 8-2) reveals the following trends: After the 1967 war, the rate of crime against person failed to reach the previous level, and there is even a significant drop in mean crime rates for this category ($t = 3.29$, $p < 0.05$). Exactly the opposite picture emerges after the 1973 war — a dramatic increase

from a mean rate of 34.7 before the war to 297.9 after the war
($t = 118.9$, $p < 0.001$).

Table 8-2 indicates an inverse trend in the rate of crime against
property. There is a significant increase in this crime category after
the 1967 war ($t = 4.06$, $p < 0.01$), while there is a decrease, though
not a significant one, after the 1973 war (from a mean rate of 344.0
prior to the war to 332.9 after the war).

For specific offenses the findings follow the trends of the more
general categories. In the case of homicide and attempted homicide,
the trend indicates increases after both wars (Figure 8-2).

Although statistically the change in the mean rate after 1967 is not
significant, after 1973 it is highly significant ($t = 13.0$, $p < 0.001$).
Theft shows the opposite trend, namely, a significant increase after
1967 ($t = 3.34$, $p < 0.05$) and a nonsignificant decrease after the 1973
war. Robbery was the only offense that showed a light increase after
both wars, though the changes did not reach statistical significance.

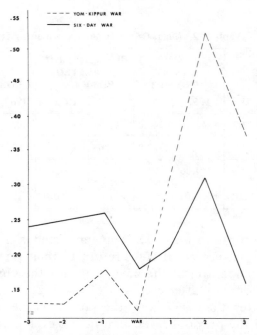

Figure 8-2. Changes in homicide and attempted homicide rates three years during
the relevant months before and after the Six Day War and the Yom Kippur War.

This may be due to the very nature of the offense, which combines elements of both crime against property and crime against person. The two seem to cancel each other out in the two time periods.

The question now, of course, is how unusual these findings are when compared with longitudinal relationships between these crime rates. In a recent study (Fishman, 1978), the crime rates in Israel were analyzed and several interesting patterns emerged. The analysis, based on data from 1951 to 1976, clearly showed that crime against person, which by definition includes homicide and attempted homicide, does not correlate at all with these two specific offenses ($r = -0.20$ and $r = -0.21$, respectively). This must lead us to conclude that, although the definition groups them together, they are nevertheless qualitatively different. In spite of this finding, crime against person as a category does behave exactly the same way as homicide and attempted homicide, increasing after the war of 1973 but not after the war of 1967. This is even more surprising if we realize that in the longitudinal study, crime against person had an extremely high correlation with crime against property ($r = 0.74$) over a period of 26 years. This trend is reversed, however, after the two wars; when there is a significant increase in crime against property, there is no change at all in the rate of crime against person, and vice versa. This of course is also true with regard to homicide, attempted homicide, and their relationship to crime against property and theft. These findings suggest that crime against person, excluding homicide and attempted homicide, and property crime (as well as fraudulent acts) together constitute what is known as traditional crime. In times of stress, social solidarity affects direct interpersonal relations. Offenses that involve this element will therefore be much more affected than other traditional forms of criminality. Hence the parallel between crime against person, homicide, or attempted homicide, a parallel that is unusual and statistically unexpected.

In order to account for these unexpected inconsistencies in the increases and decreases of various offenses before and after the two wars, the differences between these two periods should be analyzed. While the June 1967 war is considered a short event, the acts of belligerency did not cease until 1970 and the War of Attrition was intense for a long period after the official cease-fire agreement. As for the war itself, the number of casualties was relatively low (around 750). A third factor that may be relevant is the fact that the war ended a period of economic recession and brought about an economic boom. The situation in 1973 was quite the opposite. The war was not short and swift by Israeli standards, and the number of casualties was extremely high (well over 3,000). The war of 1973 came to an end rather abruptly and was not followed by any prolonged period of belligerency. Thus the shift from war to nonwar was sudden. As regards the economic situation, there is also an apparent difference. As the war ended signs of recession and economic difficulties emerged.

Over the last 26 years, crime against property has been inversely related to unemployment ($r = -0.69$), while homicide and attempted homicide are significantly and positively associated ($r = 0.72$ and $r = 0.76$, respectively). Thus it is plausible that the economic situation does affect the crime rate to a certain degree. Contrary to common belief, it seems that in times of economic hardship (as indicated by unemployment rate), crime against person and crime against property decrease while the rate of homicide and attempted homicide will tend to increase. Although the economic situation appears to influence the crime rate, its effect is limited and not all changes in crime rates can be attributed to the changes in economic conditions. Thus, while economic depression seems to correspond with the increase in homicide and attempted homicide rates, the simultaneous increase in crime against person is completely unexpected and unaccounted for by the economic situation since it correlates negatively with unemployment ($r = -0.40$). This lends further theoretical significance to our finding regarding the similarity in the patterns of crime against person, homicide, and attempted homicide after each war, and underlines the overriding importance of the war characteristics as explanatory variables.

DISCUSSION

Our findings suggest that the expectation that all crimes will follow an identical pattern after a war is based on a misconception. Uniformity exists only in the decrease of all reported crime rates during the war period. This can be attributed to the operation of common factors at such a time: mobilization of a large proportion of the criminally prone population, lack of effective law enforcement, and a strong sense of solidarity and readiness to obey the law in the midst of the perceived crisis. The postwar behavior, however, is not simply a reaction to the war as a crisis, but is also a response to new facts that have been produced by the war and that channel deviant behavior into a certain path.

According to our findings, economic crimes do not seem to be related to the war as a stressful event. They follow the expected pattern of increasing in times of affluence and decreasing during times of economic hardship. This is not the case with crimes against person, in particular homicide and attempted homicide. If it may be assumed that the amount of killing that occurs during the war brings about a corresponding reduction in the value and sanctity of human life, then the war of 1973 is obviously more likely to produce such a situation than the war of 1967. In any case, our findings support this assumption rather than the catharsis hypothesis, which would predict a reduction in crime against person, especially homicide, after crises resulting in a high death toll. Furthermore, if war is perceived as a generalized stress situation, the continuation of acts of belligerence may have a less acute effect than the onset of the crisis, but may nevertheless maintain the rate of crime against person at a relatively depressed level and at a low volume.

This brings us to a point that may account for the overall low level of physical violence in Israel. The annual homicide rate of 1.5 per 100,000 is undoubtedly extremely low by any standards, even compared to the nations in Europe. Israel, being a country of immigration and a society that has been undergoing rapid social changes, is expected to have produced much higher rates of violence. It is, perhaps, the continuous struggle for survival and the constant perceived threat that have kept the overall level of violent crime so low, with periodic fluctuations.

As expected, our findings support the conception of the war as a generalized stressor, and as the agent of cohesion and social support. All crime rates decline in wartime, but the fact that the postwar crime increase is differential requires further explanation.

It seems that a combination of two theoretical frameworks, "differential association" (Sutherland, 1956) and "differential opportunity structure" (Cloward and Ohlin, 1961), could be utilized for our purposes. In developing the theory of differential association, Sutherland actually proposes a learning approach to the problem of deviant conduct. According to one of his hypotheses, becoming a delinquent requires both the proper values and also the appropriate skills and technical knowledge to carry out the delinquent conduct. The availability of only one of these is a necessary but not a sufficient condition for delinquency. In this respect, the war furnishes both. The change in the value of human life is actually the normative change to which Sutherland refers. Norms of conduct are broken, and previously unthinkable behavior is no longer taboo. Furthermore, the war presents an excellent opportunity to acquire techniques for violent conduct.

Along the same lines, one may speculate that the property-violating behavior after 1967 might have been predicted because of the relatively massive looting and destruction of property that was so common during the 1967 war and very rare in the 1973 war. If this is plausible, then investigating the socializing effects of war and other traumatic events should be pursued further.

One by-product of any war is the increase in the amount of weaponry available to the public. In Israel, for security reasons, the acquisition of weapons by the public was officially encouraged by the government. This situation seems to provide a perfect opportunity to escalate the violence factor in any conflict. As Cloward and Ohlin indicate, the direction of delinquent behavior, as well as of legitimate behavior, is channeled and structured according to the available opportunities.

The opportunity structure is undoubtedly quite subjective and is to some extent determined by the norms and values a person holds. Thus, when pathological behavior emerges at a time of individualized stress (postwar period), it will be influenced by whether or not the sanctity of human life has been devalued (which is assumed to be linearly related with the casualty ratio). A weakening of that norm, and the accessibility of weapons, will channel the sociopathological behavior toward violence. The relative stability of the norm will reduce the significance of the availability of weaponry (as understood from Sutherland's hypothesis), and another avenue of outlet will be found. The fact that crime against property was on the increase after the 1967 war may be attributed, first, to the inappropriateness of violent response in the context of the unbroken validity of the norms and the continuation of the war of attrition and second, to the systematic relationships between property crime and economic prosperity, which existed at that time.

This brings us to the conclusion that, as Durkheim noted long ago, crime is normal and in every social situation a certain level of criminality is expected to prevail. Thus, crime rates are expected to rise after the war. What we have observed, however, is that a significant increase in one type of crime keeps another at a relatively low level and vice versa, as if the various forms of crime are trying to balance each other off, leading to a predetermined crime level.

REFERENCES

Abbott, E. Crime and the war. *Journal of Criminal Law and Criminology*, 1918, *9*, 32–45.

Abbott, E. The civil war and the crime wave of 1865–70. *Social Service Review*, 1927, *1*, 212–234.

Antonovsky, A. Conceptual and methodological problems in the study of resistance resources and stressful life events. *In*, B. S. Dohrenwend and B. P. Dohrenwend (eds.), *Stressful Life Events*. New York: Wiley & Sons, 1974.

Archer, D., and Gartner, R. Violent acts and violent times: A comparative approach to postwar monicide rates. *American Sociological Review*, 1967, *41*, 937–963.

Basowitz, H., Persky, H., Korchin, S. J., and Grinkler, R. R. *Anxiety and Stress*. New York: McGraw-Hill, 1955.

Becker, H. *Outsiders*. New York: Free Press, 1963.

Bennett, J. V. The ex-GI in federal prisons. *In, Proceedings of the American Correctional Association*, 1953, 131–136.

Bromberg, W. A. The effects of the war on crime. *American Sociological Review*, 1943, *8*, 685–691.

Calbariac, M. G. Les repercussions de la Grand Guerre Sur la Criminalite en France. *Etudes Criminologiques*, 1928, *3*, 62–70.

Cloward, R., and Ohlin, L. *Delinquency and opportunity*. Glencoe, Ill.: Free Press, 1961.

Cobb, S. A model for life events and their consequences. *In*, B. S. Dohrenwend and B. P. Dohrenwend, *Stressful Life Events*. New York: Wiley & Sons, 1974.

Durkheim, E. *The division of labor in society*. New York: The Free Press, 1968.

Engelbrecht, H. *Revolt against war*. New York: Dodd & Mead, 1937.

Ennis, H. P. Crimes victims and the police. *Trans-Action*, 1967, *4*, 36–44.

Exner, F. *Krieg und Kriminalitaet in Oesterreich*. Vienna: Holder Pichler-Tempsky, 1927.

Fishman, G. Crime trends in Israel. Paper presented in *International Symposium on Specialized Criminological Topics*, Stockholm, August, 1978.

Glueck, E. T. Wartime delinquency. *Journal of Criminal Law and Criminology*, 1942, *33*, 119–135.

Hamon, A. *Lessons of the World War*. London: Tr. B. Mall, 1918.

Leipman, M. *Krieg und Kriminalitat in Deutschland*. Stuttgart: Deutsche Verlagsanstalt, 1930.

Lemert, E. M. Some aspects of a general theory of sociopathic behavior. *Research Studies of the State College of Washington*, 1948, *16*, 23–29.

Levi, N. Statistica criminale e riforma dell legislasione Penale. *In, Scritt in Onore di Enrico Ferri*, 1929.

Lunden, W. A. *War and delinquency.* Ames, IA: The Art Press, 1963.

Mannheim, H. *War and crime.* London: Wats, 1941.

Mannheim, H. *Group Problem in Crime and Punishment.* London: Routledge and Kegan Paul, 1955.

Mannheim, H. *Comparative Criminology.* London: Routledge and Kegan Paul, 1965.

McGrath, J. E. *Social and Psychological Factors in Stress.* New York: Holt Rinehart and Winston, 1970.

Reckless, W. C. The impact of war on crime, delinquency and prostitution. *American Journal of Sociology,* 1942, *48,* 378-386.

Sellin, I. Is murder increasing in Europe? *The Annals of the American Academy of Political and Social Science,* 1926, *126,* 29-34.

Selye, H. *The Stress of Life.* New York: McGraw-Hill Book Company, 1956.

Solnar, V. La guerre mondiale et la criminalite en Tchechoslovaquie. *Revue de Droit Penal,* 1929, *9,* 858-893.

Sumner, W. G. *Folkways: "A Study of the Sociological Importance of Usages, Manners, Customs, Mores and Moral."* Boston: Ginn, 1906.

Sutherland, E. Crime. *In,* Osburn (ed.), *American Society in Wartime.* Chicago: University of Chicago Press, 1943.

Sutherland, E. Differential Association. *In,* Cohen, *et al.* (eds.), *The Sutherland Papers.* Indiana University Press, 1956.

Sutherland, E. Wartime crime. *In,* Cohen, *et al.* (eds.), *The Sutherland Papers.* Indiana University Press, 1956.

Tanter, R. International war and domestic turmoil: Some contemporary evidence. *In,* Graham and Gurr (eds.), *The History of Violence In America.* New York: Praeger, 1969.

Teele, J. E. Social pathology and stress. *In,* Levine, *et al.* (eds.), *Social Stress.* Chicago: Aladine Publishing Co., 1970.

Von Hentig, H. *Crime: Causes and Conditions.* New York: McGraw-Hill, 1947.

Welford, A. T. *Man Under Stress.* London: Taylor and Trancis Ltd., 1974.

9.
Some Effects of Stress
During Grade-School Years*

Michael Inbar
Hebrew University, Jerusalem

INTRODUCTION

Grade-school years and the latency period with which they overlap
are often regarded as tranquil years in the child's development, at
least in relative terms. The turbulence and problems of adolescence
are still ahead, and the problems and great dependency characteristics of early childhood are a thing of the past. This image of a relatively trouble-free period in the development of the child is reflected
both in the literature and in common wisdom. Elder shows, for
instance, that parents recollect this period as the most rewarding for
them (Elder, 1974, pp. 253 and 317). In a similar vein, a leaflet
distributed by the American Movers Conference expresses one brand
of common wisdom when it cautions parents about the differential
impact of moving on children in the following terms:

> Each child, because of difference in age and life experience, will
> view the move differently . . . the pre-school child can pose a
> real problem . . . .

---

*Part of this chapter is based on M. Inbar, "Immigration and Learning: The Vulnerable
Age," *Canadian Review of Sociology and Anthropology,* 1977, Vol. 14, No. 2, pp. 213–
234, and on pp. 11–49 of M. Inbar, *The Vulnerable Age Phenomenon,* N.Y.: The Russell-
Sage Foundation/Basic Books, 1976.

The grade school child has a more highly developed sense of self . . . . His developing sense of discovery may make the idea of moving exciting to him. While he will be leaving friends, they will not be the deep, vital friendships of older children . . . .

The teenager, of course, usually has enough problems even in a stable environment.   (From a leaflet of the American Movers Conference, undated, obtained by mail, March, 1976).

There is also a different view. Thus, it could be argued that the linguistic and cognitive developments that normally take place between the ages of 6 and 11 could potentially make this age span a problem-ridden one (Inbar, 1976, p. 44; Frasure and Entwisle, 1973; Entwisle and Frasure, 1974). Similarly, the Piagetan transition to autonomy between the ages of 7 and 11 is a potentially vulnerable stage of development. More specifically, Sullivan holds that the juvenile era — roughly spanning the ages 6 to 10 — is in some respects the most critical stage of development (Sullivan, 1953, pp. 227, 241–242).

A serendipitous finding that my colleague, Chaim Adler, and I were confronted with suggests there might be an important kernel of truth in this latter view. The essence of the finding is that children in about the 6-to-11-year-old age bracket may be more vulnerable to crises in their environment than either younger or older youths.

This surprising finding, which suggests the possibility of a vulnerable age (possibly socially induced), has been reported in several publications (Inbar and Adler, 1976; Inbar, 1976; Inbar, 1977; Inbar and Adler, 1977). My aim in this chapter is to summarize these reports. In the process I shall refer to a few studies and findings that have come to my attention since the publication of the finding and comment on some of their implications for the phenomenon under consideration. My primary motive in discussing the vulnerable-age effect is to invite the independent replications that are still needed to establish the effect on firmer grounds than it can be without this very necessary test.

THE FINDING: THE ORIGINAL STUDY AND ITS BACKGROUND

The immediate cause of the documentation of what Adler and myself have labeled the vulnerable-age effect was a case study by Martan

(1972) about a little village, Yad Rambam, that had been settled in 1955–6 by Jewish immigrants from Morocco. Martan was interested in the academic achievement of children as a function of the effect of the Israeli educational system on youths. To ascertain the modality of this effect, he cross-tabulated the age of the children upon immigration in 1955–6 against college attendance (1971). The expectation was that a negative relationship would be obtained between successful schooling (operationalized by percentage having attended college) and the age of the children upon immigration. This expectation was based on the fact that young children are commonly observed to learn a new language faster than older youths; moreover, language problems for adolescents translate, as a rule, into high school test failures that have a greater impact on continued school attendance than is the case for grade-school children. Furthermore, ever since the publication of the largest available survey on immigrant children at the turn of the century (Dillingham, 1911), the sociological literature explicitly or implicitly assumes an inverse relationship between age upon immigration and school achievement (e.g., Bhatnagar's *Immigrants at School,* 1970). On both intuitive and documented grounds, therefore, the anticipation was that the younger a child was when he immigrated, the better his chances for academic achievement would be.

Contrary to this expectation, however, Martan obtained what amounts to a *positive* relationship between age upon immigration and the likelihood of attending college. In particular, in his sample those children who were fourteen years of age or older upon immigration were quite likely in 1971 to have completed high school and have entered an institution of higher learning. Conversely, and quite surprisingly, their younger brothers and sisters (including those of preschool age at the time of immigration) exhibited a marked and monotonically decreasing rate of successful schooling. On the strength of his finding, Martan concluded that a process had unfolded in Israel that had hampered the educational achievements of the settlers' young children.

Quite clearly, Martan's finding could reflect a process of downward mobility. It could also be idiosyncratic to a small village for any number of reasons. In fact, most people — including Adler and myself — felt that this was the most likely explanation for the finding. Nonetheless, because at the time of Martan's report we were

Table 9-1. Percentage of Children Admitted to College, by
Age at Date of Immigration.

Age at time of families' immigration	0–5	6–11	12–15	16+
Percentage admitted to college	26	13*	25	29
	(N = 47)	(N = 77)	(N = 65)	(N = 49)

Source: After Inbar and Adler (1976, Table 4)
*Chi^2, 1 d.f. (6–11 age group versus others) = 5.23, p < 0.05.

planning a cross-cultural study on Moroccan immigrants, we decided
to take advantage of the opportunity to scrutinize the finding. Our
own impending research was about brothers and first cousins who
had settled in France and Israel; it included a control group of
Rumanian immigrants (Inbar and Adler, 1977). Our sample included
238 youths who had immigrated with their families to either France
or Israel, and who at the time of the research were old enough to
have attended college. The analyses pertaining to Martan's finding
that we performed were based on this sample. This initial study will
now be briefly summarized.

The relationship between age upon immigration and college attendance that was obtained in these data did not turn out to be the
inverse one that we had anticipated, nor did the curve resemble
Martan's. Rather, the distribution was curvilinear (see Table 9-1).
Furthermore, this relationship was obtained not only at the aggregate
level, but also within breakdowns by subsamples (see Inbar and Adler,
1976, Table 4). Of perhaps even greater interest was that at this point
the reexamination of Martan's data showed that he had mistakenly
defined one of his age categories, and that in all likelihood his data
were in fact curvilinear too (Inbar and Adler, 1976, pp. 194–196).
All of a sudden, therefore, my colleague and I found ourselves confronted with the fact that we had achieved a replication that we
had not expected, to an extent that we had not anticipated. Martan's
mistake and his unsubstantiated conclusions were no longer of importance. What was, is that an unexpected finding had emerged that
could be of some consequence.

The analyses that we carried out within the constraints of the
limited sample that was available revealed a few additional trends.
These can be summarized as follows:

1. The vulnerable-age phenomenon, while generally predominant in the six-to-eleven-year age group of immigrants, was stronger for the twelve-to-fifteen-year age group in one of the three subsamples. This suggested the possibility that chronological age and school (or social) structures may interact to produce the vulnerable-age effect; alternatively, a second problematic period − possibly independent of the first − might exist in mid-adolescence.
2. The strength of the effects was always sufficient to offset the known phenomenon of older children of immigrants (sixteen years old or more in this case) being sent to work.
3. At the same time, and quite unexpectedly, the effect was undetectable at below the college level; that is to say, with other cutting points (i.e., earlier measures) of school achievement, no trend was distinguishable. A later replication with Canadian data cast some light on this puzzling fact, as will be shortly noted.

As a tentative theoretical explanation for the vulnerable-age phenomenon, Adler and I suggested a rudimentary model. Its essence is that while school transfers are stressful for all youths, this fact is more likely to go unnoticed for grade-school children. We reasoned that the desocialization-resocialization paradigm found in many immigrant studies may be adequate to explain the vulnerable-age phenomenon (cf., Curle, 1947; Eisenstadt, 1954; Bar-Yosef, 1968). Specifically, " . . . this paradigm sees social adaptation to a new environment as involving a fundamental and usually painful process of unlearning and relearning, as well as a process which depends on social power and resources. The unlearning-relearning process, however, is probably not applicable to infants and/or very young children, at least not as far as school environment is concerned. For children of school age, however, the difficulties which accompany a radical change of school environment may be relatively similar, in any case much more similar than the resources that they marshall to ease the crisis. If so, our finding would be directly interpretable; it would simply be a consequence of differential resources under conditions of high but fairly uniform duress.

"To buttress the socialization-resocialization paradigm, consider the following. It is generally true that the older a child, the less his parents can help him directly with his school work, irrespective of country of residence. Also, however, the older the child, the more attention and power he commands inside as well as outside the family. Such factors combine to make older children better equipped to deal with school problems they face upon immigration than are younger children.

"Accordingly, in the very early years of immigration in particular, the problems encountered by young children of school age, especially grade-school children, are likely to be given low priority by many families or go unnoticed altogether. These children, in addition, are likely to have little or no independent school-related resources (e.g., peer-tutoring). The expected effect of such processes on children who are at such a stage of development would be compatible with the trend exhibited by our Israeli data." (Inbar and Adler, 1976, pp. 197–198).

The model just outlined has its logic summarized in Figure 9-1, with entries having qualitative values that follow from the discussion.

Adler and myself have stressed that this model was tentative. In the first place, at the level of types of models, we recognized that in addition to, or instead of, this environmental explanation, a developmental interference with linguistic or cognitive functions might be responsible for the vulnerable-age effect. Secondly, serious theorizing would obviously have to await such time in the future when the shape of the age-curve to be explained would be specified with greater accuracy than it was at that time. A first step in this direction would be to attempt to narrow down the 6-to-11-year age range for which the effect had been documented. We shall see that there are

	Age Range		
	0–5	6–11	12+
School duress	None	Yes	Yes
Resources (parental attention, cognitive development, peer-tutoring, etc.)	Little	Some	More
Discrepancy between school stress and resources	0	+	±

Source: After Inbar and Adler (1976, Figure 1).

Figure 9-1. Process assumed to underly the vulnerable age phenomenon.

reasons to believe that this might be feasible; indeed, there are already indications that the effect might be concentrated in the middle to upper part of the age range. Thirdly, given the lack of prior empirical and theoretical evidence, the finding could be artificial. The first task was obviously to rule out this latter possibility.

One potential artifact of importance could already be checked with the data at hand. As the reader will have noticed, the form of the trend observed in Table 9-1 suggests that the shape of the distribution could be the result of the operation of the first/later born effect. In particular, older children also being likely to be firstborn, it is conceivable that the trend observed could be due to this effect. As the analyses showed, however, this was not the case; the shape of the distribution turned out to be independent of birth order, in particular, independent of primogeniture (see Table 9-2).

This being so, a research agenda that included the following tasks suggested itself.

The first, of course, was to determine whether the finding could be replicated, particularly with North American data. Another one was to further control for possible artifacts, for example, age cohort and SES effects. A third one was to ascertain the generality of the phenomenon in terms of causal variables, population, and scope of consequences. For instance, would the effect hold for migrations? Would it hold equally for both sexes? Are variables other than college attendance affected?

In the next two sections I shall report the results of two additional studies, and the answers that they suggest to some of these and related questions.

Table 9-2. Percentage of Immigrants' Children Admitted to College by Age at Time of Immigration and Birth Order.

AGE AT TIME OF FAMILIES' IMMIGRATION	PERCENTAGE ADMITTED TO COLLEGE	
	FIRSTBORN	LATER-BORN
0–5	40 (N = 5)	24 (N = 42)
6–11	00 (N = 16)	16 (N = 61)
12–15	22 (N = 23)	26 (N = 42)
16+	36 (N = 25)	21 (N = 24)
Total	23 (N = 69)	21 (N = 169)

Source: Inbar and Adler (1976, Table 5).

ADDITIONAL EVIDENCE

The first piece of additional evidence bearing on the vulnerable-age phenomenon comes from a replication carried out with the Canadian census of 1971.*   As a background to the presentation of the results obtained with these data, a few technical clarifications are in order.

By implication, the preceding discussion has indicated that attempting to replicate the vulnerable-age phenomenon requires that a very specific set of data be available. In particular, with "crises" defined as immigration or migration, the following two conditions must be met:

1. *Sample characteristics.*   The sample must be of immigrants or migrants, and the respondents must be old enough to have had a chance to attend college; allowing for a margin of security, this means that the sample must be made of respondents who were 19 to 20 years old or more at the time of the interview.
2. *Variables and level of measurement.* (a) For each respondent it is necessary to either have information about his/her age upon immigration or migration or, alternatively, data about his/her present age and date of immigration or migration to be able to generate this information; and (b) it is also necessary to have explicit information about the respondents' college attendance.

As I shall shortly elaborate, these minimal conditions are generally not found in most available large-scale data banks. In the 1971 Canadian census, they are, at least to some extent.

The reasons for this qualified statement about the 1971 census are twofold. In the first place, there is no usable information for migrants. The analyses, of necessity, are therefore limited to immigrants only. Even for them, however, age upon entering Canada is unknown. What is available is the period of immigration coded as follows:**

1. Before 1946
2. 1946 to 1955

---

*Public Use Sample Data (Individual File for Metropolitan Areas) derived from the 1971 Canadian Census of Population supplied by Statistics Canada. The responsibility for the use and interpretation of these data is entirely that of the author.
**1971 Census of Canada, Public Use Sample Tapes, User Documentation (Draft), Statistics Canada, March 1975, p. 4.2.15.

3. 1956 to 1960
4. 1961 to 1965
5. 1966
6. 1967 to 1968
7. 1969
8. 1970
9. 1971
10. Canadian born

This variable, in combination with the age of the respondents (in 1971), can nonetheless generate the requested information. The procedure has been reported in detail in Inbar (1977): it allows a cohort analysis of the respondents who were 20, 21, and 22 years old in 1971. In particular, for each of these cohorts, age upon immigration can be determined according to three age brackets that approximate the trichotomy, 0–5, 6–11, 12+ years, in which we are interested. It should be mentioned, however, that even these categories are not without an element of imprecision. The reason is that the age of the respondents that is reported in the Canadian census is age at last birthday. That is to say, an unknown number of persons had this birthday in 1970 rather than in 1971. This incertitude generates the (trichotomized) actual age categories that are summarized in Table 9-3A; the parentheses indicate the age range of incertitude.

Clearly, the 21-year-old cohort yields the best age trichotomization for the purpose at hand. However, depending upon one's assumptions about the distribution of dates of birth, the cohorts of 20 and 22 years old also present advantages when the lower and upper boundaries of the age range with which we are concerned are considered. This being so, the analyses were always carried out twice — once for the consolidated cohort of 20 and 21 years old, and once for the consolidated cohort of 21 and 22 years old. This procedure had the additional advantages of having a built-in test for the robustness of the results, and increasing the number of cases available for the analyses, a consideration that became important when the number of cases shrank because of the introduction of control variables. The categories of age upon immigration generated when the cohorts were consolidated are presented in Table 9-3B.*

---

*Merging two consecutive age cohorts generates a one-year overlap between age categories upon immigration (see Table 9-3A); I have taken this common value to represent the modal age for the category boundaries of the consolidated cohorts.

Table 9-3. Age Categories Upon Immigration to Canada of
Three Cohorts of Respondents.

AGE AT TIME OF 1971 CENSUS		AGE UPON IMMIGRATION	
A. Individual cohorts			
20	0–(4–5)	(5–6)–(9–10)	(10–11)–(15–16)
21	0–(5–6)	(6–7)–(10–11)	(11–12)–(16–17)
22	0–(6–7)	(7–8)–(11–12)	(12–13)–(17–18)
B. Consolidated cohorts			
20 + 21	0–5	6–10	11–16
21 + 22	0–6	7–11	12–17

Source: Inbar (1976, Table 3).

With these clarifications in mind, the results of the replication can be summarized as follows (for details see Inbar, 1977).

In the first place, the U-shaped or J-shaped curve, whose replication was attempted, was obtained in each cohort (see Table 9-4). The results, however, did not reach the 0.05 level of statistical significance in any individual cohort. At the same time, as a pattern, it should be noted that the probability of the trend recurring in all three cohorts by chance is less than 0.05 (1/27).

Second, the weakness of the trend could be traced to an interaction by sexes. Indeed, controlling for this variable, no evidence was

Table 9-4. Percentage of College Attendance Among Immigrants of Both Sexes by Age Upon Immigration, and by Cohort.

COHORT (AGE AT TIME OF CENSUS)	AGE UPON IMMIGRATION		
	0–(4–5)	(5–6)–(9–10)	(10–11)–(15–16)
20	0.37	0.20	0.31
(N = 126)	(N = 43)	(N = 51)	(N = 32)
	0–(5–6)	(6–7)–(10–11)	(11–12)–(16–17)
21	0.33	0.18	0.21
(N = 151)	(N = 69)	(N = 44)	(N = 38)
	0–(6–7)	(7–8)–(11–12)	(12–13)–(17–18)
22	0.27	0.11	0.13
(N = 139)	(N = 64)	(N = 35)	(N = 40)

Source: Public Use Sample Data, Individual File for Metropolitan Areas, Canadian census of 1971.

found of a vulnerable-age effect for girls (see Table 9-5B). On the other hand, the predicted relationship recurred for boys and was in this case both sizeable and robust. In comparison with the children who immigrated during their grade-school years, younger and older male immigrants exhibited a rate of college attendance that was at least 50 percent higher; this relationship was unaffected by the combination of age cohorts that was considered (see Table 9-5A).

Third, the effect now specified for boys was shown to be independent of the mother tongue of the respondents (mostly English, followed by Italian, only some 5 percent having a French-speaking background; see Table 9-6.

Finally, the effect was shown to be independent of levels of SES (see Inbar, 1977, Table 10). At the same time, the analyses suggested that the vulnerable-age phenomenon was quite likely to be obscured by confounding factors wherever the SES background of the respondents was insufficiently controlled. This was shown to be a likely occurrence when high school measures of school achievements are used as a dependent variable, in particular high school completion (see Inbar, 1977, pp. 226–228, especially Tables 12 and 14).

In short, the finding was replicated. Moreover, it emerged from this study as being both generalized and specified. In terms of generalization, there was now evidence that the effect was not likely to be cohort, SES, or culture (language) specific. In terms of specification, the Canadian data suggested that the effect was probably restricted to boys. We shall see later that these conclusions appear to be valid — with one qualification: the vulnerable-age phenomenon, although less consistently found among girls, does not appear to be strictly limited to males.

At this point it is of interest to confront an epistemological question. Assuming that the finding is a genuine one — as obviously a successful replication makes it more likely to be the case — how could it have gone unnoticed for so long?

Interestingly, delving into the literature and searching through data banks suggested an intriguing answer to this question. The answer could even constitute, in a manner of speaking, additional evidence by default for the finding itself. Specifically, the conclusion that emerged from this search was that the effect is very difficult to document, given the manner in which the data that are required for observing the effect are usually collected and analyzed. This point is obviously of great importance and deserves to be elaborated.

Table 9-5.   Percentage of College Attendance among Immigrants, by
Sex and Age Upon Immigration.

COHORTS (AGE AT TIME OF CENSUS)	MODAL AGE UPON IMMIGRATION		
A. Males	0–5	6–10	11–16
20 + 21 (N = 106)	0.48 (N = 40)	0.18 (N = 38)	0.32 (N = 28)
	0–6	7–11	12–17
21 + 22 (N = 92)	0.40 (N = 43)	0.23 (N = 26)	0.35 (N = 23)
B. Females	0–5	6–10	11–16
20 + 21 (N = 123)	0.20 (N = 51)	0.22 (N = 41)	0.23 (N = 31)
	0–6	7–11	12–17
21 + 22 (N = 131)	0.15 (N = 59)	0.12 (N = 33)	0.08 (N = 39)

Source: Inbar (1977, Table 8).
N.B The N's for boys and girls do not exactly add up to the total N's reported in Table 4.
The reason is that in Table 4 some respondents were already heads of households. These
respondents were omitted from later analyses to allow a control by parental SES, which in
the census is only possible for nonheads of households.

Table 9-6.   Percentage of College Attendance Among Male Immigrants, by
Mother Tongue and Age Upon Immigration.

COHORTS (AGE AT TIME OF CENSUS)	MODAL AGE UPON IMMIGRATION		
A. Mother tongue: English	0–5	6–10	11–16
20 + 21 (N = 52)	0.50 (N = 20)	0.29 (N = 21)	0.36 (N = 11)
	0–6	7–11	12–17
21 + 22 (N = 47)	0.27 (N = 26)	0.17 (N = 12)	0.22 (N = 9)
B. Mother tongue: Other	0–5	6–10	11–16
20 + 21 (N = 84)	0.47 (N = 36)	0.09 (N = 23)	0.24 (N = 25)
	0–6	7–11	12–17
21 + 22 (N = 87)	0.45 (N = 42)	0.24 (N = 21)	0.29 (N = 24)

Sources: Inbar (1977, Table 11).

The Canadian census of 1971 is a good example in point. The Metropolitan tape released for public use contains 53,173 respondents. Of them 13,153 (close to 25%) are immigrants. This is an extremely high rate, which can only be expected to be found in very few modern societies. Nonetheless, the analyses I have reported were based on a few hundred cases. This stems from the fact that in the Canadian census periods of immigration have only been recorded in very rough categories, making most cases unusable. In most countries even this type of information is not available; rather, the breakdown is simply national/foreign-born, occasionally with information about country or continent of origin. Another problem is that large-scale data bases often use collapsed age categories, a frequent one being 0 to 14. The reason for this categorization is that such data are usually collected in connection with studies or surveys that focus on aspects of the labor market. The lack of information about either the precise age or date of immigration of the respondent makes it next to impossible to even attempt to observe the vulnerable-age phenomenon in most large-scale data banks that are listed.* This also holds true if one attempts to shift the focus from the effect of immigration to that of simply migrating. In this case the usual information that is available merely tells whether or not the respondent has moved in recent years. Sometimes, but not always, there is also information about the number of moves; in this case whenever the information includes dates, it is about the latest moves. The Canadian census of 1971 is a good example of some of these shortcomings. (See fields 52, 53 and 54 of the Metropolitan Area File, Statistics Canada, 1971).

Other potentially relevant data banks have an additional weakness. They focus on youths who are, at most, of high school age. In this case the problem for the analyses in which we are interested is compounded by the inadequacy of the dependent variable. As I have indicated, the vulnerable-age effect is very likely to be obscured at this level by SES factors that are particularly potent at the onset of opportunities to enter the labor market and that require, in order to be neutralized, powerful controls indeed. (See Inbar, 1977, Table

*I am extremely indebted in this respect to Mrs. Alice Robbin of the Computer Center of the Department of Sociology, the University of Wisconsin, who searched nationally and worldwide for the existence of usable data banks. It is through her efforts that I became aware of the existence of the Canadian census of 1971.

14). That is to say, in the quasi totality of the listed data banks, the vulnerable-age phenomenon could not have been observed. Documenting the effect requires not only an appropriate set of data — a very rare occurrence in itself — but also controls and nonparametric analyses that are most unlikely to be performed together if the phenomenon is not hypothesized in advance. As a result, the effect is unlikely to be easily observed.

In this respect it may be of interest to note that I did come across a couple of studies in which the finding could theoretically have been documented. What did actually occur in these studies is intriguing. First, it is noteworthy that in both cases there is evidence that the effect may have been present. In each case, however, the author either overlooked the finding or discarded it as a random fluctuation. The first case occurs in Bhatnagar's *Immigrants at School* (1970, p. 97). In this study Bhatnagar presents data about the exact age upon immigration to England of a sample of West Indian and Cypriot high school students; at one point he also relates this variable to a generalized scale of adjustment. Bhatnagar's aim was to test the usual negative relationship that is assumed to obtain between age upon immigration and school-related variables, in this case adjustment. Interestingly, he did not find evidence of such a relationship. Accordingly, and after recalling his source for the hypothesis, he concludes that past evidence "would lead to a prediction that age at the time of immigration is negatively related to adjustment. The data gathered in this study does not support the view." (Bhatnagar, 1970, p.97). Of course, should his distribution have been curvilinear, this is precisely the result that one would have anticipated, *given that the conclusion is based on correlations.* Unfortunately, Bhatnagar does not present the raw data, and neither does he elaborate on his unexpected failure to replicate a well-established relationship.

In the second study, the author explicitly noted what may be the first published evidence in support of the vulnerable-age phenomenon. However, in this case the author (Lee, 1956) chose to pursue his unrelated concern and to discard the finding as a likely random fluctuation. The study is a replication of Klineberg's finding (Klineberg, 1935) about the increase in IQ evidenced by Negro children who migrated to the North. It should be noted that the independent variable in this study is migration rather than immigration. Also, the dependent variable is not school attendance but the standardized IQ score obtained at test and retest times by the respondents. Keeping these differences in mind, the author presents in tabular form (Lee, 1956, p. 435) the IQ scores of his subjects as a function of the age (grade) at which the migrant children entered the northern school system. Lee's data span the age range 6 to 14 and are summarized in Table 9-7.

Interestingly, looking at column 9A one notes two dips in the distribution: one at ages 8 to 9.5, the other at ages 12 to 14. Because the scores are standardized, such comparisons are meaningful; at the same time it should be noted that they might be lacking validity due to the possible confounding effect of retesting. This difficulty, however, can be overcome by considering separately the results of the first test, then the results of the second test, etc.

The IQ scores obtained in the first test by all the subjects are those that appear in the main diagonal of Table 9-7. Clearly, and although the difference is admittedly small, controlling in this manner for the test-retest effect shows that the group that emerges with the lowest standardized score (86.3) is the group of children who migrated between the ages of 8 and 9.5. Furthermore, pursuing this analysis one step further, it is possible to compare among themselves those children who were retested the same number of times. For the 12-to 14-year-olds no such comparison is possible for lack of data. For the others, however, at least one comparison of this kind is feasible by considering the diagonal that runs from columns 2B to 9A. By the way Table 9-7 is set up, this diagonal is made of the scores of the children who at the time had been given exactly one retest. Inspecting

Table 9-7. Mean "IQ's" on Philadelphia Test of Mental and Verbal Ability of Southern-Born Negro Children by Age (Grade) at Which They Entered the Philadelphia School System, and by Grades at Which They Were Tested and Retested.

GRADE IN WHICH THE CHILDREN ENTERED THE PHILADELPHIA SCHOOL SYSTEM	AGE RANGE	N	1A	2B	4B	6B	9A	TEST-RETEST IMPROVEMENT BETWEEN 1ST AND 2ND TEST
1A	6	182	86.5	89.3	91.8	93.3	92.8	+2.8
1B-2B	6.5-7.5	109		86.7	88.6	90.9	90.5	+1.9
3A-4B	8-9.5	199			86.3	87.2	89.4	+0.9
5A-6B	10-11.5	221				88.2	90.2	+2.0
7A-9A	12-14	219					87.4	-

Source: After Lee (1956, p. 435, Table 1).

this diagonal clearly shows that the group of 8- to 9.5-year-olds stands out again as having the lowest IQ scores (87.2). The disutility in this sample of migrating at this age can be summarized in a single measure: the difference between the first and second test. This difference is indicative of a stable handicap; it is presented in the last column of Table 9-7.

Lee's study is intriguing on several accounts. In the first place, the age group of migrants' children that is the most affected falls well within the expected age range; it may even be a first indication that the phenomenon that we are discussing could be narrowed down in the future.* Not less interesting is the fact that the shape of the distribution did not escape Lee's attention. He chose, however, to discard the finding as an exception to the trend he was attempting to establish, without further explanation (Lee, 1956, p. 434).

It is unfortunate that the data do not allow a longer and more complete trend analysis of the IQ scores controlled for the test-retest effect. This is particularly true in the case of the 12- to 14-year-olds for which not even one retest score is available. In the light of the evidence found in one of the subsamples of the original study on the vulnerable-age effect (see second section of this chapter), it would have been intriguing indeed to find that this age group does also exhibit a lower retest score. The structural view that I shall discuss in the next section suggests, however, that we should not expect this to have been the case in Lee's data, because his study held constant the school-level subdivision. I shall elaborate this point shortly.

Be this as it may, and unless Lee's distribution is a coincidence, there are grounds to believe that the vulnerable-age phenomenon might be more general than the two immigration studies that I have discussed may suggest. The effect appears likely to be a function of migrations as well as immigrations, and if so, perhaps more generally of crises in the children's environment (e.g., divorces, parental deaths, school transfers, etc.); in turn, these crises might very well affect more than simply school-related variables. At least these are possibilities that should not be lightly discarded.

---

*We should of course be prepared for possible age shifts as a function of structural and developmental changes. Lee's study was carried out in the early 1950s and on a sample of Negro children. The vulnerable age for nonminority children and in the 1980s might conceivably be concentrated at somewhat different points of the age continuum.

Before speculating in such a manner, however, it is obviously necessary to first establish on firmer grounds than accidental evidence the fact that the vulnerable-age effect indeed holds in the case of the first conceptual step toward a generalization, i.e., in the case of migrants. In addition, the results should be further controlled for possible artifacts. This is the task addressed in the next section.

THE TALENT DATA

The second replication and the generalization of the finding to the case of migrants is based on analyses performed on the TALENT data. A few words about this data bank and about some methodological points will clarify the analyses and the discussion that will follow.

The data bank known as TALENT was started in 1960. It is a nationally representative sample of United States high school students in that year. By 1976 there had been three follow-up studies of the original sample. The last was the eleven-year follow-up that at the time of this study (1976) had been carried out for three grades: the 10th, 11th and 12th.

The master sample includes over 400,000 cases. It is kept and managed in Palo Alto by the American Institute for Research. The staff in charge of the data bank has developed weighting procedures to overcome the problem of sample mortality in the follow-ups. They have also developed various standard scales, among them an SES and an education variable.

In the following analyses we shall be concerned with the eleven-year follow-up study. The samples are those that are standardly made available to investigators by the American Institute for Research; the Ns are about 3,000 cases per grade. To be nationally representative, each sample has been calibrated by the above-mentioned weighting procedure. Details about the sample, the weighting procedures, and a copy of the questionnaires can be found in the *Handbook of the Project TALENT Data Bank* (American Institutes for Research, 1972).

For the purpose at hand it is useful to note the exact wording and coding of two key variables:

The dependent variable, years of schooling, was made available coded as follows:

Coding		*Meaning*
0	=	up to grade 8
1	=	up to grade 9
2	=	up to grade 10
3	=	up to grade 11
4	=	up to grade 12, without diploma
5	=	high school diploma only
6	=	high school diploma plus some further education (but no college)
7	=	high school diploma plus some college
8	=	college graduate
9	=	college graduate plus some graduate school education
10	=	college graduate plus Master's degree or equivalent
11	=	Beyond Master's degree but without Ph.D., M.D., or law degree
12	=	Doctorate or law degree

The independent variable, migration, was operationalized by the answers to a question that was included in the 1960 student questionnaire. The question — SIB 167 — reads as follows:

How long have you lived in this community?

1. One year or less
2. More than one year, but no more than three years
3. More than three years, but no more than five years
4. More than five years, but no more than ten years
5. More than ten years, but not all my life
6. All my life
   (American Institute for Research, 1972, p. 53)

Under the assumption that 10th graders are on the average 16 years of age, this question allows determination of the age brackets of

Table 9-8. Age Categories Upon Migration Generated by the Answers to Question
SIB167 (see Text), for the Respondents Who Were 10th,
11th, and 12th-Graders in 1960.

COHORT	ANSWERS TO QUESTION SIB167					
	1	2	3	4	5	6 (NEVER)
10th graders	15–15.5	13–14	11–12	6–10	1–5	–
11th graders	16–16.5	14–15	12–13	7–11	1–6	–
12th graders	17–17.5	15–16	13–14	8–12	1–7	–

Source: Inbar (1976, Table 8).

migration, which are reproduced in Table 9-8,* for the three cohorts
we will be concerned with.

From Table 9-8 it is apparent that the age categories in which we
are primarily interested are approximated with various degrees of
accuracy in each of the three cohorts. For instance, the pre-school
age category is best approximated for the 10th graders, and less
accurately so for the 11th and 12th graders (see Table 9-8, column
5); on the strength of Lee's study, however, this is not likely to prove
too harmful inasmuch as there are grounds to believe that the vulnerable-age effect may begin at about the age of 8. From a different
perspective, the choice of age brackets should show the effect of
moving from one level of the educational system to another, e.g.,
from elementary school to high school. Such structural transitions
are known to have an attrition effect on cohorts and should be distinguished from the vulnerable-age phenomenon (for a concrete
illustration of this point, see next section). In the United States,
transition points in the educational structure can occur at various
ages. But the consideration of importance is that the earliest commonly found transition point occurs at grade 7, that is at age 13. For a
careful test of the hypothesis at hand, it is consequently necessary
to avoid depressing the age bracket that is critical for the vulnerable-
age test by inadvertently including in it the potentially confounding
effect of the beginning of high school selection. In other words, we

*Should one prefer to assume that 10th graders are on the average 15 rather than 16 years
old, all the ages presented in Table 9-8 and in the following analyses should be reduced
by one year. Because in the forthcoming analyses the comparisons are always rational
(i.e., relative to adjacent categories), the validity of these analyses is independent of the
assumption that is chosen. It should be kept in mind, however, that given the choice that I
have made, all the vulnerable ages of transition that will be discussed represent an upper
age limit estimate of the respondents at the time of interest.

must be careful not to have 13-year-olds or older children in any of the age groups in which, on the basis of the previous studies, we expect to find evidence of the vulnerable-age effect.

Operationally, this requirement, together with the constraints of the data, means that in the TALENT samples the confirmation of the 6- to 11-year vulnerable-age hypothesis requires that dips in years of schooling be found in the following categories of Table 9-8:

1. In the 10th grade: in categories 4 and 3 as opposed to 2 and 5.
2. In the 11th grade: in category 4 as opposed to categories 3 and 5.
3. In the 12th grade: in category 4 as opposed to categories 3 and 5.

On the other hand, because in the United States the most significant transition to a higher level of the school structure occurs upon entering high school proper, that is, at the ages of 15 (in the 8-4 systems) and 16 (in the 6-3-3 systems), and because of the overlapping end of compulsory education, the selection explanation suggests that we should expect to find evidence of an independent and structurally induced dip in the following categories of Table 9-8.

1. In the 10th grade: in category 1 as opposed to category 2.
2. In the 11th grade: in categories 2 and 1 and opposed to category 3.
3. In the 12th grade: in category 2 as opposed to categories 1 and 3.

These structural predictions are obviously incidental to our main concern. They are useful, however, because they will put the findings pertaining to the vulnerable-age effect in mid-childhood in perspective and will document another possible reason for its having been difficult to observe.

With these hypotheses in mind, the aims of the analyses to be presented are fourfold:

1. To examine the extent to which the vulnerable-age finding can be generalized to the United States.
2. To examine the extent to which it holds in the case of migrations.

3. To diversify the criterion variable by using a measure of school achievement that encompasses the *whole* educational cycle.
4. To refine the findings by differentiating between effects that anticipated on the basis of the selective structure of school systems and those that require a different explanation.

We can now turn to the results of the analyses. The overall distribution of mean school levels achieved by the various groups of migrants in each of the three cohorts is presented in Table 9-9. For the reader's convenience, Tables 9-10 and 9-11 present the same data split-up according to the age ranges relevant to the test of the vulnerable-age phenomenon and the selectivity of secondary education, together with the effect predicted from these explanations.

Considering first our major hypothesis, Table 9-10 shows that, although the differences are at times small, all the predictions based on the existence of a vulnerable-age effect are consistently supported by the data, without exception. As a trend (whose probability of occurring by chance is less than 0.05 for these data alone, and infinitesimal if we consider the results of Table 9-9 together with those obtained in the Canadian study), it appears that the existence of a pre-adolescent vulnerable age is now, if not established, at least highly probable.

In terms of the magnitude of the effect, it lies between one-fifth of a standard deviation to about one standard deviation below the grand mean (of the untruncated distribution), depending on the cohort considered. In comparison to the age categories adjacent to those where the vulnerable-age phenomenon is predicted to occur, the differences are of course larger. It should be noted, incidentally, that to the extent that there is a selectivity effect from one level of the school system to another, the size of the vulnerable-age phenomenon is underestimated because of the independent dampening effect that this selection may start having on 13-year-olds (column 2 for 10th graders, and column 3 for 11th and 12th graders; see Table 9-10).

In this connection Table 9-11 shows that as far as the upper level of high school selection is concerned (i.e., for 15- and 16-year-olds), the anticipated effect is clearly documented; indeed, all the differences are in the predicted direction (see Table 9-11).

Table 9-9. Average Levels of Education Achieved by Migrants and Non-Migrants by Cohort and Age Upon Migration in Childhood.

A. Key to age categories upon migration (see Table 8)

COHORT	1	2	3	4	5
10th graders	15–15.5	13–14	11–12	6–10	1–5
11th graders	16–16.5	14–15	12–13	7–11	1–6
12th graders	17–17.5	15–16	13–14	8–12	1–7

B. Data

	1	2	3	4	5	MEAN	STANDARD DEVIATION	NEVER MOVED 6	GRAND MEAN	STANDARD DEVIATION
10th graders	6.44	6.68	6.55	6.48	6.69	6.59	0.10	6.49	6.54	0.09
(N)	(133)	(189)	(239)	(362)	(520)	(1443)		(1330)	(2773)	
11th graders	6.57	6.72	6.83	6.79	6.89	6.81	0.09	6.71	6.76	0.08
(N)	(145)	(189)	(228)	(475)	(654)	(1691)		(1537)	(3228)	
12th graders	6.85	6.77	6.85	6.82	6.95	6.88	0.07	6.72	6.80	0.09
(N)	(84)	(142)	(210)	(422)	(746)	(1604)		(1668)	(3272)	

Source: Inbar (1976, Table 10).

Table 9-10. Visual Partition of Table 9-9: Elementary School Age Range.

A. Key to age categories upon migration, and predicted dips (underlined)

COHORT	2	3	4	5	MEAN (UNTRUNCATED DISTRIBUTION – SEE TABLE 10)	STANDARD DEVIATION
10th graders	13–14	11–12	6–10	1–5		
11th graders		12–13	7–11	1–6		
12th graders		13–14	8–12	1–7		

B. Data and matching dips (underlined)

10th graders	6.68	6.55	6.48	6.69	6.59	0.10
11th grader		6.83	6.79	6.89	6.81	0.09
12th graders		6.85	6.82	6.95	6.88	0.07

Source: Inbar (1976, Table 11).

Table 9-11. Visual Pattern of Table 9-9: High School Age Range.

A. Key to age categories upon migration and predicted dips (underlined)

COHORT	1	2	3	MEAN (UNTRUNCATED DISTRIBUTION – SEE TABLE 10)	STANDARD DEVIATION
10th graders	15–15.5	13–14			
11th graders	16–16.5	14–15	12–13		
12th graders	17–17.5	15–16	13–14		

B. Data and matching dips (underlined)

10th graders	6.44	6.68		6.59	0.10
11th graders	6.57	6.72	6.83	6.81	0.09
12th graders	6.85	6.77	6.85	6.88	0.07

Source: Inbar (1976, Table 12).

In short, the image that emerges is that the vulnerable-age phenomenon and the selectivity of various levels of school structures create for learning an empirical sequence of vulnerable ages of transition. This conclusion is strengthened by a theoretically derived additional test of the hypotheses that we have just examined.

Consider the wording of the question about migrations (see p. 22). It is imprecise about the periods of migration, a shortcoming that is found in most data banks; in fact, it is fortunate that this question is as detailed as it is and that it was included in the study, otherwise the TALENT data would have been useless for the purpose at hand. But the question has another weakness: it does not allow us to distinguish between significant uprooting and trivial geographical moves; it does not allow us to distinguish either between one or repeated moves. In short, the independent variable is noisy, a fact that raises two possibilities. The first is that the results may be artifactual. The second is that the underlying phenomena may be powerful enough to be noticeable despite the inadequacies of the measure.

In an attempt to refine this measure, one could reason that the importance of moving has two major components: frequency and geocultural magnitude. The frequency variable does not require any elaboration. The geocultural continuum, on the other hand, can be conceptualized as having immigration at one of its ends and a trivial move at the other.

For lack of data, I shall have nothing to say about the frequency variable. The magnitude of the geocultural transition, however, can be estimated in all three studies where the vulnerable-age phenomenon has been documented to date. In the Israeli and Canadian immigration studies, this magnitude lies at one extreme of the continuum; in the TALENT data it lies somewhere along the continuum, in part because we are dealing with the concept of migration, but also because we have a diluted measure of this variable. Conceptually, therefore, a better definition of migrations — for instance, migrations across large geographical boundaries — should yield a magnitude that falls between these two points. In theory, we would thus expect that in this case the size of the vulnerable-age effect should also be intermediate.

Because the sets of data are not directly comparable, this test cannot be fully carried out. The TALENT data, however, allow us to determine who are the respondents for whom migration took place from one large geographical area of the United States to another. This in itself is of interest because on the basis of the foregoing reasoning we would expect that in this subsample the vulnerable-age effect should be present in a somewhat stronger form. This derivation, however, applies only to the segment of the curve where a developmental interference is suspected to have occurred. Indeed, in the case of the effect of school selection, no such accentuation of the dips can be predicted. This follows from the consideration that developmental patterns are relatively invariant, much more so in any case than school structures. Hence, the size of an interference effect on a developmental pattern may be expected to be primarily a function of the magnitude of the interference, a magnitude that in the present case is estimated by the size of the geocultural move. Large geographical subdivisions, however, do not bear any predictable relationship to the selectivity structure and policies of school systems, inasmuch as these vary no less within than across regions. Furthermore, some migrations are likely to be undertaken by parents with precisely the aim of overcoming the difficulties that high school students experience at certain selective junctions of their secondary school career. The nonspecificity of high school selectivity by region and the reactive nature of some migrations to this obstacle, along with the probable developmental nature of the problem for the 6- to 11-year-old migrants, suggest that concentrating on interregional moves should help clarify the existence of a vulnerable age in mid-childhood and, at the same time, differentiate further between the developmental and selective explanations that may apply at different points of the age curve.

This test, which will now be presented, was carried out according to a classification reported in detail in Inbar (1976, p. 33). For the purpose at hand, suffice it to note that the United States was divided

Table 9-12. Average Levels of Education Achieved by Inter-Regional Migrants by Cohort and Age Upon Migration in Childhood.

A. Key to age categories upon migration (see Table 8)

COHORT	1	2	3	4	5	MEAN	STANDARD DEVIATION
10th graders	15–15.5	13–14	11–12	6–10	1–5		
11th graders	16–16.5	14–15	12–13	7–11	1–6		
12th graders	17–17.5	15–16	13–14	8–12	1–7		

B. Data

COHORT	1	2	3	4	5	MEAN	STANDARD DEVIATION
10th graders	6.66	6.83	6.52	6.45	6.96	6.71	0.21
(N)	(37)	(48)	(59)	(80)	(114)	(338)	
11th graders	6.49	6.87	6.97	6.90	7.04	6.91	0.15
(N)	(33)	(49)	(50)	(94)	(109)	(335)	
12th graders	7.07	7.12	7.11	6.82	7.33	7.12	0.20
(N)	(15)	(42)	(48)	(84)	(124)	(313)	

Source: Inbar (1976, Table 13).

Table 9-13. Visual Partition of Table 12: Elementary School Age Range.

A. Key to age categories upon migration, and predicted dips (underlined)

COHORT	2	3	4	5	MEAN (UNTRUNCATED DISTRIBUTION – SEE TABLE 13)	STANDARD DEVIATION
10th graders	13–14	11–12	6–10	1–5		
11th graders		12–13	7–11	1–6		
12th graders		13–14	8–12	1–7		

B. Data and matching dips (underlined)

10th graders	6.83	6.52	6.45	6.96	6.71	0.21
11th graders		6.97	6.90	7.04	6.91	0.15
12th graders		7.11	6.82	7.33	7.12	0.20

C. Comparative size of the effect relative to adjacent category

10th graders (whole sample)a	+0.13	–	–	+0.21
10th graders (present sample)	+0.31	–	–	+0.51
11th graders (whole sample)a		+0.04	–	+0.10
11th graders (present sample)		+0.07	–	+0.14
12th graders (whole sample)a		+0.03	–	+0.13
12th graders (present sample)		+0.29	–	+0.51

a. See Table 10.
Source: Inbar (1976, Table 14).

into six regions. Focusing then on the subsample of respondents who migrated from one of these regions to another, Table 9-12 presents the overall distributions that were obtained in their cases. For visual convenience, these data are again split up according to the age range that is relevant to the test of the vulnerable-age phenomenon (Table 9-13) and to that of the selectivity of secondary education (Table 9-14). Each of these two tables also presents the magnitude of the migration effect (relative to the adjacent age categories) for the whole sample (from Tables 9-10 and 9-11) and in the present case.

Considering first the vulnerable age in childhood, Table 9-13B shows that the predicted effect recurs among the interregional migrants. The critical test, however, lies in the magnitude of the effect. Table 9-13C shows that without exception the effect is magnified for

Table 9-14. Visual Partition of Table 9-12: High School Age Range.

A. Key to age categories upon migration, and predicted dips (underlined)

COHORT	1	2	3	MEAN (UNTRUNCATED DISTRIBUTION – SEE TABLE 13)	STANDARD DEVIATION
10th graders	15–15.5	13–14			
11th graders	16–16.5	14–15	12–13		
12th graders	17–17.5	15–16	13–14		

B. Data and matching dips (underlined)

	1	2	3	MEAN	SD
10th graders	6.66	6.83		6.71	0.21
11th graders	6.49	6.87	6.97	6.91	0.15
12th graders	7.07	7.12	7.11	7.12	0.20

C. Comparative size of the effect relative to adjacent category

	1	2	3
10th graders (whole sample)a	–	+0.24	
10th graders (present sample)	–	+0.17	
11th graders (whole sample)a	–	–	(+0.26, +0.11) b
11th graders (present sample)	–	–	(+0.48, +0.10) b
12th graders (whole sample)a	+0.08	–	+0.08
12th graders (present sample)	–0.05	–	–0.01

a. See Table 11.
b. Category 3 relative to categories 1 and 2, respectively.
Source: Inbar (1976, Table 15).

all three cohorts. Thus, in the case of interregional moves, the 12th graders who migrated at ages 1–7 and 13–14 achieved a level of schooling that was respectively 0.51 and 0.29 points higher than that of children who migrated during the vulnerable-age period (see Table 9-13C); in the case of the whole sample, these differences are only 0.13 and 0.03 points, respectively. The same pattern obtains for 11th and 10th graders. In particular, in the latter case the children who made an interregional move at ages 1–5 achieved a level of schooling that is 0.51 points above that of the 6- to 10-year-old migrants, and the children who moved at ages 13–14 achieved a level that is 0.31 points above that of the 11- to 12-year-old migrants; the comparable differences in the case of the whole sample are only 0.21 and 0.13 points, respectively.

In short, and to the extent that interregional moves subsume greater disruptions in the children's homes and environments than lesser moves, the finding would seem to lend strong additional support to the existence of a vulnerable age in mid-childhood.

Turning now to the selection effect of schools, Table 9-14 shows that in this case no consistent trend emerges. In the first place the selection pattern itself is inconsistent. In particular, in the case of the 12th graders the empirical dip does not occur in the predicted category (see Table 9-14A and 9-14B). As will be noted shortly, this is due to an interaction effect. More importantly, where the effect does recur (in the cohorts of 10th and 11th graders), its relationship to magnitude of migration is erratic. Thus, in the whole sample of 10th graders, those respondents who moved at age 13–14 achieved a level of schooling that is 0.24 points higher than that of the 15- to 15.5-year-old migrants. In the case of interregional migrations, no accentuation of the effect is noticeable; on the contrary, it is now only 0.17 (see Table 9-14C). In the case of the 11th graders (for the whole sample), the 12- to 13-year-old migrants achieved a level of school education that is 0.26 points highers than that of the 16- to 16.5-year-old movers, and 0.11 higher than that of the 14- to 15-year-old migrants (see Table 9-14C); for interregional movers, the comparable differences are 0.48 and 0.10, respectively. In one case we find an accentuated effect, in the other, not.

In short, no demonstrable relation exists between size of geographical mobility and variations in the effect of the selectivity of schools. If anything, the data would suggest a mild inverse relationship. Such a trend would be consistent with a reactive interpretation of the cause of migrations in the case of some parents of high school students. It would also, and especially, be consistent with what would be expected if most parents were aware of the selection problem. On psychological grounds the salience of this problem is not unlikely to be a function of the geographical size of the move contemplated, and the magnitude of migrations may well therefore be related to the efforts that are made to overcome the anticipated difficulties.

Be this as it may, the vulnerable-age effect and the effect of school structures bear a predictable relationship to migrations. These effects are analytically different and appear to be empirically distinguishable. This is clearly an important result that should help avoid confusions in the future.

Table 9-15. Average Levels of Education Achieved by the Cohort of 10th Graders (Interregional Movers) by Parental SES, and by Age Upon Migration in Childhood.

A. Key to age categories, with vulnerable-age predictions (underlined twice), and school selection predictions (underlined once)

	1	2	3	4	5	MEAN	STANDARD DEVIATION
	15–15.5	13–14	11–12	6–10	1–5		

B. Data and matching dips (underlined)

SES Level

	1	2	3	4	5	MEAN	STANDARD DEVIATION
low	5.05	5.95	5.31	5.21	5.42	5.40	0.29
(N)	(14)	(17)	(12)	(23)	(27)	(93)	
medium	6.59	6.82	6.40	5.89	6.82	6.47	0.39
(N)	(5)	(13)	(20)	(27)	(35)	(100)	
high	7.50	7.58	6.97	7.56	7.92	7,57	0.34
(N)	(20)	(20)	(30)	(32)	(55)	(157)	

Source: Inbar (1976, Table 16).

As in the case of the Canadian study, no systematic pattern of effect by SES emerged in the present data. However, Table 9-15, which presents the SES distributions for the cohort of 10th graders (interregional movers), documents a shift that is of interest. This shift occurs in the vulnerable-age range for high SES respondents, between categories 4 and 3 (see Table 9-15); the shift seems also to be characteristic of boys, as we will shortly see.

Because of the constraints of the data, the trend can only be documented in the case of the 10th graders and is therefore difficult to interpret. It could be indicative of maturation differences among levels of SES (or sexes), or of earlier entrance into junior high school. It could also indicate, however, that the vulnerable-age phenomenon is concentrated in the upper part of the 6- to 11-year age range, and that the reversal in the rank order of the two categories that span the vulnerable-age period is a function of fluctuations in dates of birth (and perhaps also of maturation) within, say, the age range 8 to 11. Which of these or other interpretations is the correct one is a question that must await further research.

Another interesting result consists of the partial replication of the finding documented in the Canadian study about sex differences. As it turns out, in the TALENT data too the results of interregional

Table 9-16. Average Levels of Education Achieved by Male Interregional
Migrants, by Cohort and Age Upon Migration in Childhood.

A. Key to age categories, with vulnerable-age predictions (underlined twice), and school
selection predictions (underlined once)

COHORT	1	2	3	4	5	MEAN	STANDARD DEVIATION
10th graders	15–15.5	13–14	11–12	6–10	1–5		
11th graders	16–16.5	14–15	12–13	7–11	1–6		
12th graders	17–17.5	15–16	13–14	8–12	1–7		

B. Data and matching dips (underlined)

	1	2	3	4	5	MEAN	STANDARD DEVIATION
10th graders	6.53	7.25	6.63	7.12	7.77	7.21	0.47
(N)	(19)	(27)	(30)	(41)	(60)	(177)	
11th graders	6.77	7.59	7.35	7.02	7.41	7.25	0.24
(N)	(14)	(19)	(25)	(50)	(59)	(167)	
12th graders	7.31	6.85	7.51	7.42	6.68	7.47	0.25
(N)	(6)	(18)	(27)	(41)	(66)	(158)	

Source: Inbar (1976, Table 17).

migrations — upon which much of my argument is based — hold
consistently for boys, with only one exception. This occurs among
the 11th graders and concerns the effect of school selection; specifically, the expected dip occurs only among the 16- to 16.5-year-olds,
rather than both among them and the 14- to 15-year-olds. The
relevant data are presented in Table 9-16.

For girls, the picture is more complex. The vulnerable-age effect
in mid-childhood is present among 12th graders. It is also present
among 10th graders; in this case, however, it is limited to the 6- to
10-year age group. Among 11th graders, finally, it is absent. With
regard to school selection, the effect is only present in the case of
the 11th graders. The relevant data are presented in Table 9-17.

Two conclusions appear to be warranted by the analysis by sex.
The first is that, as the Canadian study has suggested, there are important sex differences for the phenomenon under consideration.
The second is that these differences are less pronounced for the
vulnerable-age phenomenon in mid-childhood than is the case for
the effect of school structures. I shall return to the question of sex
differences, in particular for the vulnerable-age phenomenon, in the
following section.

The last finding of interest is that in all three cohorts the average
level of schooling achieved by nonmovers is consistently lower than

Table 9-17. Average Levels of Education Achieved by Female Interregional
Migrants, by Cohort and Age Upon Migration in Childhood.

A. Key to age categories, with vulnerable-age predictions (underlined twice), and school
selection predictions (underlined once)

COHORT	1	2	3	4	5	MEAN	STANDARD DEVIATION
10th graders	15–15.5	13–14	11–12	6–10	1–5		
11th graders	16–16.5	14–15	12–13	7–11	1–6		
12th graders	17–17.5	15–16	13–14	8–12	1–7		

B. Data and matching dips (underlined)

	1	2	3	4	5	MEAN	STANDARD DEVIATION
10th graders	6.79	6.30	6.41	5.75	6.07	6.16	0.32
(N)	(18)	(21)	(29)	(39)	(54)	(161)	
11th graders	6.28	6.41	6.59	6.77	6.60	6.57	0.16
(N)	(19)	(30)	(25)	(44)	(50)	(168)	
12th graders	6.91	7.32	6.59	6.25	6.94	6.76	0.37
(N)	(9)	(24)	(21)	(43)	(58)	(155)	

Source: Inbar (1976, Table 18).

that of the migrants. This trend can be observed in Table 9-9, by
comparing the average of the respondents who never moved (category 6) with the average of the movers, which appears two columns
to the left of category 6. In part, of course, this difference reflects
an SES effect. Controlling for levels of SES, however, does not
completely reduce the differences (data not presented); in any case,
never does the average of nonmovers rise above that of the migrants.
This finding may be due to an insufficient control of the respondents' socioeconomic background. It could also reflect the frequently documented fact that adult migrants are a better motivated group
than nonmigrants (see, for example, Spilerman and Habib, 1976, pp.
804–805). Even within SES levels one could expect that their
children should also be better motivated, even scholastically (see
next section for a qualification). The finding, however, could also
have a very different kind of explanation. It could stem from the
fact that moving has an *enrichment* effect at certain points of the
age curve. In fact, some experts believe that the most important
learning experience during puberty — roughly around the ages of 12
to 13 — consists of being exposed to cultural and social stimuli
(Maeroff, 1975). Migrations obviously mediate such experiences,
and the shape of the age curves that we have examined could therefore reflect this process, as well as those that we have discussed. I

shall not presently elaborate on this possibility, although it is obviously useful to keep it in mind.

THEORETICAL INTERPRETATIONS

It is probably fair to say that one conclusion that emerges from the evidence that we have reviewed is that a vulnerable-age effect in midchildhood is clearly and recurrently observable for boys; for girls, too, the effect is noticeable, although not invariably so. A school selection effect is distinguishable as well; however, its impact on migrants is somewhat less predictable for boys, and even less so for girls, than is the vulnerable-age phenomenon proper.

These, then, are the major trends that require a theoretical explanation. In this section I will attempt to provide a few plausible explanations of this kind. I wish to stress, however, that I will engage in this task with the utmost caution. My motive is to avoid repeating some of the mistakes made in the context of another serendipitous finding — the firstborn effect. As is well known, the effect, although of great importance in itself, does not hold for only children, and hence much of the early theoretical explanations are groundless. The lesson is, of course, that the first task with a serendipitous finding is to specify its exact nature. In our case this means that the first order of priority is to determine the exact shape of the age curve that has to be explained. Before this is done, theoretical explanations can only be speculations. The point of this remark is that we are at the earliest stage of the documentation of a finding. We are therefore moving on uncharted territory. The cues presently available are not only few in number but also noisy, due to both the limited number of replications performed and the imperfections of the age categories that were available for the analyses. Accordingly, what is presently needed above all are replications.

The task of reliably specifying the age curve that will ultimately have to be explained (perhaps a different one for different societies), is likely, however, to take years of concerted effort. Some theoretical guidelines, no matter how tentative, are therefore necessary along the way. The following ideas are offered to fulfill this function. They are of a general nature by design.

Theoretically, then, the explanations that might account for the vulnerable-age phenomenon fall into two categories: one is based on developmental factors, the other on environmental ones. I shall illustrate in turn the form that these explanations could take.

One developmental process whose disruption might conceivably account for the vulnerable-age effect in mid-childhood could be the cognitive process. Specifically, recent research suggests that language and cognitive development may interact in an as yet unspecified but important way between the ages of 6 and 11. As opposed to the long-held belief that fundamental syntax and grammar are acquired by age 5, the latest studies show that a considerable amount of improvement occurs between ages 5 and at least 9 (Frasure and Entwisle, 1973; Entwisle and Frasure, 1974). It should be noted that the age of 9 does not constitute a ceiling; it simply represents the age limit that has presently been investigated. In future research the true limit may have to be extended to the age of 10, or perhaps even 11. To an extent that remains to be determined, the vulnerability of children in mid-childhood to significant crises and changes in their social or school environments may therefore reflect an interference with language development that might be quite general.

Another developmental explanation could be social in nature. It was advanced more than two decades ago by Harry Stack Sullivan. Sullivan (1953) suggests that one stage of development, the juvenile era, is critical. As he puts it, "the importance of the juvenile era can scarcely be exaggerated, since it is the actual time for becoming social" (Sullivan, 1953, p. 227). As noted in the first section, this era lasts from about the age of entry into school to around the age of 10; it is bounded by the chum period with which it overlaps from around ages 8.5 to 10. The juvenile era is a prerequisite for establishing fundamental patterns of social adjustment. Sullivan has spelled out how the disruption of this era usually comes about:

"One of the things which time and again has shown itself to have been quite disastrous in the history of patients, was the social mobility of the parents, which took the juvenile from one school to another at frequent intervals . . . . Other things being equal, if one is getting on at all fortunately in juvenile society, it is a very good thing to stay in that group of juveniles throughout the period, or certainly until near the end of the juvenile era . . . continuous upheavals in schooling − and this is strikingly true with service personnel − is apt to leave a very considerable handicap in this and subsequent development." (Sullivan, 1953, pp. 241−242).

In other words, as far as the number of environmental disruptions and school transfers are concerned, there is both evidence and a theory for the existence of a vulnerable age at almost precisely the points of the age curve with which we are concerned. It is entirely conceivable, of course, that a single but very drastic change of social and/or school environment should have all or part of the effects that milder repetitive changes or transfers have. Furthermore, it is noteworthy that for the age range 8.5 to 10, Sullivan explicitly states that on the basis of his data his generalizations hold *for males only* (Sullivan, 1953, p. 248; also p. 249). Because Sullivan does not elaborate, neither can I. Nonetheless, the relevance of Sullivan's remark for the finding under discussion is evident.

Still another developmental explanation could be related to the disruption of the transition to autonomy — the acceptance of co-operation and social control through socially agreed-upon rules — which has been identified by Piaget as occurring between the ages of 7 and 11 (Piaget, 1965). Because in this section my aim is notional, I shall not attempt to go into the details of this explanation. It is, how-ever, of interest to note that for this process there would again appear to be important sex differences; for girls the transition is more rapid and seems to be over by age 8, almost at the onset of the stage of cooperation (Piaget, 1965, p. 80). Of course, for the purpose at hand it might very well turn out that Sullivan's and Piaget's interpretations are the two sides of the same coin. Indeed, from the standpoint of the vulnerable-age phenomenon, Sullivan would appear to have stressed the independent variable and Piaget the dependent one. In substance, however, and granting small variations, it is intriguing to note how much their observations agree in form and content, down to specific sex differences that in the light of the empirical findings that we have discussed, are obviously of great interest.

Turning now to environmental factors, Table 9-18 illustrates the type of effect that one might anticipate this class of variables to have. This table presents the survival and transition rates in high school, year after year, of two selected cohorts. The data are from Germany and are taken from the sequence of fifteen cohorts pre-sented by Boudon (1974, p. 57, Table 3.11). The cohorts are the first and last for which there is complete information from the seventh grade to graduation.

Table 9-18. Survival and Transition in Secondary School, for Two
Selected Cohorts, Germany.

	1952		1959	
	SURVIVAL RATES	TRANSITION RATES	SURVIVAL RATES	TRANSITION RATES
NUMBER OF STUDENTS	14,077		10,170	
"Quarta" 7th grade	100		100	
		89.1		90.7
8th grade	89.1		90.7	
		87.7		91.2
9th grade	78.1		82.7	
		93.3		94.1
10th grade	72.9		77.8	
		62.7		86.1
11th grade	45.7		67.0	
		93.4		92.5
12th grade	42.7		62.0	
		94.4		93.7
"Oberprima" 13th grade	40.3		58.1	
		95.5		95.9
High school degree	38.5		55.7	

Source: After Boudon (1974, p. 57, Table 3.11).

A feature of this table is that for the 1952 cohort there is a clear drop in transition rates between the 10th and 11th grades. In the 1959 cohort, on the other hand, the drop is almost unnoticeable. The reason for this difference is that "a traditional turning point, the *mittlere Reife* (literally, middle maturation), underwent drastic change over the period . . . . (Up to about) 1955, the *mittlere Reife* was perceived by many students as a terminal point, but some years later it had become just an intermediate step" (Boudon, 1974, p.56).

The sociological explanation of this phenomenon is that from the standpoint of the students and their families, each year is a decision point where success in school (marks) and socioeconomic costs and opportunities are taken into account to decide whether or not to remain in school. Transitions from one formally or normatively defined level (or sublevel) of schooling to another are also decision points of this kind, only more so. This fact is well documented for nonmovers in all educational systems, as Table 9-18 illustrates. It stands to reason, therefore, that the effect should also be found among migrants and immigrants, although in this case, it is reasonable to anticipate that it should be magnified.

In other words, the theoretical expectation is that all age curves, including, of course, those of migrant or immigrant adolescents, should exhibit one or more vulnerable ages of transition, the specific ages being a function of the formal and normative structures of the school systems under consideration.

It should be noted that, given the structure of the selective process in school systems, we would expect the school structure effect to apply only to teenagers.*

Additionally, this structural effect may conceivably be accentuated by a developmental interference; however, I have not yet found in the literature a clear-cut set of consequences that one could expect from school disruptions occurring within a specific age range during adolescence. This question obviously deserves further theoretical attention.

In any case, we have seen that there is some evidence of a structural effect of schools in the TALENT data. This segment of the curve, however, was not of primary interest in the studies that I have carried out and was consequently the least analyzed. Nonetheless, the results clearly point to one additional reason that is likely to account for the fact that the vulnerable age in mid-childhood is easy to overlook. Indeed, depending on the number and intensity of the selection points and on random fluctuations in the data, the segment of the curve pertaining to high school years clearly can at times overshadow the vulnerable-age effect and even impart to the whole curve a shape that makes unavoidable the conclusion that schooling and age upon immigration are inversely related. In this sense, the Israeli and Canadian data may have been fortunate occurrences.

THE PRESENT STATE OF THE FINDING

Since the publication of the findings and discussions reviewed above, few advances have taken place in the study and understanding of the

---

*However, I should like to mention a variant of a structural explanation that might have some bearing on the vulnerable-age phenomenon in school. In certain schools what has been learned in a given grade is reviewed in the next grade at the beginning of the school year; in certain schools it is not, or there is one or more breach of continuity – one often noted occurring in the 3rd grade. It could be that in such school systems being transferred at this juncture constitutes a handicap of some consequence. For another variant of an explanation that is environmental in nature, see in the second section the original interpretation advanced by Adler and myself.

vulnerable-age effect.   Indeed, the developments of which I am aware are very few in number and include a set of studies that were carried out before the effect was reported, but that were brought to my attention later.*

The first of these investigations is some twenty years old. It was reported by Gordon & Gordon (1958) in a paper entitled "Emotional Disorders of Children in a Rapidly Growing Suburb." Table 1 of this study shows a definite relationship between the boy/girl ratio in psychiatric referrals and community mobility in five New Jersey and New York counties. Boys consistently outnumber girls, although census figures show total numbers of boys and girls to be about equal in all counties. In most areas there was a relatively greater number of boy patients at younger than older ages (the age ranges of the two groups studied were 4–11 and 12–17).

Additionally, counties that had the highest migration rate also had the greatest boy/girl ratio, especially in the 4–11 age group, which was greater than in the 12–17 age group. Moreover, in further findings, it was shown that response to brief psychotherapy had a differential effect between migrants who were ages 4–11 versus those who were 12 and over at the time of therapy. Of all the children and teenagers who did well in brief therapy, 64% of those were under-12-year-old migrants. This was in contrast to the 24% of the older age group (12–17) who were migrants, and who did well in brief therapy.

Clearly, these trends are very consistent with the existence of a vulnerable-age effect.

Another set of researches was conducted in Sweden. These studies are important because of the light that they cast on some of the subprocesses included in what Sullivan has called the process of becoming social. The results of this program of research are reported in summary form in Schaller (1975). I can do no better than to quote directly from this report:

"The studies summarized in this paper were carried out with a project called 'Geographic mobility and its relation to different aspects of school adjustment.' ... The present paper summarizes work on the cross-sectional part of the project, reported in full in six articles, four of them based on empirical studies.

---

*I am most grateful in this respect to Bernard Finifter and Thomas L. Woods, who called my attention to the relevance of these studies.

"The attitudes towards newcomers of 458 pupils in 22 classes were studied one week before a new pupil was expected . . . . The findings of the study may be summarized in the following way:

"Twenty-nine percent of the answers were classified as positive, 17% as neutral, and 54% as negative. Newcomers who were girls elicited somewhat more positive and fewer negative responses than newcomers who were boys.

"Boys were more negative than girls to newcomers of their own sex. Boys responded more negatively to newcomers, irrespective of sex, than girls did.

"It is quite clear from these results that pupils, especially boys, in grades four and five are to a great extent negative to newcomers, when their attitudes are measured by the techniques used in this study.

"Children's reactions to moves were studied in two samples comprising 335 and 514 pupils . . . .

"Most worries about a hypothetical move concerned making new friends after the move, least were about the new teacher . . . .

"From these results it is quite clear that the worries pupils have and the adjustment problems they expect before a move mostly concern social relations — to give up the old relations and to establish new ones. The nature of mobility is primarily social.

"Geographic mobility and children's perception of their school situation were studied in a group comprising 440 children in grades five and six . . . .

"Mobility was significantly related to the factor 'Peer adjustment.' Pupils who had moved once or never reported better peer relations than pupils who had moved twice or more.

"The results of the four empirical studies suggest that children who move should be given special consideration." (Schaller, 1975, pp. 185–187).

The compatibility and at times the similarity of some of these findings and conclusions with those discussed in the previous sections is quite obvious. While it could be argued that Schaller's findings do not have the representativeness of those based on the analyses of the two large-scale data banks that we have discussed, their specific contribution is nonetheless very great. Indeed, conceptually speaking, Schaller's studies and those reported in this chapter come very close to constituting independent replications and extensions of each other.

As a result, the Swedish program of investigations can legitimately be regarded as adding validity to, as well as insights into, the processes that may account for the findings that we have examined. In this connection, it is especially interesting to note that these studies do not only replicate the sex differences that we have recurrently noted, but they also provide the first researchable clue about this puzzling effect. Specifically, Schaller's investigations strongly suggest that the sex differences stem, in part at least, from different norms and peer relations within as well as across the sex groups of preadolescent children.

Schaller also reports certain interactions and trends that may be idiosyncratic to his sample, or which may require, if replicated in the future, that certain conclusions I have advanced be qualified or rephrased. In addition, he documents (Schaller, 1976) that when they were investigated (in grade 9), the movers in one of his main studies had a lower grade-point average than the nonmovers. The point, however, is that the former group already had a lower grade-point average in grade 3, before any move took place. Clearly, therefore, in highly developed countries (even if unusually homogeneous and stable), relatively large-scale processes of geographical mobility can also be either a low SES phenomenon, or perhaps, in part, a reaction to school difficulties, on a scale as yet unsuspected.

Whichever of these explanations, or a different one, is found in the end to account for some specific trends and interactions reported by Schaller, the substantive importance of these studies for the understanding of the vulnerable-age phenomenon does not need to be elaborated.

The next development to be considered is a study by Schrader (1978). This study is concerned with children of immigrants from south and southeast Europe to the Federal Republic of Germany. As in the case of the Swedish program of research, the present investigation was carried out independently of the findings pertaining to the vulnerable-age effect that we have discussed. In contrast to the Swedish studies, however, Schrader has reported his findings by reference to the vulnerable-age effect. Because of the limitations of his data, Schrader could not examine the whole age-range of interest, but had to concentrate on the lower age limit of the phenomenon.

Schrader's overall conclusion is that his findings are compatible with those presented in the original report of the vulnerable-age effect. Specifically:

"In the context of successful or unsuccessful adaptation, it can be said that the crucial age for foreign children in Germany begins at age six. Our data and analysis do not permit, however, establishing an upper limit of that age. With regard to the lower limit of what Inbar and Adler (1976, p. 197) call the Vulnerable Age, our findings are consistent with theirs.

"Inbar and Adler hypothesize that the vulnerable age of a child is the age between six and eleven years. This hypothesized time span is dually supported. First, Claessens' socialization theory may be used to identify the crucial age as the age at which the process of enculturation takes place. Second, as far as the beginning of this age is concerned, our results bear out that it coincided with the age mentioned by Inbar and Adler." (Schrader, 1978, pp. 228 and 229).

Schrader, however, questions the theoretical interpretations of the finding. He argues that the ability to mobilize outside resources and help, like peer tutoring, also depends on peer-group links forged prior to entering grade school and on assumptions about the degree to which the socialization process is otherwise intact. Consequently, he believes that a different theoretical framework is more appropriate. He suggests adopting the conceptualization advanced by Claessens (1967). According to Claessens' views, the developmental process is usefully broken down into three phases — the "socialization," "enculturation," and "secondary social fixation" stages — that span approximately the ages 1-5, 6-12, and 13+. In this light, Schrader believes that what Adler and myself have called the vulnerable-age phenomenon, is more adequately conceptualized as the disruption of the enculturation stage.

Another study similarly presents independent findings explicitly examined in the light of the vulnerable-age effect. The study is Crain and Mahard's review of the literature on the effect of integration in schools. To quote these authors:

"Although most of the conclusions drawn from our review of the desegregation research are debatable, on one aspect the results are clear and unmistakable: the earlier the grade at which desegregation occurs, the more positive the impact on achievement . . . .

"As a further test of the hypothesis, we related the impact of desegregation on achievement reported in the different studies to the grades that were tested. The results of this analysis support the conclusion that desegregation in the early grades is more successful in terms of achievement gains than is desegregation in later grades. Of twelve studies of desegregation undertaken at the junior high school, and high school level, five showed negative effects, while none of ten studies of desegregation undertaken in the first and second grades showed negative results . . . .

"The critical point, as indicated by the data . . . is at the second or third grade, since only 12 of the 24 studies of desegregation that occurred in grades three or four showed positive achievement results. These grades are at the center of an age range that Inbar has called the 'Vulnerable Age.' . . .

"It has been frequently urged that desegregation begin in the early grades. It is gratifying to see empirical evidence support the conventional wisdom so clearly — although if the Inbar finding is pertinent, even third grade may not be early enough." (Crain and Mahard, 1978, pp. 34–38).

The data to which Crain and Mahard refer are presented in their Table 4 and exhibit an overall negative trend, that is, the younger the child at the time of integration, the better the consequences of integration. At the same time, the fluctuations in the data are compatible with a vulnerable-age interpretation in the third to fourth grades or fifth to sixth grades, depending on the set of studies considered. I surmise that the authors base their conclusion regarding the third and fourth grades on their familiarity with the studies reviewed. This assumption appears reasonable, given that the authors explicitly mention at times that they give differential weights in their judgments to the studies reviewed, according to such considerations as quality of design and analysis, kind of effect observed, etc. Under this assumption, the secondary analysis of over sixty studies by Crain and Mahard and the conclusion that this study suggests to them takes on an obvious significance.

An additional development, although on a different scale, is a study that is presently being carried out by my colleague, Chaim Adler. Adler is investigating the dynamics of the life situation of young immigrants and migrants, which could explain the vulnerable-age effect. The research is an anthropological type of study from which Adler has been kind enough to communicate to me a case. This case provides an illustration of the concrete form that some of the mechanisms mediating the vulnerable-age effect may actually take in real life. The following is a vignette summarizing the field notes on the case:

222 III/ISRAEL AS A STRESS LABORATORY

"The Does are a family of four. The parents and their two children — two boys aged 15 and 9 — arrived in Israel eighteen months ago from Eastern Europe. They are living in X, a development town where immigrants are settled in newly built houses. X is located twenty miles away from the nearest established Israeli urban center.

"The family lives in a two-bedroom apartment. Its income is partly made up of wages, and partly of support that newcomers get under certain conditions (Peter, the father — a clerk in his country of origin — works occasionally at unskilled jobs. Mary, the mother, takes care of the home; she has never been gainfully employed in Israel).

"The family's home is rudimentarily furnished; it looks cold, almost empty. Several unpacked suitcases can still be seen lying around the living room. The impression one receives anew at each visit, is of tenants on the move.

"The Does have applied for a visa to immigrate to a number of western countries. This step summarizes their extreme maladaptation to the country. It is also reflected in the daily life of the family.

"Fred, the eldest child, is particularly vehement. He has problems with the language. Added to this, the program of studies is very different from what he was used to, especially in such subject matters as history, geography, and biblical studies. And to top it all, he cannot pursue the musical studies he started in school abroad, for there is no violin teacher in the school or for that matter in the whole development town. He attempts to keep up by travelling twenty miles, three times a week, to the urban center where he has worked out some arrangement to have lessons. He is under great stress and is extremely frustrated by the situation. Fred shares overtly his parents' wish to leave the country.

"Ronald, the youngest son, projects a completely different image. He likes his teacher and reports getting along well with his new school friends. He has no particular complaints and is quite happy. He appears, however, to like playing alone, for he has been observed engaged in lonely activities while he was supposed to be with his little friends." (By courtesy of Chaim Adler).

This sketch does not purport to demonstrate anything, of course. Based as it is on actual observations it does, however, illustrate how the generative process underlying the vulnerable-age effect might operate in part. Specifically, behind the complaints of the eldest son one can clearly discern serious attempts, not altogether unsuccessful, at coping with a difficult situation. By comparison, it is probably safe to hypothesize that the youngest child is happy more because of the level of aspirations that he has developed under the new circumstances than because of his integration into his environment. Other things being equal, one would probably not be surprised to find that ten or twenty years later, in a large sample of such pairs of children, a statistical trend should emerge showing the younger child to have been more adversely affected than his adolescent counterpart by the disruptions experienced by both, but at critically different stages of development and with different resources for coping effectively with the difficulties.

From a different perspective, there is a reanalysis of our original data that casts light on the adequacy of the simple analyses on which the inference of a vulnerable age was based. This reanalysis was carried out by Coleman, who, in an illustrative application of the technique that he presents (Coleman, 1981, chapter 2, Tables 2.7, 2.8), shows that submitting the data to a multivariate analysis yields results consistent with the vulnerable-age effect. It appears, therefore, that the vulnerable-age effect exhibits some robustness across methods of analysis, a fact whose implications are obvious.

Lastly, there is a study by Dohrenwend and de Figueiredo (1978). This study is of special interest for three reasons. The first is that it comes from psychiatry, a tradition of research that is completely independent of that underlying the studies just discussed. Secondly, it proposes an additional mechanism that could explain the vulnerable-age effect — the impairment of self-esteem at a critical period of development. Thirdly, it provides indirect evidence for the vulnerable age finding by means of a test of one of its possible implications.

The study is about the effect of remote events on the ability to cope with stress later in life. The respondents are a sample of New York City adults. The specific traumatic event that the investigators have focused on is the loss of parents in childhood. The review of the literature cited by the authors shows previous research to indicate that "it is the loss of one or both parents before age 11 rather than later in childhood that appears to be important" (Dohrenwend and de Figueiredo, 1978, p. 3). Accordingly, the investigators chose age 11 as a cutoff to distinguish earlier from later bereavement during childhood.

The results of the study can be summarized as follows: On the one hand, type of family structure during childhood and separation from parents for causes other than death were found not to be related to the measure of maladaptive response to stress used in the study. On the other hand, there was clear evidence to support the hypothesis that the loss of one or both parents before age 11 increases the vulnerability to stressful events later in life. Contrary to what is implicit in the literature, however, the researchers found that the outcome was as likely for deaths of fathers as of mothers. Such a result creates a problem of interpretation insofar as the usefulness of existing theories is limited to explaining either or both the effect of losing one's mother or the effect of parental loss through about age 5 (Dohrenwend and de Figueiredo, 1978, p. 18).

In an attempt to resolve this difficulty, the investigators decided to try to build on the vulnerable age finding that had just been brought to their attention. They reasoned that the financial loss and logistics of remarriage would be more likely to lead to disruption of schooling in the case of deaths of fathers than of mothers. But this explanation would be more likely to hold if the child were 6 or more years old at the time of the father's death than if the child were younger. This follows from the fact noted above that as a rule the mother is the most significant agent and potential loss for the child. In addition, before the child has reached school age, the socioeconomic changes likely to follow the father's death cannot (by definition) readily translate into the kind of disruptions in the child's life, and especially in the school environment, that the vulnerable-age effect subsumes in part.

To test the validity of this explanation, Dohrenwend and de Figueiredo divided the respondents who had suffered a bereavement in childhood into two subsamples: those who showed evidence of a maladaptive response to later stress and those who did not. The results were striking: fully 86% in the former subsample had lost their mothers before age 6 and/or their father between ages 6 through 10, as opposed to only 38% in the latter case. On the strength of their findings the authors conclude:

"Overall, our results provide a possible explanation of why some researchers like Brown, Harris and Copeland (1977) have found loss of mother before age 11 to be important while others have found loss of fathers to be important as well (e.g., Birtchnell, 1972).

Specifically, our findings point to loss of mother before age 6 and/or loss of father between ages 6 through 10 . . . .

"We would like to close by venturing our tentative conclusion. Where maladaptive responses by adults to contemporary stressful events involving loss take the form of marked subjective distress, there are at least two sets of childhood deprivations that may be involved as predisposing factors. One is loss of mother by death during the first five years of formal schooling. In the first, loss of maternal love and nurturance during childhood induces the vulnerability to later loss. In the second, disruption of the early process of formal education is the culprit. It is quite possible that each provides a different way to render an individual's self-esteem unusually vulnerable to losses later in life. (Dohrenwend and de Figueiredo, 1978, p. 19).

This application of the vulnerable-age effect and the surprising finding it led to completes the review of the studies I am presently aware of that either directly bear on, explicitly refer to, or build on, the vulnerable-age effect.

As noted above, these studies are few in number and, additionally, of limited scope. They certainly do not amount to the replications that are still needed to firmly establish the vulnerable-age effect and clarify its generative process. However, it is probably fair to say that these developments, limited as they are, add weight to the call for replications with which Adler and myself ended the original reports that we authored.

In an age when geographical mobility keeps growing, and given the increased evidence that is now available, this call appears even more justified today than it was five years ago.

POSTSCRIPT

After this chapter went to press, I received a copy of Professor Frank Jones' report on his unsuccessful attempt to replicate the vulnerable-age finding in Canada (F. E. Jones, "Age at Immigration and Educational Attainment." *The Canadian Review of Sociology and Anthropology.* Forthcoming, 1981). The census data that he describes appear to be superior to those I used (in the sense of being more representative of the Canadian population of immigrants). His conclusion is that while both the relationship between age upon immigration and education achievement is indeed nonmonotonic, the shape of the curve that obtains does not support the vulnerable-age explanation. It is noteworthy, however, that this conclusion is based on an analysis that does not control for cohort effects. When such controls are introduced in the analysis, Jones notes that some limited evidence for girls does emerge in support of the vulnerable-age effect.

In the light of Jones' study and findings, the need for more research, just noted, hardly requires additional emphasis.

REFERENCES

American Institutes for Research, *The Project TALENT Data Bank: A Handbook*, Palo Alto, California, April, 1972.

American Movers Conference, *Moving and children*. Undated leaflet, A.M.C., Suite 806, 1117 North 19th Street, Arlington, Virginia.

Bar-Yosef, R. Desocialization and resocialization: The adjustment process of immigrants. *International Migration Review, 12* (Summer, 1968), 27–45.

Bhatnagar, J. *Immigrants at School.* London: Cornmarket Press, 1970.

Birtchnell, J. Early parent death and psychiatric diagnosis. *Social Psychiatry,* Vol 7, 1972, 202–210.

Boudon, R. *Education Opportunity and Social Inequality: Changing Prospects in Western Society.* New York: John Wiley & Sons, 1974.

Brown, G. W., Harris, T., and Copeland, J. R. Depression and loss. *British Journal of Psychiatry, 130,* 1977, 1–18.

Census of Canada, *Public use sample tapes. User documentation (Draft).* Statistics Canada (March, 1975).

Claessens, D. *Familie und Wertsystem. Eine Studie zur "zweiten, soziokulturellen Geburt" der Menschen und der "Kernfamilie".* Berlin: Duncker und Humbolt, 3rd revised edition, 1967.

Coleman, J. S. *Qualitative Data Analysis: Cross Sectional and Longitudinal.* New York: Basic Books, 1981.

Crain, R. L., and Mahard, R. Desegregation and black achievement: A review of the research. *Law and contemporary problems,* Vol. 42, No. 3, 1978, 17–56.

Curle, A. Transitional communities and social reconnection. *Human Relations, 1,* No. 1 (1947), 42–68.

Dillingham, W. P. *The children of immigrants in school,* Vol. 1. Reports of the Immigration Commission, Sixty-first Congress (3rd Session), December 5, 1910–March 4, 1911. Senate Documents, Vol. 13. Washington, D.C.: Government Printing Office, 1911.

Dohrenwend, B. P., and de Figueiredo, J. M. Remote and recent life events and psychopathology. Paper presented at the meeting of the Society for Life History Research in Psychopathology, University of Cincinnati, Cincinnati, Ohio, April 7–8, 1978.

Eisenstadt, S. N. *The Absorption of Immigrants.* London: Routledge & Kegan Paul, Ltd., 1954, p. 6.

Elder, Jr., G. D. *Children of the Great Depression.* Chicago, Ill: The University of Chicago Press, 1974.

Entwisle, D. R., and Frasure, N. E. A contradiction resolved: Children's processing of syntactic clues. *Developmental Psychology, 10,* No. 6. (1974), 854–857.

Frasure, N. E., and Entwisle, D. R. Semantic and syntactic development in children. *Developmental Psychology, 9,* No. 2 (1973), 236–245.

Gordon, R. E., and Gordon, K. K. Emotional disorders of children in a rapidly growing suburb. *The International Journal of Social Psychiatry, 4,* No. 2, 1958, 85–97.

Inbar, M. *The Vulnerable Age Phenomenon.* N.Y.: Russell-Sage/Basic Books, 1976.

Inbar, M., and Adler, C. The vulnerable age phenomenon: A serendipitous finding. *Sociology of Education, 49,* No. 3 (July, 1976), 193–200.

Inbar, M. Immigration and learning: The vulnerable age. *The Canadian Review of Sociology and Anthropology, 14,* No. 2 (May, 1977), 218–234.

Inbar, M., and Adler, C. *Ethnic Integration in Israel: A Case Study of Moroccan Brothers Who Settled in France and Israel.* New Brunswick, N.J.:Transaction Books, 1977.

Klineberg, O. *Negro Intelligence and Selective Migration.* New York: Columbia University Press, 1935.

Lee, E. S. Negro intelligence and selective migration: A Philadelphia test of the Klineberg hypothesis. *In,* J. J. Spengler and O. D. Duncan (eds.), *Demographic analysis: Selected readings.* Glencoe, Ill.: The Free Press, 1956, 432–437.

Maeroff, G. I. Junior high is not easy to handle. *The New York Times Week in Review,* December 14, 1975.

Martan, M. *Comparative study of the communities of Yad Rambam in Israel, and Sarcelles in France.* Paper presented at the World Congress of North African Jew, Jerusalem, 1972.

Piaget, J. *The moral judgement of the child.* New York: The Free Press, 1965.

Schaller, J. Geographic mobility as a variable in ex post facto research. *British Journal of Psychology, 46,* 1976, 341–343.

Schaller, J. The relation between geographic mobility and school behavior. *Man-Environment Systems, 5,* 1975, 185–187.

Schrader, A. The "vulnerable" age: Findings on foreign children in Germany. *Sociology of Education, 51,* No. 3, July 1978, 227–230.

Spilerman, S., and Habib, J. Development towns in Israel: The role of communities in creating ethnic disparities in labor force characteristics. *American Journal of Sociology,* 81 (January, 1976), 781–812.

Sullivan, H. S. *The interpersonal theory of psychiatry.* New York: W. W. Norton & Co., 1953.

10.
Life Events: Stressful Ordeal or Valuable Experience?

Shlomo Breznitz and Yohanan Eshel
University of Haifa

The study of life events is based to a great extent on the assumption that stress is cumulative. A great number of stressful events can amount to a critical mass of stress, leading to physiological or psychological symptoms of illness (Rahe and Arthur, 1978).

Research on life events seems to indicate that a wide variety of ailments are indeed contingent on the amount and nature of life events preceding the negative change in physical or mental health. Death resulting from heart disease (Rahe and Lind, 1971), deterioration of chronic illness (Wyler, Masuda, and Holmes, 1971), pregnancy complications (Gorsuch and Key, 1974), or symptoms of depression (Vinokur and Selzer, 1975), were some of the criteria employed. All these and a substantial number of other variables have been found to be correlated with the quantity or the nature of previously experienced life events. Essentially the same trend was found in data obtained by means of personality inventories. Thus, Constantini, Braun, Davis, and Iervolino (1974) report positive correlations between life events and insomnia, headache proneness, hypochondriasis, and other somatic complaints.

While the assumption of growing vulnerability to stress due to the experiencing of many life events is related to the Selye idea of exhaustion, the particular emphasis on *recent* life changes introduces a major departure from that line of thinking. Whereas in Selye's formulation exhaustion is the ultimate expression of cumulative exposure to stressors during the entire life time of the organism, the focus on recency of life events assumes a gradual reduction in the impact of stressful events with time. The recent life changes tradition is likewise very different from the psychodynamic notions of early trauma and vulnerability in the first years of life. It is conceivable, however, that these departures from the mainstream theories of adjustment were seen by many scholars as the main advantages of this approach. Its strength is in its simplicity; however, there also lies its weakness.

The explanatory or predictive value of life events, in spite of their systematic vindication, is, however, rather small. Even when statistically significant, the actual size of the effects are usually small. This need not come as a great surprise considering the crudeness of this measure. There is an obvious need to go beyond the simple counting or weighting of life events and investigate the mediating mechanisms between life events and their consequences.

One mechanism of psychological importance, which was mentioned in the beginning of this research tradition, is the problem of *adjusting to change.* Events in one's life history, even if they are positive, introduce a new element into one's personal ecology and thus make it necessary to change certain behavioral patterns. It is this need to change, to leave well-tested ways of coping and look for new ones, that can be seen as one of the stressful aspects of any life event. The need to readjust thus becomes a limitation to adjustment. It is on the basis of this reasoning that both positive and negative life events are used in the same basic inventory. While they may obtain different weights in terms of their disruption of one's life, it is not the direction of the change but rather the change itself that is the critical factor.

Change, however, does not operate in a vacuum. Its detection and significance depend on the background to which it is introduced. Like a signal, if it is imposed in a situation of great noise, change can pass undetected. The potency and uniqueness of an event cannot be judged without taking the background into consideration. The same event, if taking place within the context of an uneventful life, will have a much greater impact than if occurring amidst many other different changes. If a person lives a very active and hectic life, it takes more for an event to be eventful. There is no need to assume that habituation is at work; suffice it to say that the definition of an event, particularly an event associated with a change in one's life, depends on the amount of contrast between it and its background. When stressful events are routine, they may still be stressful, but not because they are events.

THE ACUTE IN VIEW OF THE CHRONIC

The Israeli scene provides a rather unique opportunity for studying stressful life events and their impact on coping with subsequent stressful conditions. The long and varied list of woes to which Israelis are exposed has often been mentioned, and there is no need to repeat it here. It can be safely assumed that a higher baseline of pressures and stressors is characteristic of a large part of the Israeli population. It is not at all clear, however, how this should affect the impact of life events in general, and recent life events in particular. The voluminous research in this area does not touch on this problem at all. Clearly, this problem goes beyond the question of a specific population as such, and is central to any sophisticated evaluation of an individual's life history. Indeed, if the significance of an event depends on the number and kind of other events to which a person has been exposed, the simple equation based on assumptions of additivity, algebraic summation, and linearity would have to be abandoned rather soon. In the broader social context, there were many claims made that the weight assigned to life events by members of different cultures are very similar to each other. The study of life events was seriously enhanced by the claim that it is culture-free. Various studies have reported correlations, with regard to ratings of weight assigned to life events, ranging from 0.80 to 0.90 between members of entirely different societies, age-levels, etc. (e.g.: Masuda and Holmes, 1967; Miller, Bentz, Aponte, and Brogan, 1974; Rahe, 1969). While some differences between national groups have been reported (Rahe, Lundberg, Bennett and Theorell, 1971), they were often explained away as measurement errors.

The cross-cultural studies mentioned above tend to assume that no systematic response bias is expected to influence the findings when large enough samples are employed. This assumption may be quite unwarranted insofar as it disregards the possibility that populations vary in the total amount of stress to which they are exposed. Thus, for instance, in harsh climates disasters can become quite frequent and treated accordingly, whereas in milder climates even a slight change in the weather can be treated as an event. It is therefore a nontrivial question whether a population like that of Israel, which for a long period of time has been exposed to frequent intense stressors, would view the impact of various life events in the same way as, for instance, the American population. In this context two possibilities can be mentioned: On the one hand, one can argue that the frequent exposure to intense stress will produce some sort of habituation, and thus lead to an overall reduction in the weights ascribed to various events. On the other hand, it is quite possible that because of the exposure to stress, certain differences will be perceived as less important, resulting in decreased differentiation between the various items. Such reduced differentiation would be in line with theories both in the context of level of adaptation (Helson, 1964), as well as classical learning theories. The latter will assume that a high general level of tension will necessarily lead to a greater generalization gradient, thus producing much the same effect (e.g.: Jenkins, et al., 1958; Rosenbaum, 1953).

The above analysis relates to what one might expect to take place in the ratings of the various life events by Israelis. But what should one expect in the actual individual reports concerning life events? Is there anything that follows from the systematic exposure to frequent life events that one would predict about the individual responding to the biographical questions? We submit that if one lives in a situation that is characterized by frequent and often extreme stresses, the definition of what constitutes a stressful event will be changed and fewer events will pass the higher definitional threshold. Thus, one would predict that living in a country like Israel would make individuals more stringent in what constitutes a stressful event for them, and thus they will actually report fewer events than people living under less stressful conditions.

There is yet another argument that leads to nearly the same conclusion, namely, the effect of interference on memory. If someone is exposed to frequent events, all of which pass the definitional threshold, it is safe to assume that the more recent ones will inevitably interfere with the memory of those that preceded them. We thus hypothesize that Israelis report on fewer life events than they should. In other words, they do not necessarily report fewer events than other populations, but considering what they are experiencing, it should be possible to show a certain deficit in life events reporting.

The issue of interference is directly related to the issue of recency. While one can in principle argue the case of proactive inhibition, most of the effect due to interference should be retroactive. It is the constant influx of new events that covers up the memory and perhaps the impact of those that preceded them.

The life events research is quite unique in stressing the recency of the effects investigated. It is argued that if a large number of changes requiring extensive investment of energy for readjustment take place over a rather short period of time, their impact on the individual's health is bound to be more prominent. While the amount of data that supports this overload notion is quite impressive, there is no agreement on the definition of recency. Three weeks, six months, twelve months, and eighteen months are some of the proposed definitions (Cleary, 1974). Holmes and Masuda (1974) believe that a period of twenty-four months best defines the range of time in which the subject is "at risk" after the life-changing clustering.

Theoretical considerations should have determined the effect of time on the pathogenic impact of life changes. Such a model should have specified whether effects of life events are gradually diminished with time or whether they interact with new events in a more complex fashion. Unfortunately, there is no such model in the vast literature on stressful life events, and thus the role of time as a moderating variable in predicting illness remains to be totally vague. It might very well be that the focus on recent changes represents an empirical convenience rather than a theoretical point of view. At least two studies indicate that life change scores computed for a period of a few years give larger correlations with the criteria used than scores computed over one year only (Thurlow, 1971; Lloyd, Alexander, Rice and Greenfield, 1980). In the absence of a theory there is necessarily some ambiguity as to what is gained and what is lost by limiting the research to recent life changes and ignoring earlier events. This issue is particularly relevant in the context of this study, which investigates the impact of life events in a population that has many of them. The interference argument by necessity gives prominence and visibility to recent life changes, without at the same time questioning the possibility of long-term effects evident even if those events were not recalled or just not reported.

SELECTIVE FORGETTING

Living a highly eventful and stressful life was seen as possibly leading to a variety of consequences, such as reduced differentiation in the weight given to various events and reduction in the number of life events reported. It should be pointed out that these predictions were made on the basis of some rather simple psychological principles. We can now proceed one step further in the level of complexity of our analysis by introducing a dynamic consideration. For a person or a group of people living in a situation of continuous and frequently dramatic stress, it should be of some psychological value to filter these events and their potential impact. This filtering can take place on two levels: on the one hand, one cannot attend to certain information or actively deny it while it is first entering the system; and on the other hand, once there, it is possible to distort it in certain ways, to give it very specific meaning, or even to simply forget it. These various ways of defense can protect an individual from the overwhelming impact of his surroundings. There is no argument made here, however, that this protection is always a successful and worthwhile one. Quite the contrary, as psychodynamic theories often claim, it is by virtue of repression and selective forgetting that we cause ourselves additional trouble. The context of this limited study does not allow, however, the analysis of this fine and crucial point. Suffice it to say that a person may resort to selective forgetting more frequently if there are too many stressful events rather than when there are fewer. This intrusion of motivational factors into the assumed simplicity of the life events method is, of course, of great import.

Most of the existing psychological scales were designed to examine feelings, attitudes, comparisons with others, or evaluations, all of which are highly subjective. The life changes method attempts to overcome this shortcoming by tapping actual events in the history of the respondent. In principle, it is even possible to validate these reports and determine whether or not a brother was born, a relative deceased, or a change in residence has taken place. It is further assumed that since subjects have no reason, or perhaps no way to conceal or deny these life events, very little bias should be expected in the data collection procedure. Several investigators even went further and tried to identify reports of change with the actual events that presumably took place. It is suggested that "the consistency of recall may well be an indicator that the event or some facsimile did (or did not) occur in the life situation" (Casey, Masuda and Holmes, 1967, p. 246).

Careful reading of the available research leads one to believe that the subjective rather than the objective aspects of recalling prior life events are perhaps the important ones both for empirical predictions and for the theoretical understanding of the relationships between these changes and the ability to cope with subsequent stress. This has found expression in various methodological discussions in this area. Thus, it was suggested, that getting sick may increase sensitivity to previous stressful life events, perhaps because of a need to justify being ill. The consistent correlation between life changes scores and various forms of maladjustment may reflect, therefore, the salience of past events caused by an illness rather than being its cause (Brown, 1974; Dohrenwend, 1973; Hudgens, Robins and Delong, 1970; Johnson and Sarason, 1978). More direct evidence was presented by Thurlow (1971), who found that items more subjective in nature predict illness rates better than the more objective items.

It is of some interest to note that in reporting life events, over-reaction was a possible bias. Very little attention was devoted to the possibility that these reports may represent selection processes determined by repression or denial, leading to systematic forgetting. This omission is even more salient in light of the findings that indicate that deniers of change stand a better chance of surviving a heart attack (Hackett, and Cassem, 1975), and experience a lower level of physiological upheaval in a coronary care unit (Hackett, Cassem and Wishnie, 1968; Klein, Garity and Gelein, 1979).

The study of life events in Israel allows us to pursue this point a little further. We would thus predict that the intensive exposure to rapid and frequent stressors will push the Israelis toward a greater selectivity, filtering, and biased forgetting. In order to facilitate the testing of the selective forgetting assumption, certain specific changes have to be introduced into the list of life events themselves. Thus, those events that are phrased in terms of change only would provide more information if they were separated into positive changes and negative changes. We would then predict that Israelis will report positive changes more frequently than negative ones. Such a finding, if documented, could not indicate a true state of affairs, because it would imply that things are necessarily getting better all the time, which, unfortunately, is far from being the case.

There is a logical jump that must not be covered up. It is the jump from selective forgetting to selective reporting. The life events methodology is too crude and too simple, and indeed its whole utility is in its simplicity, to be able to go beyond the simple report aspect of the issue. We shall view selective reporting as an indicator of selective forgetting without at the same time being able to prove it.

LEARNING FROM STRESSFUL EXPERIENCE

We now come to the heart of the matter. During the last fifteen years, indeed from the very beginning of the life events methodology, the implication of frequent experiences was seen almost exclusively as negative. As a matter of fact, there has developed an equation between life events and stressful life events, as if the two were synonymous. This was seen as the major thrust of this research to the extent that there was no need at first even to distinguish between positive and negative events. Even now, after years of research and virtually hundreds of published scientific articles, in spite of a growing sophistication in the methodology used, the basic idea remained unchanged. An individual who experiences an event in his or her life has to utilize certain resources to adjust to the change implied by that event, and thus he or she can come out of the experience slightly weakened. The weakness is in the basic Selye's (1956) tradition; namely, that there is a finite amount of resources that a person has, and the greater the need to use them, the more replenished they become. Even though Selye himself has recently moved away from this rather simplistic notion (Selye, 1974), it did not yet lose much ground in empirical research. Changes, so goes the argument, even positive ones, are necessarily stressful. In view of the growing body of evidence relating life events to a variety of symptoms, a person would be better off leading a quiet and uneventful life. This will clearly be the case if longevity rather than quality of life is the central criterion for adjustment.

The above argument, and the line of thinking on which it is based, is, however, in sharp contrast to another recently evolving research tradition. I refer here particularly to the area that goes under the name of *stress inoculation*. Numerous scholarly papers reporting on a variety of psychological techniques and procedures have reported that exposing an individual to a specific stress can, sometimes, better prepare him to deal with similar subsequent stressors in the future (e.g.: Janis, 1981; Meichenbaum and Novaco, 1978; Novaco, 1977; Turk and Genest, 1979).

As the name stress inoculation suggests, the central conception is that of preparing the person to deal with certain kinds of stressors by exposing him or her to similar stressors, preferably in a milder form, and providing him or her with certain tools to cope with the problem. These "psychological antibodies" will then serve the person in future instances.

Like in the case of biological immune systems, this psychological immunity is most effective if the first encounter is a mild one. Some stress inoculation techniques suggest, however, this need not be so.

How can these two opposing ideas be reconciled? The proponents of the stressful life events tradition will presumably point out that the stress inoculation was not just an exposure to stress, but provided a learning experience as well. The subject in these procedures learned something new about himself or herself and the best ways to cope with certain stressful situations. But "there's the rub," for is it not true that every life experience, whether stressful or not, whether positive or negative, implies some form of learning? After all, most of our learning comes from life experiences. A life filled with events, whether stressful or not, is at the same time a life rich with experience.

Next, consider the issue of military training. The whole idea on which such training is based is that soldiers exposed to stressful conditions during their training will be better able to cope with the much harsher stresses of combat. Here again the simple life event approach will argue exactly the opposite. By subjecting the soldiers to stressful events during their military training, they then become more vulnerable to subsequent stresses.

Learning theory broadly defined as well as simple common sense maintain that past experience, painful as it may be, is a necessary condition for better adjustment in the future, and for improved coping with the stress of life. Life events models, on the other hand, claim that this very experience leads to deteriorated coping potential. Should we assume then that learning principles do not apply to behavior under stress? Or, perhaps, is one of these approaches simply wrong?

We submit that the resolution of these two opposing views lies in the criteria for adjustment that they employ. Whereas the life events tradition employs the onset of symptoms as the major criterion for problems of adjustment, stress inoculation as well as the more general learning traditions use entirely different criteria. The effectiveness of learning or preparing for a certain situation is best measured by performance in situations that approximate the training situation as much as possible. But this is surely a totally different approach. Consider the life events approach testing the impact of symptoms or partial symptoms on subsequent symptoms. This is not at all, however, what they do. As a matter of fact, the main advantage and in many ways the greatest appeal of the life events approach to stress is in the greater conceptual jump from the antecedent conditions to the actual outcomes. We thus claim that there is no intrinsic contradiction between these two approaches, that they rather focus on two different parts of the same complex issue. Learning as such, while of tremendous value in some instances, would be entirely irrelevant when no performance is actually required. Thus, there is little doubt that heart conditions are indeed related to the accumulation of stressful events, but students of this field have failed to mention that there is very little that the patient can do about it. Much the same is true for most health criteria that have been used. Even if people do learn from experience how to cope with stress, this learning would be quite irrelevant insofar as the above criteria are concerned. When no active coping is possible, learning would seem to be of little value indeed.

In What Ways Can A Stressful Experience Help?

The adjustment equation is a highly complex one and any attempt to break it down into simple formulations is bound to fail. At the same time, however, any theoretical attempt, particularly during its initial stages, requires a certain amount of simplification. Bearing that in mind, we can then point out three complete areas in which an experience, even a stressful one, can actually help an individual to better cope with similar situations in the future.

Emotion Management. Any stressful life event by definition produces a certain amount of emotional response. While the specific quality of the emotion will of course depend on the exact situation, some kind of elevation in the emotion would always take place. The stress inoculation procedure attempts to insure that the quality of the emotion to which the subject is exposed during the training situation is as similar as possible to the emotion to which he will presumably be exposed later, and in response to which he wishes to perform adequately. In a nutshell, the argument is that by experiencing a particular emotion very often a person gains a certain amount of familiarity, and perhaps a certain sense of mastery as well. This can occur either through habituation, or through acquisition of self-confidence and a sense of competence (Kern, 1966, Keinan, 1980). This is of course much in the minds of proponents of military training. It is the hope of the trainer that exposure to frightening and anxiety-provoking situations can progressively reduce the detrimental psychological impact of anxiety and thus increase the effectiveness of the soldier. This can happen either automatically, or by virtue of some specific techniques that the individual may develop in order to better manage his or her own emotions. This refers to what Lazarus (1966) called palliation. In the absence of active coping, palliation can play a major role in one's efforts to deal with stress.

Acquisition of Specific Skills. We now deal with the nonemotional aspects of stressful life events. These are of special relevance if the individual has access to certain behaviors that may help him or her to effectively cope with the situation. The importance of this facet of experience depends almost entirely on the issue of control. To the extent that the individual has control over the outcomes, previous experience is important. In the absence of alternatives, learning has very little to contribute.

Experiencing the same or very similar stressful events more than once can help in the area of acquisition of specific cognitive skills, motor skills, or social skills, as the case may be. One learns what to expect, and what some of the options are. The first confrontation with any major event, and particularly if it is a stressful one, rarely allows a person to utilize his or her potential resources adequately. On second or third occasions, however, this may be possible.

"Wisdom" and "Maturity." Any experience has a nonspecific contribution as well. The fact that psychologists visibly neglected the exploration of wisdom, as contrasted with simple intelligence, need not deter us from giving it its due. People who have been through a lot often claim that in some sense they have profited by gaining insights and understanding they lacked before. They have, so to speak, become more mature. We submit, then, that in addition to chronological age and mental age, one ought to consider the importance of *experiential* age as well.

There is vast literature, unfortunately most of it anecdotal rather than hard empirical evidence, illustrating the impact of a major stressful period in life, such as participation in war. Those that leave for the front as boys return from it as men. This epigrammatic statement refers to something that people in different countries in different periods of time have sensed, namely, that exposure to intense stress can accelerate maturation. Is it maturation, or ageing? Here we are again in close touch with Selye's theory of the general adaptation syndrome. He would clearly argue that exposure to frequent stressors leads in a short time to the same biological effects as if the organism were exposed to the same amount of stressors over a longer period of time. Accelerated ageing or proximity to exhaustion would be the usual phrases used in this context.

We submit, however, that ageing and maturation are not mutually exclusive terms, and in many spheres of behavior they are closely related. It was not long ago that the elders of the community instead of being viewed as past their prime were actually seen as the bearers of cumulative wisdom and experience for the benefit of all. This was documented in all societies prior to the introduction of writing. Literacy allows younger members of the community to acquire knowledge that would normally have been acquired only through a lifetime of experience. These informational shortcuts, however, do not necessarily deduct from the importance of experiential age. There are items of information that cannot be obtained the easy way through reading or other forms of indirect acquisition of knowledge, but only through direct personal experience. Stressful events in particular are of this kind, as indirect exposure necessarily reduces their emotional impact. Without speculating further about the importance of experiential age, we would thus submit that stressful life events contribute to a person's orientation to life through adding to his or her maturity and perspective. This is viewed as a nonspecific effect, which will influence behavior in situations that are only distantly related to the original experience.

The above analysis indicates that the life events research had conspicuously neglected the possibility of a positive impact of stressful life events. With few exceptions in the area of academic success (Cohler, Gruenbaum, Weiss, Robbins, Shader, Gallant and Hartman, 1974; Harris, 1972; Wildman, 1978; Clinard and Golden, 1973; Lloyd, Alexander, Rice, and Greenfield, 1980), the virtually hundreds of studies all employed criteria of illness. Even the above-mentioned studies on academic performance approached the problem from the negative side, namely, they all assumed that experiencing many life events should inevitably lead to poor performance in college. In the study reported here, we attempt to make a first limited step in the direction of ascertaining a possible positive impact of life events.

Being ourselves part of the Israeli scene certainly plays a significant role in the evolvement of our thinking. On the basis of the currently predominant ideas in the area of stressful life events, one would expect that all Israelis without exception would be very close to exhausting their adaptational resources. Considering the life-style of people who live in this country this could hardly be otherwise, unless something is wrong with the theory. Clinical and epidemiological evidence does not present the picture of a country made of individuals close to physical breakdown. In spite of major difficulties, Israelis exhibit a vitality and coping far beyond what would be expected on the basis of their own individual experience. Individually we like to think of ourselves as being strengthened by our hardships, so why not try to test it out empirically?

To sum up, we hypothesize that Israelis will be less differentiating in allocating weights to different life events, they will recall fewer events than actually took place, they will recall selectively more positive events than negative ones and, finally, we hypothesize that life change unit scores will be positively related to coping with certain stressful episodes in their lives.

METHOD

Instrument

The first part of this study was based on Israelis' judgments of the life change unit weights that have to be given to various items. To allow comparability with other studies, the list was based on the original 43 SRE items (Holmes and Rahe, 1967). Six items that were irrelevant to the Israeli scene, such as "Christmas," were, however, excluded.

In the second part of our study we aimed at greater differentiation. Thus, general items such as "Death of a family member" were divided into two or more items respectively, such as death of siblings and death of parents. Additional items reflecting specific aspects of life in Israel, and particularly the stressful aspects, were also included. These included such items as participation in war, drastic changes in reading newspapers, etc. All in all, 80 items were included in the final form of the life event questionnaire (see Appendix 10.1). Our interest in the effect of frequency and interference upon the recency question made it necessary that our subjects be instructed to point out when they experienced each of the life changes in the past, and how many times they experienced them.

RESULTS

How Stressful are Life Events for Young Israelis?

The first issue to be discussed are the weights assigned to life changes by Israeli, as compared to American, subjects.

Cross-cultural comparisons require samples that are both large and representative of the population investigated. It would be presumptuous to claim that our data are based on a sample fulfilling these conditions. We prefer, therefore, to consider the following as preliminary results requiring further support in future research.

Several studies indicate a high degree of similarity in cross-cultural evaluations of life events. In light of the above discussion, weights were assigned to the Life Events Questionnaire (LEQ) items using the Life Change Unit (LCU) method suggested by Masuda and Holmes (1967). We preferred this method since group means are more adequate for the purpose of the present analysis.

One hundred forty-three subjects participated in the first phase of the present study. This group is composed of 85 students and 58 young people not studying in universities. Sixty of them were females and 83 males, their ages ranging from 19 to 25. The subjects were group-administered the LEQ, using the standard LCU procedure: They were instructed to assign a value of 500 Life Change Units to the life event of "marriage," and to rate the remaining items around this basis. Geometric means comparing young Israelis to young Americans are presented in Table 10-1.

Examination of the data in Table 10-1 indicates that as hypothesized, young Americans tend to use extreme scores, both at the upper and at lower ends of the weights sequence, more often than Israelis. Mean scores in Table 10-1 suggest that about 900 points were required by the American sample to encompass the scope of the life events presented, while only 500 were used by their Israeli counterparts. Separating the first and the second halves of the items appearing in Table 10-1 according to the median rank order of the American sample, we found that 14 out of the first 18 life events considered by the Americans to be of greater importance are scored significantly lower by the Israelis.

The four items not conforming to this rule are death of a close family member or of a friend, addition of a new family member, and start or end of formal schooling.

The opposite trend is indicated for the 17 low ranking items. Fourteen out of these were rated higher by the Israeli sample than by the U.S. sample. Thus, for example, while church activities and vacation are low ranking items for both groups, Israelis, however, attribute them greater importance in absolute terms. A median test applied to this data indicated that the differences between the two groups were highly significant (X^2 = 10.362, d.f. = 1, p<0.001).

Additional items specific to the Israeli scene reflected the same phenomenon of reducing the perceived importance of any life change that is of significance. Thus, being injured in battle was allocated only a mean of 386 LCUs, a prolonged period of service in the reserve forces obtained 294 units, and participating in war only a 258 LCU value!

The data thus clearly support our hypothesis. Israelis, who as a group are exposed to frequent stressful events, reduce their differentiation between events as a result. It is conceivable that the overall higher "baseline" leads to diminished perceptual and/or emotional uniqueness of certain episodes in life. One possible interpretation of this finding can be that beyond a certain amount of stress, any additional stress has much the same impact. It is as if the frequency and quality of stress rather than its exact nature become the predominant factors.

Table 10-1. Mean Weighted Scores Assigned to Life Events by Americans and Israelis.[†]

ITEM	YOUNG AMERICANS		YOUNG ISRAELIS	
	RANK	SCORE	RANK	SCORE
Death of spouse	1	914*	2	514
Divorce	2	640*	10	301
Marital separation	3	536*	7	320
Death of close family member	4	507	1	570
Marriage	5	(500)	3	(500)
Detention in jail	6	484*	5	394
Major personal injury or illness	7	404*	11	290
Being fired from work	8	365*	18	230
Marital reconciliation	9	351*	28	164
Sexual difficulties	10	348*	8	316
Death of a close friend	11	334	6	356
Major change in health of family member	12	316*	17	238
Major change in financial state	13	294*	16	245
Major change in arguments with wife	14	292*	12	285
Addition of new family member	15	285	4	425
Changing to different line of work	16	261*	19	212
Start or end of formal schooling	17	219	13	275
Major change in work responsibilities	18	212*	20	211
In-law troubles	19	194*	22	192
Mortgage or loan over $10,000	20	171	15	260
Wife starting or ending work	21	156	26	173
Trouble with boss	22	154*	31	149
Outstanding personal achievement	23	136	9	305
Major changes in living conditions	24	135	14	262
Changing to a new school	25	126	22	192
Major change in working conditions	26	120*	34	105
Major revision of personal habits	27	114	25	183
Major change in social activities	28	102	24	184
Major change in recreation	29	100	32	115
Change in residence	30	92	22	192
Major change in church activities	31	88	30	151
Major change in family get-togethers	32	74	27	169
Major change in sleeping habits	33	66	35	79
Major change in eating habits	34	64*	36	57
Vacation	35	51	33	111
Minor violation of the law	36	26	29	158

*American weighted score is higher than Israeli score.

[†] American weights are derived from Rahe, et al. (1971).

There is, however, yet another way to look at these results. Young Israelis can be compared to older Americans in terms of their experiential age. On closer scrutiny of Rahe, et al. (1971), one finds that older Americans indeed exhibit less differentiation than younger ones when judging the stressfulness of events. It is of interest to note that this phenomenon is stronger among young Israelis even when compared with older Americans. The impact of age suggests that recency does not play a major role in producing the effect since the hectic Israeli way of life, even when spread over a longer duration, like in the older American subjects, tends to produce reduced differentiation.

Selective Reporting of Life Events

In our next step, we attempted to determine whether certain items were systematically missing from life events reports, assuming that if found this would indicate more than mere negligence.

Eight hundred forty-seven subjects divided into three samples were tested. The first sample consisted of 434 high school boys between the ages of 17 and 18; the second group included 90 enlisted army men with an age range of 19 to 20, and the third group consisted of 323 university students, of which 129 were male and 194 female, who ranged in age from 20 to 30 years. Each of these samples was group-administered the Life Events Questionnaire described above.

Certain characteristics were common to most of these subjects: all of them had formal schooling of no less than ten years, and they had a fair chance of experiencing academic success or failure more than once. The older among them could hardly avoid being exposed to changes regarding recreation and family get-togethers, as well as in eating and sleeping habits, during their military service.

Percentages of subjects claiming to experience these life events are presented in the bottom part of Table 10-2 for each sample separately; the top part of Table 10-2 presents some typical Israeli-specific items. The data presented in Table 10-2 indicate the following:

1. A substantial proportion of the examined population has experienced some of the more stressful life events that are associated with living in Israel. In spite of their young age, over 27% of the whole sample have lost a close friend or have a friend who is seriously injured; and over 50% of the student subjects have actively participated in war.

This confirms the assumption on which the entire present argument is based. Namely, Israelis do indeed experience frequent and often dramatic stressful events. While we were confident that this assumption was warranted, it is comforting to see it supported by the data.

2. Life events experienced by most of the respondents seem to be forgotten, repressed or denied. Keeping in mind that all the subjects are actively involved in some educational system, a somewhat higher percentage of either passing or failing exams could have been expected. The fact that about 48% of the total sample did not mention passing an important exam, and no more than 18% could recall failing an exam, seems to indicate that either the memory span for life events is rather short, or that stressful life events tend to be selectively remembered. In the same vein, similar selectivity is indicated on the part of both soldiers and ex-soldiers: Major changes enforced by army life on personal habits, eating, sleeping, recreation, or social interaction seem to be minimized by subjects of the present samples. Even the obvious changes in social framework caused by either being enlisted or released

Table 10-2. Percentages of Subjects Reporting Various Life Events.

ITEM	HIGH SCHOOL STUDENTS	SOLDIERS	UNIVERSITY CANDIDATES
Death of a close friend	13	20	21
A close friend injured	10	14	10
Major personal injury	18	14	8
Participation in war activities	—	—	52*
Increase in listening to radio news	35	17	35
Increased rate of reading newspapers	44	18	39
Major change in family get-togethers	11	7	7
Major revision of personal habits	11	23	18
Major change in recreation	21	13	28
Major change in sleeping habits	10	33	26
Major change in nourishment	9	26	18
Major increase in social activities	31	23	23
Major change in social framework	22	32	27
Failing an important examination	20	10	16
Passing an important examination	52	37	57

*Males only.

from the army are not mentioned by about 70% of the respondents. This tendency is even more pronounced when the rates of change reported by the older groups are compared to those of the younger and presumably less experienced group. The gaps between this group, which had not left home by the time the study took place, and the other two groups, which already had a marked life history behind them, are in most cases practically negligible.

Additional estimates for a selective tendency expressed by reports of life events could be derived by comparing the mean number of events characteristic of Israelis and Americans. An average of 25 life changes was found for a sample of American soldiers (Rahe, 1974), as compared to an average of 22 for Israelis in the present sample (corrected for the total number of parallel items in the Israeli questionnaire). While the difference between the samples seems to be rather small, it should be kept in mind, however, that the Israeli score includes both recent and earlier life changes. A mean score computed for the present soldiers' sample on recent events only, that is, items taking place within two years prior to the administration of the LEQ, indicates a rather different picture. No more than 5 life changes are reported on the average by Israeli soldiers to have occurred recently. There is little reason to assume that lives of young Israelis are less eventful than those of comparable American peers. The decreased number of life changes in the present sample may be attributed, therefore, to processes of selection in perception, memory interference, or reporting.

If motivational factors play a role in this trend to underreport life changes, it should be expected that positive changes will be recalled more frequently than negative ones. Such a comparison is not feasible with the original SRE items, but the more detailed LEQ, which includes items tapping both positive and negative changes within the same domain, lends itself more easily to examining this effect. Table 10-3, presenting percentages of elicited responses for such comparable pairs of items, indicates a systematic bias in favor of changes for the better in both soldiers and students.

Both the present data and earlier findings seem to suggest that being exposed to a greater number of stressful life events is not necessarily reflected in more detailed reports. Moreover, there seems to be a negative relationship between richness of experience and

Table 10-3. Percentages of Recalled Positive and Negative Life Events.

ITEM	HIGH SCHOOLERS PERCENT	SOLDIERS PERCENT
Passing an important examination	52.1	36.7
Failing an important examination	19.8	10.0
Starting going steady	47.7	43.3
Not going steady any more	32.0	25.6
Increase in social activities	30.9	23.3
Decrease in social activities	7.1	15.6
Outstanding personal achievement	25.3	25.6
Outstanding personal failure	7.6	8.9
Major increase in family get-togethers	14.1	7.8
Major decrease in family get-togethers	7.4	5.6
Major positive change in financial state	12.4	20.0
Major negative change in financial state	6.9	10.0
Increase in work responsibilities	9.0	20.0
Decrease in work responsibilities	0.0	2.2
Major decrease in arguments with spouse	7.6	4.4
Major increase in arguments with spouse	8.8	2.2
Mean positive	24.9	22.6
Mean negative	11.2	10.0

total life events scores on a group basis: The richer the stressful life history, the lower the frequency of life events recalled.

This suggests that a research strategy focusing on items that are conspicuously missing from the subjects' reports rather than those reported may provide a clue to the underlying psychological mechanisms at work. In this way life events questionnaires can take us beyond the simple factual statements to the area of coping and defense.

Positive Effects of Life Events

The life events tradition of research is totally dominated by criteria of maladjustment. We now proceed to evaluate the possible impact of stressful experience on active coping in stressful situations. Two such situations were chosen: University Admission Examinations, and leadership under simulated stress.

The Haifa University admission examination is similar to an intelligence test having subtests such as arithmetical problems, analogies,

Table 10-4. Correlation Between LEQ Items and University
Admittance Scores (Pearson r).[†]

ITEMS INCLUDED IN THE SRE	r
Start of formal schooling	0.200***
Changing to a new school	0.206***
Vacation	0.157**
Change in residence	0.228***
Major change in living conditions	0.178***
Major revision of personal habits	0.117*
Major negative change in financial state	-0.186***
Marriage	0.197***
Addition of new daughter to family	0.127*
Increase in family get-togethers	-0.119*
Decrease in family get-togethers	0.120*
Change to different line of work	0.141***
ITEMS NOT INCLUDED IN THE SRE	
Outstanding monetary expenditure	0.215***
Buying a car	0.110*
Going abroad	0.269***
Failing an important examination	0.135*
Moving to another city	0.145**
Resignation from work	0.141*
Participation in war activities	0.229***
Total LEQ score	0.222***

*p < 0.05; **p < 0.01; ***p < 0.001.
[†]Only items having correlations significant at 0.05 level and over are included.

reading comprehension, vocabulary, current information, and matrices. The test is used both for selecting candidates and for determining cutting points for admission to each department. Candidates taking this test often reveal a high level of anxiety, which is further augmented by its competitive nature. A random sample of 323 candidates was group-administered the LEQ. The correlations between each of the life event items, the total LEQ score, and admittance test scores were computed, and the significant ones are presented in Table 10-4.

The most striking feature of the data are the plus signs of the correlations. The more life events indicated, the higher the rate of success in the admittance test. Getting married, change in residence or in school, revision of personal habits, living conditions, or line of work — all of these life changes positively contribute to successfully coping with this kind of stressful condition. Only two items are negatively correlated with this criterion, namely, "Major negative change in financial state" and "Increase in family get-togethers." It is interesting to note that participation in war, traumatic as it may be, is also positively related to successful test performance. Since there is no reason to believe that young married people who changed school and residence, travel abroad, and have taken part in warfare are necessarily more intelligent than their peers, it seems reasonable to assume that in one way or another these life changes enrich human experience, making the individual more prepared for intellectually stressful and demanding conditions.

A second study was conducted to further examine this issue. Seventy-nine enlisted army men who volunteered to participate in leadership assessment tests were group-administered the LEQ in groups of seven or eight members. Leadership assessments were conducted by a crew of six experienced army psychologists using three sources of information: (1) a battery of personality tests, (2) performance in a group discussion requesting subjects to reach agreement on an issue debated with other members of the group, and to convince the group to accept their respective views on the subject, and (3) personal interviews by the psychological staff. Each subject was rated on a nine-point scale ranging from no leadership ability at one extreme, to a recommendation for a leadership position at the other. The examinations were conducted in a realistic military setting, and the volunteers were led to believe that their performance would seriously affect their chances of becoming future officers. There was general agreement among the six judges that under these conditions subjects appeared to be under marked stress.

It was found that the arithmetical sum of LEQ items reported as well as most of the items were again positively correlated with leadership scores. Unlike in the former study, the correlations did not, however, reach statistical significance.

The data derived from both studies indicate that a standard pool of items is less than optimal for predicting a rather specific criterion for coping with stress. Additional research is required if scales are to be derived that will be more effective in predicting specific criteria. At the same time, even the present list of items was quite successful in conjunction with a multiple regression analysis, as suggested by

Rubin, Gunderson, and Arthur (1969). Regression analyses done on the data in both studies have led to similar results: A substantial increase in the percentages of explained variance that is greater than the correlation with a single total score.

Effective Recall Span

By definition, life changes take place throughout one's life history. The research in this field, by focusing on recent changes and excluding earlier events, reflects one of two beliefs: Either memory span regarding life events is relatively narrow, leaving little or no room for changes that have taken place long ago, or earlier life events have little bearing on behavior under current stress. While both of these assumptions are empirically testable, very little research has been conducted on them so far.

Our LEQ was designed to tap both recent and former life changes and register their time of occurrence. It was found that the distributions of the indicated times are quite skewed for all of the items. Table 10-5 presents, therefore, the median recall span for each of the LEQ items that were derived from the original SRE.

The data offer some interesting evidence concerning the recency of spontaneous recall of life events. Very few items appearing in the table are confined to a stringent definition of recency. Twenty percent of the items at the lower end of the distribution are characterized by a median time span of no more than 10 months. Another 20 percent widen the median range to no more than 12 months. About 40 percent of the life events presented in Table 10-5 have taken place 2 years or more before the administration of the questionnaire, the highest median score being 155 months.

Insofar as free recall is concerned, the data provide no support for the claim that life events should be confined to the last year or two preceding the administration of the test. It is quite clear that either the decision to limit the study of life events to a period of two years only (Rahe, Meyer, Smith, Kjaer, and Holmes, 1964) has been somewhat arbitrary, or that there is something different in the Israeli context. Table 10-5 indicates a substantial number of items that are reported to happen within two years. A sizeable number of life events are, however, recalled mainly from earlier periods.

Table 10-5. Median Time Spans in Months of LEQ Items for
High School Students and Enlisted Army Men.

ITEM	SOLDIERS	STUDENTS
Start or end of formal schooling	155	47
Addition of new family member	150	138
Change in residence	59	70
Death of close family member	58	66
Changing to a new school	53	43
Major change in financial state	50	21
Major change in family get-togethers	45	17
Major change in arguments with wife	39	21
Being fired from work	37	2
Son or daughter leaving home	36	22
Major change in church activities	30	36
Major change in living conditions	27	27
Trouble with boss	27	12
Major change in recreation	26	15
Minor violation of the law	24	2
Major personal injury or illness	24	35
Changing to different line of work	20	2
Major change in work responsibilities	19	24
Death of a close friend	18	14
Major change in health of family member	12	19
Mortgage or loan over $10,000	12	18
Outstanding personal achievement	12	10
Major revision of personal habits	12	11
Major change in social activities	12	17
Major change in sleeping habits	12	12
Major change in eating habits	12	22
Vacation	9	8
Major change in working conditions	8	12
Detention in jail	8	12
Marital reconciliation	6	6
In-law troubles	6	3

Table 10-5 further suggests that some life events are retained in
memory for a short period of time, while others are not forgotten
for many years. A comparison of Tables 10-1 and 10-5 indicates
that the long-remembered events are also assigned higher weighted
scores by judges. A comparison of the weights attributed to the
least recent ten items to the weights given the intermediate most
recent ten items in Table 10-5 shows their mean weights to be 274,
225, and 178, respectively.

DISCUSSION

Theoretical Shortcomings

The simple and direct method for assessing the magnitude of stress is perhaps the most important contribution of life changes research. It may be argued, however, that this innovative methodology is the source of both the strength and the weakness of this tradition. The majority of life events studies lean heavily on an assumed monotonous relationship between the volume of change and decreased resistance to stress (Holmes and Masuda, 1974). In line with Selye's physiological model of stress (Selye, 1956), it is hypothesized that accumulation of stressful life events, requiring an investment of energy for readaptation, would eventually lead to increased vulnerability to stress, and to enhanced predisposition towards the development of disease.

In spite of its rich theoretical background, the study of life events in relation to stress may be described quite accurately as empirical data in search of a theoretical framework. Major issues such as personality and mediating variables, conditions leading to vulnerability or to immunity to stress, the role of recent as compared to earlier life events, the factual versus the subjective components of change scores, or the issue of effective recall time are frequently discussed in reviews of this domain. These discussions, however, have had no significant effect on methods of investigating life changes nor did they change the dominant research paradigms. This omission is summarized in rather strong terms by Rabkin and Struening (1976), who claim that "although conceptual and theoretical orientation should play an important preparatory role in the design and execution of empirical studies, this does not often appear to be the case in the literature reviewed on the relation of life events, stress, and illness" (p. 1019). It may well be that the relative empirical success in relating life history changes to states of sickness has played an important role in hindering further search for both new research methods or more refined theoretical models.

At least two theoretical issues have to be discussed in order to establish the nature of relationships between life changes and susceptibility to stress. The first should delineate the process through which perceived life events are transformed into physiological symptoms, and through them into various forms of illness. The second ought to explain the phenomenon of subjects experiencing very elevated life change levels without becoming ill within a reasonable period of time. The most extensive attempt to answer these questions has been offered by Rahe and his associates (Rahe, Flistad, Bergan, et al., 1974; Rahe and Arthur, 1978). This model assumes several diversion and selection phases. Life events are: (a) selectively perceived, (b) selectively denied or repressed, (c) somehow translated into a variety of physiological responses, (d) selectively managed or "absorbed" to prevent the development of organ dysfunction, and (e) lead to certain bodily symptoms when not "absorbed."

There exist ample data suggesting that the model's steps indeed represent major phases in the investigated process. A close examination reveals, however, that neither the first nor the second issues are satisfactorily answered. No specification is offered in terms of either individual or event characteristics as to what changes would cause illness, for what people, and under which conditions. No clear answer can be deduced concerning the nature of the life changes that are more likely to be selectively remembered, diverted, or denied, not to evoke physiological response, or what psychophysiological expressions are bound to be filtered or "absorbed," not becoming "illness" behaviors.

General and descriptive terms have been used to answer these questions. The prevailing approach linking life changes to stress focuses on the role of readjustment: "As defined, social readjustment measures the intensity and length of time necessary to accommodate to a life event, regardless of the desirability of the event" (Holmes and Masuda, 1974, p. 49). Another approach using even more general terms assumes that changes and crises could be evaluated by their impact on the respondent as measured by the time span of the experiences (Antonovsky, 1974). In both cases it is maintained that accumulation of recent life changes may create a psychological or physiological overload leading to crises, and through them to onset of illness. However, attempts to specify the pathway between changes and disease tend to focus on existing correlations rather than on process variables. A well-known description of the process involved goes as follows: "Changes in significant social or interpersonal relationships are very often accompanied by changes in habits, changes in patterns of activity, changes in intake of food and medication . . . . They are also frequently associated with changes in mood, and with physiological changes directly mediated by the central nervous system. Any or all of these might affect the frequency or severity of illness" (Hinkle, 1968, p. 243).

An extensive review of life change research has estimated that attempts to derive a theoretical model from the available data may be somewhat premature. "The hypotheses are not sufficient to provide a basis for resolving the overall issue of the pathogenic power of stressful life events for they leave this term undefined" (Dohrenwend and Dohrenwend, 1974, p. 318). In spite of the considerable development in the studies in this field, this statement still seems to accurately describe the current state of the art (Johnson and Sarason, 1978).

Perhaps the most badly needed element in life change models is the translation of correlations into process terms (e.g. Lazarus, 1978). Rules of transformation and possible mechanisms should also be spelled out, suggesting how psychological variables, such as experience of change, turn into physiological dysfunction.

Coping with High Levels of Stress

Life in Israel can be characterized as existence under continuous stress. While for most people this stress is not strong enough to cause severe psychological or physiological crises, it is strong enough to influence certain modes of behavior. The incessant stream of stressful life events calls for development of some adequate modes of adjustment, based on learning from this experience. Reporting life changes already indicates one part of such a process. Rather than being a straightforward presentation of past events, these reports seem to represent the respondents' way of perceiving (or misperceiving) their life history. Both repression and sensitization have been pointed out as typical responses to stress. The present data indicate that as a group, young Israelis seem to be on the repressive side. The need to manage the overstimulation of stressful life experiences superimposed upon an already high base level, triggers processes of filtering and denial. In the present study these processes take the form of both selective recall and a very low absolute rate of recently reported changes. Such possibly far-reaching effects of a denial bias, while mentioned by Cobb (1979), were never yet demonstrated on a group level.

The data suggest that life events are accumulated in complex ways, determining the way subsequent stressful events are evaluated and perceived. Relatively high and constant stress has a distinct impact on evaluating the significance of life changes in a rather systematic way. Israeli subjects respond as if some of their capacity for emotional involvement in significant stressful events has been exhausted, or as if they could not afford to be shocked by every case of illness, monetary loss, and even death.

On the other hand, it is conceivable that more trivial items may serve as compensation for the unexpressed feelings evoked by more crucial life events.

Israelis tend to systematically avoid reporting life changes that most probably did occur to them. The rule seems to be that the more frequent the changes, the less change is perceived. This effect, which is characteristic of older people, is prevalent among younger Israelis. While people aged 60 seem to report half as many life changes as those under 30 (Rabkin and Struening, 1976), Israeli soldiers report about one-fifth of the number of events elicited by American soldiers of the same age level. The items that are not reported by the Israeli sample do not seem to share a common denominator of content or severeness, with the exception of the division into positive and negative events.

We believe that a better understanding of how base rates of stress are established may lead to a clearer definition of antecedents of reported life changes. A better formulation of these elements may reveal the nature of processes linking life changes to behavioral, psychological, and physiological outcomes.

Stressful Events as a Valuable Experience

Of all our findings the one of potentially the greatest importance consists of the positive correlations between stressful life events and success in performance in future stressful situations. It should be emphasized that here we have a truly prospective study, where the criterion follows not only the life events themselves, but their reporting as well. As was already pointed out in the results section of this chapter, it would be presumptuous to expect a standard list of items to give good predictions of outcomes in other areas of experience. At the same time, however, the significant positive correlation of many items, as well as the total score, are more than suggestive of the potential of this approach. This finding, however, raises more questions than answers. Particularly on the background of available research, we ought to raise the issue of the mechanisms involved. How is it possible that life events that were found to be related only to negative consequences do indeed exhibit some positive effects? Does this necessarily contradict the rest of the findings? Do we deal here only with some random insignificant variance? Or perhaps there are ways to integrate our findings with the many other results obtained so far?

We submit that it is possible to integrate our findings with the rest of available knowledge in this area. In order to do so certain points must be made clearer: Firstly, we are dealing with healthy young individuals, rather than with populations at risk. Secondly, we did not at all investigate susceptibility to illness. It is quite possible that those subjects that had higher total scores of life events were indeed more susceptible to illness, as one would expect on the basis of the research tradition in this area. This does not exclude, however, the possibility that the same subjects, because of their life experiences, are better able to deal with a certain set of stressful events in the future. In short, we raise the possibility that stressful life events can have both positive and negative consequences. For some odd reason, the positive aspects were simply not tested so far, and that is why they couldn't be discovered.

There is another facet that is different in our research from most of the other studies in this area. This relates to the criteria used, namely, success in a very short span of time, such as an entrance examination or a leadership test for officers selection. The criteria themselves are, therefore, events in their own right. Rather than trying to predict something that is a long-term phenomenon, such as growing vulnerability to an illness or even academic performance over a year or more of studies (Harris, 1972; Wildman, 1978; Clinard and Golden, 1973; Lloyd, Alexander, Rice and Greenfield, 1980), the criteria used in our studies reflect behavior during hours, not days, weeks, months, or years. It is possible to suggest, therefore, that life events can sometimes prepare for subsequent events. Stated differently, we submit that experience with many different and stressful changes can help a person to better deal with changes as such.

The above need not be seen as an absurb statement in view of the fact that changes, and particularly stressful ones, have something in common; namely, the arousal component. It is by virtue of gaining some experience to one's own emotional behavior that a person can gain a certain amount of control. Thus, going through many examinations and other "thousand natural shocks that flesh is heir to," a person can learn to take these situations somewhat less seriously than without the experience. Maybe it is not such a strange finding that university candidates who have been exposed to ordeals of real battle do not find the entrance examination such a terrifying and incapacitating ordeal. It is then through anxiety management that the positive correlation with success could be obtained. By being better able to control their emotions, they can better concentrate on the task at hand.

One must not, however, forget the possibility of the nonspecific contribution of varied and rich life experiences. Whether in the cognitive domain or the social domain, the experiences as such may contribute to the wisdom of one's decisions, and to a generally more mature outlook on life. The finding that young Israelis judge the stressfulness of events as if they were much older in comparison to other nationalities, is in itself a pointer in that direction. Experiential age is indeed a concept that ought to be given a fair chance in future research.

The possibility still exists that individual differences rather than any other consideration are the critical variables in our dilemma. While some individuals may respond to certain stressors with growing vulnerability and predisposition to physical or psychological illness, others may respond in a totally different manner, one more conducive to health and coping. Any formulation in this respect must await a great deal of additional research. In the absence of critical data bearing on this point, our own bias is that stressful life events are a package deal, and the same factors that help in one situation can lead ultimately to exhaustion and disease.* It is also conceivable that there are certain critical threshold effects that determine whether it will be the positive or the negative contribution of stressful experience that will be predominant in influencing behavior. The nonlinearity of cumulative life events clearly emphasizes the viability of such a theoretical position.

---

*It is of some interest to note that Clinard and Golden (1973) found that greater life change was associated with positive outcomes (promotions and raises) as well as with negative outcomes (personal injuries or illnesses). What they considered to be mixed results could indeed be meaningful clues to our present analysis.

REFERENCES

Antonovsky, A. Conceptual and methodological problems in the study of resistance sources and stressful life events. *In*, B. S. Dohrenwend and B. P. Dohrenwend (eds.), *Stressful Life Events: Their Nature and Effects.* New York: Wiley, 1974, 245–258.

Brown, G. W. Meaning, measurement and stressful life events. *In*, B. S. Dohrenwend and B. P. Dohrenwend (eds.), *Stressful Life Events: Their Nature and Effects.* New York: Wiley, 1974, 217–244.

Casey, R. L., Masuda, M., and Holmes, T. H. Quantitative study of recall of life events. *Journal of Psychosomatic Research*, 1967, *11*, 239–247.

Cleary, P. J. *Life events and disease: A review of methodology and findings.* Stockholm: Laboratory for Clinical Stress Research, 1974.

Cobb, S. A model for life events and their consequences. *In*, B. S. Dohrenwend and B. P. Dohrenwend (eds.), *Stressful Life Events: Their Nature and Effects.* New York: Wiley, 1974.

Cohler, B. J., Gruenbaum, H. W., Weiss, J. L., Robbins, D. M., Shader, R. I., Gallant, D., and Hartman, C. R. Social role performance and psychopathology among recently hospitalized and nonhospitalized mothers. *Journal of Nervous Mental Disorders*, 1974, *159*, 81–90.

Constantini, A. F., Braun, J. R., Davis, J. E. and Iervolino, A. The life change inventory: A device for quantifying psychological magnitude of changes experienced by college students. *Psychological Reports*, 1974, *34*, 991–1000.

Dohrenwend, B. S. Life events on stressors: A methodological inquiry. *Journal of Health and Social Behavior*, 1973, *14*, 167–175.

Dohrenwend, B. S. and Dohrenwend, B. P. (eds.), *Stressful Life Events: Their Nature and Effects.* New York: Wiley, 1974.

Gorsuch, R. L. and Key, M. K. Abnormalities in pregnancy as a function of anxiety and life stress. *Psychosomatic Medicine*, 1974, *36*, 352–361.

Hackett, T. P. and Cassem, N. H. Psychological management of the myocardial infarction patient. *Journal of Human Stress*, 1975, *1*, (3) 25–38.

Hackett, T. P., Cassem, N. H. and Wishnie, H. A. The coronary-care unit: An appraisal of its psychologic hazards. *New England Journal of Medicine*, 1968, *279*, 1365–1370.

Harris, P. W. The relationship of life change to academic performance among selected college freshmen at varying levels of college readiness. Unpublished Doctor of Education thesis, East Texas State University, Commerce, Texas, 1972.

Helson, H. *Adaptation-level Theory: An Experimental and Systematic Approach to Behavior.* New York: Harper & Row, 1964.

Hinkle, Jr., L. E. Occupation, education and coronary heart disease. *Science*, 1968, *161*, 238–246.

Holmes, T. H. and Masuda, M. Life change and illness susceptibility. *In*, B. S. Dohrenwend and B. P. Dohrenwend (eds.), *Stressful Life Events: Their Nature and Effects.* New York: Wiley, 1974.

Holmes, T. H. and Rahe, R. H. The social readjustment rating scale. *Journal of Psychosomatic Research*, 1967, *11*, 213–218.

Hudgens, R. W., Robins, E. and Delong, W. B. The reporting of recent stress in the lives of psychiatric patients. *British Journal of Psychiatry*, 1970, *117*, 635–642.

Janis, I. L. Stress inoculation as a means of preventing pathogenic denial. *In*, S. Breznitz (ed.), *The Denial of Stress*. New York: International Universities Press, 1981.

Jenkins, W. O., Pascal, G. R., and Walker, Jr., R. W. Deprivation and generalization. *Journal of Experimental Psychology*, 1958, *56*, 274–277.

Johnson, J. H. and Sarason, I. G. Recent developments in research on life stress. Office of Naval Research, Arlington, Virginia. N 00014-75-C-0905, NR-170-804. 1978.

Keinan, G. The effects of personality and training variables on the experienced stress and quality of performance in situations where physical integrity is threatened. Ph.D. Thesis. Tel Aviv University, 1980.

Kern, R. P. A conceptual model of behavior under stress with implications for combat training. HUMRRO Technical Report 66-12, 1966.

Klein, R. F., Garity, T. F. and Gelein, J. Emotional adjustment and catecholamine excretion during early recovery from MI. *Journal of Psychosomatic Research*, 1979, *18*, 425–435.

Lazarus, R. S. *Psychological Stress and the Coping Process*. New York: McGraw-Hill, 1966.

Lazarus, R. S. and Launier, R. Stress-related transactions between person and environment. *In*, L. A. Pervin and M. Lewis (eds.), *Perspectives in Interactional Psychology*. New York: Plenum, 1978, 287–327.

Lloyd, C., Alexander, A. A., Rice, D. G., and Greenfield, N. S. Life change and academic performance. *Journal of Human Stress*, 1980, *6*, 15–25.

Masuda, M., and Holmes, T. H. The social readjustment scale: A cross-cultural study of Japanese and Americans. *Journal of Psychosomatic Research*, 1967, *11*, 227.

Meichenbaum, D., and Novaco, R. Stress inoculation: A preventive approach. *In*, C. Spielberger and I. Sarason (eds.), *Stress and Anxiety*, Vol. 5. Washington: Hemisphere, 1978.

Miller, F. T., Bentz, W. K., Aponte, J. F., and Brogan, D. R. Perception of life crisis events: A comparative study of rural and urban samples. *In*, B. S. Dohrenwend and B. P. Dohrenwend (eds.), *Stressful Life Events: Their Nature and Effects*. New York: Wiley, 1974, 259–274.

Novaco, R. A stress-inoculation approach to anger management in the training of law enforcement officers. *American Journal of Community Psychology*, 1977, *5*, 327–346.

Rabkin, J. G. and Struening, E. L. Life events, stress and illness. *Science*, 1976, *194*, 1013–1020.

Rahe, R. H. Multi-cultural correlations of life change scaling: America, Japan, Denmark and Sweden. *Journal of Psychosomatic Research*, 1969, *13*, 191.

Rahe, R. H. The pathway between subjects' recent life changes and their near-future illness reports: Representative results and methodological issues. *In*, B. S. Dohrenwend and B. P. Dohrenwend (eds.), *Stressful Life Events: Their Nature and Effects*. New York: Wiley, 1974, 73–97.

Rahe, R. H., and Arthur, R. J. Life changes and illness studies: Past history and future directions. *Journal of Human Stress*, 1978, *4*, 3–15.

Rahe, R. H., Flistad, I., Bergan, T., et al. A model for life changes and illness research. Cross-cultural data from the Norwegian Navy. *Archives of Genetic Psychiatry*, 1974, *31*, 172–177.

Rahe, R. H. and Lind, E. Psychosocial factors and sudden cardiac death. *Journal of Psychosomatic Research*, 1971, *15*, 19–24.

Rahe, R. H., Lundberg, U., Bennett, L., and Theorell, T. The social readjustment rating scale: A comparative study of Swedes and Americans. *Journal of Psychosomatic Research*, 1971, *15*, 241–249.

Rahe, R. H., Meyer, M., Smith, M., Kjaer, G., and Holmes, T. H. Social stress and illness onset. *Journal of Psychosomatic Research*, 1964, *8*, 35–44.

Rosenbaum, G. Stimulus generalization as a function of level of experimentally induced anxiety. *Journal of Experimental Psychology*, 1953, *45*, 35–43.

Rubin, R. T., Gunderson, E. K. E., and Arthur, R. J. Life stress and illness patterns in the U.S. Navy. III. Prior life change and illness onset in an attack carrier's crew. *Archives of Environmental Health*, 1969, *19*, 753–757.

Selye, H. *The Stress of Life*. New York: McGraw-Hill, 1956.

Selye, H. *Stress Without Distress*. New York: Lippincott Co., 1974.

Thurlow, H. J. Illness in relation to life situation and sick-role tendency. *Journal of Psychosomatic Research*, 1971, *15*, 73–88.

Turk, D. C., and Genest, M. Regulation of pain: The application of cognitive and behavioral techniques for prevention and remediation. *In,* P. C. Kendall and S. D. Hollon (eds.), *Cognitive-behavioral interventions*. New York: Academic Press, 1979.

Vinokur, A., and Selzer, M. L. Desirable versus undesirable life events: Their relationship to stress and mental distress. *Journal of Personality and Social Psychology*, 1975, *32*, 329–337.

Wildman, R. C. Life change with college grades as a role-performance variable. *Social Psychology*, 1978, *41*, 34–46.

Wyler, A. R., Masuda, M., and Holmes, T. H. Magnitude of life events and seriousness of illness. *Psychosomatic Medicine*, 1971, *33*, 115–122.

APPENDIX 10-1. LIFE EVENTS QUESTIONNAIRE (LEQ).

1. Outstanding monetary expenditure.
2. Minor violation of the law.
3. Purchasing a car.
4. Immigrating to Israel.
5. Start of formal schooling.
6. End of formal schooling.
7. Change to a new school.
8. Start of advanced studies.
9. End of advanced studies.
10. Traveling abroad.
11. Winning a lottery.
12. Passing an important examination.
13. Failing an important examination.
14. Increase in reading newspapers.
15. Decrease in reading newspapers.
16. Increase in listening to broadcasted news.
17. Decrease in listening to broadcasted news.

18. Car accident.
19. Vacation.
20. Major change in eating habits.
21. Major change in sleeping habits.
22. Major change in religious activity.
23. Major change in recreation.
24. Change in residence.
25. Transfer to another town.
26. Major change in living conditions.
27. Major revision in personal habits.
28. Major improvement of standard of living.
29. Outstanding personal achievement.
30. Outstanding personal failure.
31. Loan over $10,000.
32. Being deeply in debt.
33. Major positive change in financial state.
34. Major negative change in financial state.
35. Sexual difficulties.
36. Operation.
37. Major personal illness.
38. Major personal injury.
39. Detention in jail.
40. Death of spouse.
41. Death of father.
42. Death of mother.
43. Death of brother.
44. Death of sister.
45. Death of other family member.
46. Marriage.
47. Divorce.
48. Marital reconciliation.
49. Birth of son.
50. Birth of daughter.
51. Birth of brother.
52. Birth of sister.
53. Major increase in arguments with spouse.
54. Major decrease in arguments with spouse.
55. Son or daughter leaving home.
56. In-law troubles.
57. Wife (husband) starting work.
58. Wife (husband) ending work.
59. Major increase in family get-togethers.
60. Major decrease in family get-togethers.
61. Major change in health of family.
62. Changing to a different line of work.
63. Being fired from work.
64. Resigning from work.
65. Promotion.
66. Major increase in work responsibilities.
67. Major decrease in work responsibilities.
68. Start of interesting job.
69. End of interesting job.
70. Trouble with boss.
71. Major change in working conditions.
72. Serious injury of a close friend.
73. Death of a close friend.
74. Major increase in social activity.
75. Major decrease in social activity.
76. Major change in social framework.
77. Marital separation.
78. Participation in war.
79. Serious injury in battle.
80. Parachuting.

Part IV
Stress as a Way of Life

11.
The Noble Challenge of Stress

Shlomo Breznitz
University of Haifa

"May you lead an interesting life!"
Ancient Chinese curse

Stress is part of life, an everpresent companion. Rarely controllable, from varying distance it shadows our movements, our very existence. Having many faces its image is elusive and continuously changing. Whether we succumb to it or challenge its attempts to dominate our lives is, however, not entirely outside our personal sphere of influence. We can and often do muster the necessary strength to challenge its supremacy. This is particularly so when there is no better available alternative. Necessity is a mobilizing force par excellence.

The wisdom of resistance to stress is not always self-evident. "Fight for your highest attainable aim, but never put resistance in vain," teaches Selye. Thus it is in the gray area between the possible and the futile that the battle of coping with stress has to be fought. This volume represents barely a single page in the annals of that continuous struggle. Like Jacob wrestling a force greater than himself, we wait for the morning to give us pause.

The very name of Isra-El (He that wrestled God) appropriately dates back to that night-long struggle that never truly ended. While nobody has a monopoly over stress, some have much more of it than others. Israel, unfortunately, claims a lion's share. As such, it provides a concentrated focus on the complexity of the issue.

IMMUNIZATION VERSUS EXHAUSTION

Within the restricted context of health and adaptation, the main question is this: What are the cumulative effects of long exposure to a variety of stressors? Two dramatically opposed answers present themselves.

On the one hand, there is the notion that people get used to anything, even extremely difficult conditions. Like steel forged out of fire, so runs the argument, a person coming from a difficult ordeal more or less unharmed is toughened up by the experience and should be better able to deal with subsequent difficulties.

The idea of immunization has a fantastic psychological appeal. There is something elegant and intellectually rewarding, which makes its appeal almost irresistible. Like its biological prototype, it raises images of psychological antibodies, implying that there is a reward for suffering; one doesn't only get older and wiser, but at the same time emotionally stronger.

It is of some interest to note that to the superficial observer the Israeli scene appears to be precisely that. The Israelis give the overwhelming impression of being tough, and unconcerned by their predicament. They go about their business in a normal way, they are interested in the arts, in sports, and they invest in the future. They have children, which is another indication of their belief in the future. In short, it is business as usual.

Some chapters in this volume probe underneath this superficial facade and present a much more complex and balanced picture. At the same time, however, the belief in psychological immunization is itself a source of strength and as such cannot be easily discarded. Even if proven essentially wrong, it would probably persist. Through it, one need not envy people who lead much easier lives.

The second possible answer to the question of long term effects of stress is based on Selye's (1956) notion of finite adaptation energy. Every individual has a finite quantity of adaptational resources that, once spent, are irreplaceable. Each exposure to stress taxes these resources, and by adding more and more stress the individual must eventually "break down." Instead of immunization, exhaustion is inevitably expected. The pace at which the adaptational energy is used up is a direct function of the frequency, intensity, and duration of stressors. A brief hectic life is comparable to a long uneventful one.

As there is no direct way to measure the hypothetical adaptation energy, breakdown under stress is practically impossible to predict on an individual basis. The gradual exhaustion is latent until its dramatic manifestation. An interesting feature of Selye's General Adaptation Syndrome is that short of manifest exhaustion, during the "stage of resistance," a person may appear actually better adjusted than before the stress started. This misleading external adaptation stands in sharp contrast to the underlying weakening of resources and growing vulnerability. While Selye and his many followers did not address themselves specifically to the human organism subjected to the particular psychological stressors that interest us here, any extrapolation from that tradition of research inevitably predicts that long periods of multiple stressors must sooner or later produce exhaustion. Although some studies of soldiers who broke down under the strain of prolonged warfare lend support to the above model, much additional evidence is needed before even a tentative statement would be justified.

What then are the long-term effects of living under conditions such as those prevailing in Israel? Is it immunization or exhaustion? Growing strength or progressive vulnerability? Vitalization or premature ageing? This volume suggests that rather than trying to simplify the issue, we can gain better insights by complicating it. One such complication relates to the analysis of the potential cost of adaptation.

THE COST OF ADAPTATION

Just like stress itself, the cost of adapting to it exhibits a richness of variety that defies description. Moses (1981), using the psychoanalytic vantage point, clearly made the case for the need to look beyond the usual epidemiological statistics. There are indications that Israelis are, as a group, a population at risk in relation to physical, psychosomatic, and psychological symptoms. The evidence is, however, rather incomplete, and the difficulties of obtaining an adequate comparison group are practically insurmountable. In any event, there are many other kinds of cost, entirely outside the classical epidemiological domain.

Certain aspects of adaptational cost are impossible to quantify and must remain in the descriptive-qualitative mode. Rarely reaching expression, they are firmly locked in the privacy of one's personal world, fantasies, dreams, and games children play.

Consider the following true story I heard from a colleague investigating creativity in children. In one of the creativity items a child was asked: "What can you do with a shoe?" The immediate answer was: "I can throw it at a terrorist!" This rare and creative answer clearly indicates the degree of preoccupation with the threatening content of terrorism. This too is part of the cost that children pay, but how is it possible to adequately measure these things? How to learn about the turmoil inside a child's soul? Visiting the children that live in border settlements exposed to occasional shelling, one is struck by their "normal" appearance. As Raviv and Klingman point out, however, a closer scrutiny of the children's games, fantasies, and dreams yields a variety of disturbing factors. These factors are often signs of coping and in that sense are clearly positive. And yet, there is this continuous need to cope with these extras in addition to the many other problems that children have. This too is part of the cost that must be taken account of.

Next, consider the quality of life, broadly defined. For the benefit of comparison with his or her familiar scene, the reader may wish to take the life-style of the university student in Israel as an example.

To start with, the Israeli students are older than their North American or European counterparts. Having served in the army first, they start at least two years later for girls and three years later for boys. Being older, they are practical minded, and want to finish their studies as quickly as possible in order to enter the job market. They are often already married and sometimes have children. About 80% of the students have to work to support themselves. With an inflation rate of 120% per annum, this is a difficult proposition. The studies are not easy. In addition to work they serve many weeks and sometimes months on reserve duty in the army. This can lead to a lost semester, or a lost vacation. Considering the pace and the load with which the Israeli students have to cope, a lost, much-needed vacation may well be more damaging than prolonging the studies. Then there is no time for extracurricular activities, no time for just playing with ideas and sampling from varieties of knowledge, and no time for sports, hobbies, and recreation. Life for these students is too heavy, too serious. This is also a cost.

The high tension in social contact also extracts a cost. Israelis don't have time, and they are high-strung and nervous. Their many worries keep them much too preoccupied and self-centered.

Israel is a natural laboratory for stress research. This much is agreed on by medical, social, and behavioral scientists, and indeed an entire section of this volume is based on the above assumption. The attempt to turn our situation into scholarly pursuit for the benefit of people everywhere, while a worthy venture, rates a distant second in Israeli psychological studies. Who wants to be a natural laboratory for stress research? Why not, as the song goes, specialize in the study of birds who pass through this beautiful country twice a year? Look at the themes in which Israeli behavioral researchers are at the forefront of knowledge: the study of orphans, widows, psychiatric combat casualties, prisoners of war, and, of course, death itself.

Smilansky (1980) found that Israeli children attain a more advanced concept of death earlier than American children. This surely is a cost. Why should our children be among the first to comprehend the finiteness of life? They will have enough of this when they grow up.

The many memorial days dedicated to those killed in the many wars follow each other and keep the issue of death salient in the minds of young and old alike. On these days the beautiful sad songs are sung again and again. I hoped to include a chapter on the content analysis of Israeli songs and poems but was not successful. This, to my mind, illuminative cultural indication must await future occasion.

Some costs will surface only years from now. As Inbar, when discussing the vulnerable-age phenomenon, demonstrated, the lives of children who went through the upheaval of an immigration or migration during the early years of grade school were less fully realized ten to fifteen years later. And immigration, in the Israeli context, is just immigration. What about the rest?

Children are particularly vulnerable for a variety of obvious reasons. Not least important among them is the danger that their plight will be overlooked by those who can lend them the much-needed support. Raviv and Klingman (1981), as well as Inbar (1981), mention this quite explicitly. The high frequency of exposure to critical stressors may lead the parents and teachers to the illusory conclusion that young children habituate easily and are in smaller need for help than older ones who more readily voice their concerns.

Just as there is now a growing number of studies indicating the effects of the holocaust experience on the second and third generations of children, so the effects of stress of life in Israel cannot be properly evaluated without the perspective of a few generations of longitudinal research.

Last but not least, there is an adaptational cost related to socialization. The shoe as a defensive weapon is just a symptom. Education for certain universal human values becomes so much more difficult in a country that has "enemies." It is a natural breeding ground for prejudices that ought to be overcome. This, perhaps, is the most difficult aspect of man-made, as opposed to natural disasters. To raise peace-loving individuals who, in spite of everything, do not hate other people, is the noble challenge of stress research.

COPING STRATEGIES

Denial occupies a prominent position among the variety of coping devices and strategies. While there are many different kinds of denial (Breznitz, 1981), they are all involved in the active reduction of an external threat. Of some obvious short-term advantages (Lazarus, 1981), in the long run denial is bound to be problematic. Rofe and Lewin (1980, 1981) documented that children living in particularly dangerous areas close to the border expressed less aggression and anxiety than those living in relatively more secure areas. Others reported a similar phenomenon, indicating the operation of denial. The greater the threat, the higher the chance that some sort of denial will take place. It is the answer, alas, a partial and often inadequate one, to the greater need for psychological defense.

Behavioral scientists themselves attempted to deny stress the status of a legitimate and interesting research theme. Until the Yom Kippur War, with the exception of some "neutral" basic research on stress (Breznitz, 1967, 1968, 1971; Kugelmass, 1966) and studies of morale and social integration during the Six Day War (Kamen, 1971), very little was done in this area. By contrast, what followed during and in the wake of the Yom Kippur War can best be described as a flood of interest in researching the various facets of that trauma. This dramatic change tempts one to look for psychological reasons for both the earlier absence of interest and its subsequent eruption. If I am allowed a speculation in this matter, I submit that there was a deliberate attempt to deny the existence of stress on the part of both the population at large and the behavioral scientists in particular. With the sudden outbreak of the most frightening of all our wars, denial was not tenable any more as a coping device. In a matter of days it turned into massive preoccupation with psychological stress, preferably in the emotionally neutral disguise of objective research. Thus, for many Israeli scholars, researching the tragedies in the midst of which they found themselves, became, I believe, a convenient strategy for coping.

A rather similar development took place in relation to study of the holocaust. For years Israeli scholars were visibly absent in much of the research of survivors of the holocaust, in spite of the many obvious advantages in conducting the work in Israel. The entire topic was taboo until the beginning of the Eichmann trial in 1961. Then too, all at once, further denial became impossible and was replaced by active preoccupation by both the general public and scholars from the various relevant disciplines. Being part of a scene dominated by anxieties, it is perhaps only natural that as scientists we orient ourselves to such anxiety-inducing topics, at least in part, according to our personal psychological needs.

The International Conference on Psychological Stress and Adjustment in Time of War and Peace, which took place in Tel Aviv during January, 1975, attracted thousands of professional and paraprofessional participants. It became the focus for many who attempted during the Yom Kippur War and in the period following it to be involved in the various helping programs, most of which were initiated by volunteers. There was an obvious need to discuss these experiences, reflecting underlying psychological mechanisms at work. These efforts have now been published in a separate volume (Milgram, Spielberger and Sarason, 1981).*

In addition to denial and active preoccupation, there are, however, many other coping strategies. *Passive detachment* is clearly one of them. It implies an attitude of "taking things as they come," the ups and the downs. This is particularly relevant to habits of listening to and reading the news. While many Israelis follow the news every hour on the hour, the cumulative effect of it all is sometimes the deliberate switching off of interest and involvement.

Detachment for purposes of "psychological recuperation" is, in itself, I believe, a symptom of fatigue. One of its outcomes is the

---

*The last section is based on a similar discussion that appeared in chapter 6 of *Selye's Guide to Stress Research* (1980). I am grateful to Dr. Selye for permission to quote from that material.

dramatic fluctuation in morale; the extreme ecstasies and the deep depressions. A single item in the news has the power to achieve that. Another outcome is the occasional distancing from the perennial discussions of "the Israeli situation." People often prefer simply not to talk about the issues, and if possible not to think about them.

THE VITAL HOPE

One of the most dramatic and illustrative examples of the ability of hope to help individuals adequately cope with intense and prolonged stresses is the story of American bombers who flew on dangerous missions over Germany (Janis, 1949). The high casualty rate of these nightly missions led to many psychiatric breakdowns among the crew members, particularly the old-timers. Psychologically, they interpreted their chances of being hit by the enemy as growing continuously, and with so many of their friends dying it was only a question of time when their own turn would come. If not today then tomorrow, but sooner or later it would inevitably happen to them as well.

When the pilots were told in advance that they would have to fly a fixed number of missions, a fascinating transformation took place. They started to count backwards the missions left, and their subjective estimates of surviving increased, rather than decreased with each mission. It was still the same subjective stress, the same rate of casualties, and yet their psychological impact was drastically reduced and the frequency of psychiatric breakdowns greatly reduced. What had happened?

By interpreting the objective situation in a way that was psychologically more conducive to hope, the individuals could better cope with their difficulties.

If the Israelis had been told in 1948 that they would have to fight five wars before reaching peace, nobody would have believed it. But after each war there would at least have been the sense of "one less to go." Such a perspective would have made a tremendous difference, but it was and still is totally unrealistic.

In order to be effective, hope must be realistic. If based on denial of threatening reality, it is bound to be shattered with the realization of the illusion. The psychological benefits of realistic hope cannot, however, be overstated. It is of some interest to note that Guttman and Levy (1981) found that "in contrast to mood, the post-war negative assessment (of Israel's situation) never returned to the pre-war level, with the very temporary exception during a few days following Sadat's appearance in Jerusalem." (p. 159). Thus, the relatively high level of mood is not based on unrealistic assessment of the situation, but rather in spite of it.

It is by virtue of "cognitive appraisal" (Lazarus, 1966) that a difficult reality can be construed either as a threat or a challenge. Once so subjectively defined, much of the rest follows. The issue of immunization versus exhaustion may thus depend upon whether or not one's cognitive appraisal leads to hope.

We started with the exposition of stress as an opportunity, and the last chapter again indicated that stressful life events may have positive as well as negative effects. In this vein, Inbar (1981) and Maeroff (1975) saw that immigration in addition to the stressful impact of dislocation can also produce enrichment. We have now made a full circle only to discover that stress is indeed a package deal. So is life in Israel. It combines the worst with the best that stress can offer, and in line with the ancient Chinese curse that appears at the beginning of this chapter, it is a uniquely interesting life.

REFERENCES

Breznitz, S. Incubation of threat: Duration of anticipation and false alarm as determinants of fear reaction to an unavoidable frightening event. *Journal of Experimental Research in Personality*, 1967, *2*, 173–180.

Breznitz, S. 'Incubation of threat' in a situation of conflicting expectations. *Psychological Reports*, 1968, *22*, 755–756.

Breznitz, S. A study of worrying. *British Journal of Social and Clinical Psychology*, 1971, *10*, 271–279.

Breznitz, S. The seven kinds of denial. *In*, S. Breznitz (ed.), *The denial of Stress*. New York: International Universities Press, 1981.

Guttman, L, and Levy, S. Dynamics and varieties of morale: The case of Israel. *In*, S. Breznitz (ed.), *Stress in Israel*. New York: Van Nostrand Reinhold, 1981.

Inbar, M. Some effects of stress during grade-school years. *In*, S. Breznitz (ed.), *Stress in Israel*. New York: Van Nostrand Reinhold, 1981.

Janis, I. L. Problems related to the control of fear in combat. *In*, S. A. Stouffer, *et al.* (eds.), *The American soldier, Vol. 2., Combat and its aftermath*. N.J.: Princeton University Press, 1949.

Kamen, C. S. Crisis, stress and social integration. The case of Israel and the Six Day War. Doctoral dissertation, The University of Chicago, 1971.

Kugelmass, S. Reactions to stress. Research report to the U.S. Air Force, The Hebrew University, Jerusalem, 1966.

Lazarus, R. S. *Stress and the Coping Process.* New York: McGraw-Hill, 1966.

Lazarus, R. S. The costs and benefits of denial. *In,* S. Breznitz (ed.), *The denial of Stress.* New York: International Universities Press, 1981.

Maeroff, G. I. Junior high is not easy to handle. *The New York Times Week in Review,* December 14, 1975.

Milgram, N., Spielberger, C. D., and Sarason, I. G. (eds.), *Stress and Anxiety,* Vol. 8. New York: Hemisphere Publishing, 1981.

Moses, R. Emotional response to stress in Israel: A psychoanalytic perspective. *In,* S. Breznitz (ed.), *Stress in Israel.* New York: Van Nostrand Reinhold, 1981.

Raviv, A., and Klingman, A. Children under stress. *In,* S. Breznitz (ed.), *Stress in Israel.* New York: Van Nostrand Reinhold, 1981.

Rofe, Y., and Lewin, I. Attitudes toward an enemy and personality in a war environment. *International Journal of Intercultural Relations,* 1980, *4,* 97–106.

Rofe, Y. and Lewin, I. The effect of war environment on dreams and sleep habits. *In,* N. Milgram, C. D. Spielberger, and I. G. Sarason (eds.), *Stress and Anxiety,* Vol. 8. New York: Hemisphere Publishing, 1981.

Selye, H. *The Stress of Life.* New York: McGraw-Hill, 1966.

Smilansky, S. The concept of death of Israeli children. *In,* A. Raviv, A. Klingman and M. Horowitz (eds.), *Children under Stress and in Crisis.* Tel Aviv: Otsar-Hamoreh Publishing House of the Teachers' Union in Israel, 1980 (in Hebrew).

Index

Israeli stereotype of toughness, 39–41, 43,
　　62–63
　can change occur?, 62–63
　dilemma of need for "virtuous" strength,
　　61–62
　pressure toward heroism, 40–41, 47–53,
　　57
　　male more than female, 41
　price of heroism, 41, 53–57
　　alienation, 54–55
　　ontological insecurity, 55–57
　reaction to former Diaspora-Jewish
　　stereotype, 40
　roots of the phenomenon, 57–61
　　blocking feelings of fear and despair,
　　　59–60
　　fear of death and injury, 58–59
　　strength a denial of weakness, 60–61
　sheer need for survival, 40
　see also Gestalt therapy groups in Israel;
　　Stress of living-with-war

Janis, Irving L., 5, 21, 33, 36, 38, 119–120,
　　236, 272
Jenkins, W.O., et al., 231
Johnson, J.H., and Sarason, I.G., 234, 254
Jones, Professor Frank E., 225–226
Jordanians, 127
Juliard, A.L., and Juliard, A.S., 67

Kaffman, M., 143, 144
Kaffman, M., and Elizur, E., 145, 146, 148,
　　150, 151
Kamen, C.S., 270
Kark, S.L., and Mainemer, N., 117
Kastenbaum, P., 33–34, 37
Keinan, G., 238
Kern, R.P., 238
Kernberg, O., 130
Klein, R.F., Garity, T.F., and Gelein, J.,
　　234
Klineberg, O., 194
Klingman, A., 156, 157, 158
Klingman, A., and Ayalon, O., 157
Klingman, A., and Ninio, J., 157
Klingman, A., and Wiesner, E., 141, 152
Kohut, H., 130
Kringlen, E., 116
Kubler-Ross, E., 34, 35

Kubovy, D., 157
Kugelmass, S., 270

Laing, R.D., 42–43, 52, 53, 55, 58
Larsen, K.S., and Giles, H., 66
Lazarus, R.S., 238, 254, 270, 273
Lee, E.S., 194–195, 199
Leipman, N., 168
Lemert, E.M., 166
Levav, I., 116
Levi, N., 168
Levy, S., and Guttman, L., 106
Lieblich, A., and Haran, S., 74
Lieblich, Amia, 6–7, 44, 45
Life Change Units (LCU), 241–242
Life events in Israel, stress and: further
　　study needed on coping with
　　high stress levels, 254–255
　experience value of stressful events,
　　255–257
　selective forgetting of events, 233–235
　　positive changes vs. negative ones, 234
　　or selective reporting, 235
　stress characteristic of Israeli population,
　　230–232, 254
　　ailments due to, 230
　　interference on memory, 231–232
　　rating of various life events, 230–232
　　recency, effects of, 231–232
　study of, 240–242
　study results, 241–251
　　effective spontaneous recall of events,
　　　250–251
　　selective reporting of events, 244–247, 254
　　stressfulness of events for young
　　　Israelis, 242–244, 254
　　successful coping relative to number
　　　of life events, 247–250
　see also Stress: learning from stressful
　　experiences
Life Events Questionnaire (LEQ) [Appendix
　　10-1], 241, 244, 246, 248, 249,
　　250, 260–261
Life-threatening war experiences, study of
　　effects of, 3, 7–38
　existential crisis involved, 33–38
　　explanations for and of, 33–37
　　letdowns from personal growth
　　　feelings, 37